FUNDAMENTAL THEOLOGY

SACRA DOCTRINA SERIES

Series Editors

Chad C. Pecknold, *The Catholic University of America*

Thomas Joseph White, OP, *Dominican House of Studies*

FUNDAMENTAL THEOLOGY

Guy Mansini, OSB

The Catholic University of America Press
Washington, D.C.

Library of Congress Cataloging-in-Publication Data
Names: Mansini, Guy, author.
Title: Fundamental theology / Guy Mansini, OSB.
Description: Washington, D.C. : The Catholic University of America Press, 2018. |
Series: Sacra Doctrina Series | Includes bibliographical references and index.
Identifiers: LCCN 2017023819 | ISBN 9780813229850 (pbk. : alk. paper)
Subjects: LCSH: Catholic Church—Doctrines.
Classification: LCC BX1752 .M255 2018 | DDC 230/.2—dc23
LC record available at https://lccn.loc.gov/2017023819

CONTENTS

FUNDAMENTAL THEOLOGY

INTRODUCTION

Theology is a word about God—talk about God. When it is simply our talk, purely human talk about God, it can be philosophical, something we find in Aristotle's *Metaphysics*. More originally, there is God's talk about God. Before the foundations of the world were laid, there is the eternal Word of God, the Word that St. John says was "in the beginning" (Jn 1:1). Since God's Word expresses not only the infinite intelligibility of God, but contains the original pattern of every created thing, it already encompasses within itself all true human speech about God, including true philosophical speech about God. Moreover, "every truth by whomever it be spoken," St. Thomas says, "is from the Holy Spirit"; and he means that every true speaking is provoked by the Spirit of Truth.[1] However, the Trinitarian horizon of all truth does not make it that true human speech about God is God's own word to us, in such a way, that is, that he comes forth as the very speaker. But when God turns his Word to us, so as to make us hear Him, then there is the Word made flesh. And when Jesus speaks of his Father, himself, and his Spirit, then we have God's talk about God in human words, at once the most accessible and the most authoritative talk about God there ever could be in the world.

1. St. Thomas Aquinas, *Summa theologiae*, ed. Peter Caramello (Rome: Marietti, 1952), I-II, q. 109, a. 1, ad 1. For an English translation, see St. Thomas Aquinas, *Summa Theologica*, trans. Fathers of the English Dominican Province, 5 vols. (Westminster: Christian Classics, 1981). This is a reprint of the Benziger Brothers edition of 1948, itself a reprint of the original 1911 English edition.

For us to hear the Word made flesh, however, there is required a prior word of God spoken through the prophets, and this is so that we can recognize the Word made flesh. There is required also a consequent apostolic and missionary word of God, a sort of necessary reverberation of the Word made flesh, without which it would fall into silence. All these are words of revelation, the opening of the divine mind in a humanly accessible way. Then there is the Church's subsequent talk about God, recapitulating and interpreting the law and the prophets and psalms, the Gospels and the apostolic letters, in her preaching, catechesis, and dogmatic definition. Finally, there is the Christian talk about God that is called "theology," or "revealed theology," *sacra doctrina* in the form of a school discipline, professed by teachers, learned by students. Today, this is mostly called "systematic theology." That is the theology whose footings are to be laid down in a "fundamental" theology, foundations upon which the edifice of theology proper can be erected in the great tracts devoted to the Trinity, Christology, the Church, and the Sacraments. The created and historical presuppositions of these four great tracts are addressed in Theological Anthropology, their consequences for action are detailed in Moral Theology, and their implications for prayer are counted up in Spiritual Theology.

If there is no revealed theology without revelation, the word of God addressed to us and culminating in the Incarnation, neither is there such theology without faith, which is man's response to revelation in Christ. Faith is how revelation makes its home in us, and so faith and revelation are most immediately identifiable as "foundations" of theology and considerations of both are rightly included in fundamental theology.

The various instantiations of revelation already mentioned also have a place in fundamental theology. Originally, revelation occurs in and through the history of Israel, Christ, and the apostolic Church. This history is woven of both words and deeds, especially the words and deeds of Jesus, where the deeds accomplish the design of God for our salvation, and the words explain the deeds.[2] The record of both the words and the

2. See Vatican II, *Dogmatic Constitution on Divine Revelation (Dei Verbum)*, in *Decrees of the Ecumenical Councils*, vol. 2, *Trent to Vatican II*, ed. Norman P. Tanner, SJ (London: Sheed and Ward, 1990), no. 2.

deeds meets us authoritatively in Scripture, according as it is interpreted by the Church's doctrine within the framework of Tradition. Scripture, Tradition, dogma, and the Church's "magisterium" or competence to teach, are all places to be visited by fundamental theology. These things follow on from revelation, keeping it available to us, and so we do not have a complete understanding of how revelation really meets us here and now without considering them at least in some measure. In fact, it was just disagreement about the nature and relations of Scripture, Tradition, and the Church that elicited the emergence of fundamental theology in the sixteenth century.

Where it is our talk about God's word to us, theology is often characterized as faith seeking understanding. This implies that faith and understanding are distinct things. It belongs to fundamental theology to think about their relations. Especially today, when prior to catechesis we are taught to distinguish faith from reason as the irrational from the rational, we have to think more carefully. Evidently, the God who creates reason does not ask us to sin against this created good when he invites us to faith in revelation. The understanding of revelation that faith seeks will be concordant with all other understandings of created reality even if revelation is more fundamental and comprehensive than any other understanding, even when all the others are taken together.

The theological relations of faith and reason can be temporally distinguished. The understanding faith seeks is a work of reason contemplating what is revealed and also how it is revealed (since that is interesting in itself and also tells us something about the "what"). Here, the work of reason comes *after* faith. *Prior* to faith reason is concerned with the *praeambula* of faith. The *praeambula* are those things coming before ("walking before") faith, things logically presupposed to faith that reason can determine, even independently of faith, things that must be true if there is such a thing as God speaking to us and our hearing him. *Concomitant* with faith, reason must be able to apprehend revelation as credible. The credibility of revelation has to do with its suitability to address our capacity reasonably to recognize the fact and anticipate the form of revelation. Part of this credibility is the historical reliability of Christian records. Another part is the beauty of Christian doctrine. With the *praeambula*, reason functions independently of revealed truth, meaning merely that it does not invoke revealed truths as premises in its arguments, and metaphysically; with the issue of credibility, it functions more epistemologically and historically; where faith seeks understanding, all the human disciplines surrender their results to the judgment and use of theology understood as a share in the divine wisdom.[3]

The list of topics to consider may already seem unmanageable. But in what follows the organization of thought will be perfectly plain. Since faith is a response to a spoken word, we have to begin with what it responds to: revelation itself (chapter 1) and how it meets us in Tradition (chapter 2), Sacred Scripture (chapter 3), and the Church (chapter 4). Then we turn to faith. We first excavate some of the presuppositions of faith—the *praeambula* (chapter 5). These fall into two lots, the first dealing with God and his capacity to speak and to say something that needs to be said, especially about our end, and the second lot dealing with man and his capacity to hear. Next we consider revelation as immediately related to faith, that is, we consider its "credibility," its worthiness to be believed, and its call—a moral call—to be embraced by faith (chapter 6). Then we turn to faith itself, the reception of revelation, according to its structure and properties (chapter 7). Last, we turn to why and how faith flowers into theology (chapter 8).

There are two key apologetic moments in this treatment of fundamental theology, one historical and one philosophical. As to history, it is crucial to defend the historical reliability of Christian records, especially as giving us trustworthy news of Jesus of Nazareth. We treat this in the chapter on credibility. As to philosophy, it is imperative explicitly to consider the nature of man and his knowledge as escaping the strictures of positivism or scientism. We treat this with the *praeambula*. These issues are salient for a contemporary fundamental theology, which has to work in a milieu skeptical of and indifferent to history and blinkered by materialism. It might be argued that they should be treated first. But the course of topics will keep to a sort of dialogical organization: God speaks; we hear.

Fundamental theology, as its title declares, is a peculiar kind of theol-

3. St. Thomas Aquinas, *Summa theologiae*, I, q. 1, a. 6.

ogy. The theology of the Trinity, or of Christ, or of the Church uses the data of Scripture and Tradition, including the Fathers of the Church and the Magisterium, in order first to establish what God has truly revealed about the Trinity, Christ, or the Church, and then second to come to some imperfect understanding of the revealed mystery both in its intrinsic intelligibility and as related to the other mysteries and to the end of man. In fundamental theology, the aim is to come to the knowledge of what has been revealed about revelation, Scripture, Tradition, the Magisterium, and the relations of faith and reason. And it perforce must do this very thing on the basis of … revelation itself as inscribed in Scripture and Tradition, and as these things are expounded by the Magisterium, and with the very reason that faith illumines, but where revelation itself again declares the scope and the nature of the illumination it brings to reason. There is, therefore, a sort of reflexive character to fundamental theology; it is theology thinking about itself.

Fundamental theology is fundamental because it is about how we see the mysteries of God, his Christ, the Church, and the sacraments of the Church. It is about how these things show themselves—how God shows them—to the eyes of faith. If Christ and the Church are things shown, fundamental theology is about the very showing itself. If we talk about the showing and lose sight of the things shown, however, we will be at risk of drifting off into abstractions. Keeping an eye on the things shown prevents that and will answer many of the questions that arise when we ask about the nature and necessity of Scripture and Tradition, Magisterium and Dogma, Faith and its *praeambula*. There will be more to say on this in the chapter on theology.

PART I

GOD SPEAKS

REVELATION

The second paragraph of *Dei Verbum*, the *Dogmatic Constitution on Divine Revelation* (1965) of the Second Vatican Council, provides a helpful outline of things to be treated in considering Revelation.[1] The paragraph begins with a declaration of the end of revelation, to wit, that the Father so reveal himself through Christ and in the Holy Spirit that we can draw near to him (Eph 2:18) and share in the divine nature (2 Pt 1:4). Thus we become friends with God (Jn 15:14–15), and God enters into our life. Second, it turns to the nature of this revelation. "The pattern [*oeconomia*] of this revelation unfolds through deeds and words intrinsically connected to one another [*intrinsice inter se connexis*] in such a way that the works achieved by God in the history of salvation show forth and corroborate

---

1. See Francis Martin, "Revelation and Its Transmission," in *Vatican II: Renewal within Tradition*, ed. Matthew L. Lamb and Matthew Levering (Oxford: Oxford University Press, 2008), 55–75, for the first three chapters of the constitution, on revelation itself, its transmission, and Scripture and inspiration; and see Henri de Lubac, SJ, *La Révélation divine*, 3rd ed. (Paris: Cerf, 1983), for chap. 1 of the constitution. There is a complete commentary on the constitution in *Commentary on the Documents of Vatican II*, vol. 3, ed. Herbert Vorgrimler (German, 1967; New York: Herder and Herder, 1969), with chaps. 1 and 2 entrusted to Joseph Ratzinger.

the doctrine and the realities signified by the words, and the words proclaim the works and illuminate the mystery contained in them."[2] Just after this, third, the constitution asserts that Christ is "at once the mediator and fullness of revelation."[3] All of these things are developed in the constitution, and can serve us, too, in thinking about revelation. First, as to the nature of revelation materially considered: why must revelation take place through the mutual connection of words and deeds? Second, what is meant by the economy or form or pattern of revelation? Third, how is Christ related to this form, and fourth, how is he the mediator and agent of revelation? Last, how should we more fully characterize revelation's end?

Words and Deeds Intrinsically Connected

Words

It is easier to see the necessity of words in God's revelation of himself and his intentions to us than the necessity of deeds. There is a general anthropological reason, a reason specific to the revelation of the divine, and a reason specific to the revelation of the Trinity.

A General Consideration   How else do human beings communicate with each other, and how would one communicate with a human being, except with language? Theologians sometimes lament a propositional or "merely propositional" view of revelation, and there may be some point here if the deeds of which the council's constitution also speaks are ignored. But really, there is no substitute for language in human communication. Suppose two of us are examining a new car in the showroom, and I want my friend to admire the finish. How can I do that without words? I can indicate the car, the whole of it by walking around it and gesturing—and after all, we went to the showroom to see cars. If I go up to the car, gesturing for him to follow and look, I can touch the finish. I can move my hand over it, and then look up and raise my eyebrows twice. But how does my

2. Vatican II, *Dogmatic Constitution on Divine Revelation (Dei Verbum)*, in *Decrees of the Ecumenical Councils*, vol. 2, *Trent to Vatican II*, ed. Norman P. Tanner, SJ (London: Sheed and Ward, 1990), no. 2. I have modified the translation.
3. Ibid. I have modified the translation.

companion know I want him to notice the finish, and not the color, or not the carbon fiber material of which the hood is made? Or the peculiar swell of the hood, or …? The same visual and tactile experience cannot discriminate what I want my friend to notice. I have to use words.[4]

Especially, we need words for absent realities. In fact, words are precisely those signs that let us negotiate presence and absence. Smacking the lips might mean the beer on hand is good, and a cry may indicate present danger, but such signals exhaust their scope in communicating present bodily satisfactions or threats. On the other side of immediate animal interests, there is the cool consideration of things just in themselves, and independently of their immediate availability, independently even of their utility. Such consideration is indifferent to the sensory presence or absence of the things, and it is names that enable this consideration.[5]

Without the ability in language to manage the presence and absence of ordinary things, we could never manage to deal with that most absent thing, that uniquely absent thing, God, who is not just a distant part of the world, but also not in the world at all. It is the name of God that lets us do that, and so God tells us his name.[6] A non-linguistic, non-propositional theory of revelation cannot get us out of our own sensorium.[7]

Naming God   How do we fix our reference to God and know we really are referring to him? Reference to material objects within the sensorium of two human beings can seem to be accomplished by gesture and the more complete bodily motion of walking to and walking around. But without words, how can I indicate to another person that I am thinking of God and want him to think about God? Pointing to the sky, or waiting for a thunderstorm will not do it. For this reference to be success-

4. For an introduction to arguments from the indeterminacy of the physical to the nature of meaning, see Edward Feser, *Philosophy of Mind* (London: Oneworld, 2006), 198–205.

5. On names, see Robert Sokolowski, *Presence and Absence: A Philosophical Investigation of Language and Being* (Bloomington, Ind.: Indiana University Press, 1978), chaps. 1–3.

6. The Lord gives, as it were, his proper name to Moses at Exodus 3:14, on which see St. Thomas Aquinas, *Summa theologiae* I, q. 13, a. 11. This name reflects back on what we take "god" (*deus*), a common name, to mean; for which, see q. 13, aa. 8 and 9.

7. See John R. T. Lamont, *Divine Faith* (Aldershot, UK: Ashgate, 2004), chap. 2; and Mats Wahlberg, *Revelation as Testimony: A Philosophical-Theological Study* (Grand Rapids, Mich.: Eerdmans, 2014), chaps. 2 and 3.

fully made, there are two quite special words that are deployed or at least which must be able to be deployed; and they work together in directing our mind to God. They are the words "all" or some equivalent thereof— "everything" or "the whole of things" or "the world" or the "collection of all things in the world and all possible worlds" or some such—and the word "not." To refer to God exactly, I have to sum up the world with the language of "all" and the "whole" and so on, and then I have to say, "And now I am talking about what is not a part of the world and does not belong to this whole, but what transcends it and makes it." Without this kind of use of language, there can be no reference to God.

This is exactly the kind of language that is deployed in the Bible in order to speak about God. It is found in well-developed and practically philosophical form in the last books of the prophet Isaiah: "For my thoughts are not your thoughts, neither are your ways my ways, says the Lord" (55:8). It is deployed narratively in the opening chapters of Genesis: there, God exists, alone, and all other things, all things not God, are subsequently said to be made by God, and purely and alone by his "word." His word, his naming, traverses and so manifests that most original distance between him and what is not him. Thus his transcendence to the world is established in the story of Creation. But the point here is that it is established with words and cannot be established any other way, and the remarkable thing is that this the very first story in the Bible gives us to think about a more original word than ours, a word of God, that, so to speak, from his side, establishes the real distinction between God and the world. His word establishes the world, and only subsequently can he condescend to speak to us in our words, whose pattern is his Word.

The peculiarity of naming God, the difficulty for human beings of having a name for God, is anticipated by God who gives us his name in Exodus 3:14. It is not enough for Moses to identify God for the people of Israel merely relationally, as the "God of your fathers." He must have a name, a more potent, more exact conveyance of the identity and reality of God. And after all, St. Thomas says, names are fashioned in order "to signify the natures or essences of things."[8] "What is your name?" Moses asks. God an-

---

8. St. Thomas Aquinas, *Summa Contra Gentiles, Book One: God*, trans. Anton Pegis (Notre Dame, Ind.: University of Notre Dame Press, 1975), chap. 22, para. 10.

swers with a play on the verb "to be." Moses is to tell them he has been sent by one who, in J. C. Murray's paraphrase, names himself as "I shall be present as the one who I am shall I be present."[9] God will be present within the history of the people for their good. But he will not be present as one subject to history, subject to the fate that befalls men and nations. No, he will be present precisely in his transcendence to the world, as "the one who I am," determined and determinable by nothing except himself, the providential master of fate. Has he given a name or has he refused a name at Exodus 3:14? He has refused any name such as makes present the intelligibility, the essence or nature of worldly things to us. He gives us a name that indicates our inability to know his nature. When Exodus is read in Greek and Latin in a world that has taken the invitation to think beyond cultural limitations—the invitation to think philosophically—then the name will tell us that God is beyond the distinction of essence and existence, and his name will declare to us that he alone gives intelligibility to the things of the world, both in their natures and in their existence.[10]

When the divinely named God is subsequently said to figure in this, that, and the other actions and words which the Bible records him as doing and saying, then we can be said to know him historically. That is to say, we know him as acting in a story, and so we come to know his character, his goodness and justice and mercy, just as they are revealed in his relations to us. At the same time, we also come to know him precisely as the one whose nature cannot be conveyed to us in this way and so cannot be defined. We come to know him as the one the full knowledge of which can only be conveyed to us in the vision promised us at the close of the age, when the many words give way to the one Word and hearing itself to sight.

To sum up, no reality is possessed in the way proper to man without words. This is especially evident when we deal with absent reality. God, however, is more absent than other absent things. His absence from the world, his not being part of the world, defines him for us. Words, however, give us mastery over presence and absence. And even the absence—the

9. John Courtney Murray, SJ, *The Problem of God* (New Haven, Conn.: Yale University Press, 1964), chap. 1. See further Robert Sokolowski, "God's Word and Human Speech," *Nova et Vetera* (English) 11 (2013): 202–3; Olivier-Thomas Venard, OP, "Scriptural Hermeneutics and the Thomistic Making of a Doctrine of God," *Nova et Vetera* (English) 12 (2014): 1093–96, 1102–4.

10. St. Thomas Aquinas, *Summa theologiae* I, q. 13, a. 11.

transcendence of God—can be negotiated by words. The first word of revelation in Scripture, in Genesis, is that whatever words we have to speak about God are subsequent to his word of creation and so parasitic on that word. We will return to this in chapter 5. For now, let us note merely the historical fact that God and his most proper name are first known via his word of revelation. St. Paul and the Book of Wisdom teach that God should be manifest to us from the world (Rom 1:19–20; Wis 13:1–9). But this knowledge was not actualized in any history of any culture that we know, high or low, gentile or Greek, prior to an encounter with the word of revelation.[11]

Naming the Triune God   There is, third, the matter of the revelation of the Trinity.[12] Expressing our knowledge of the Trinity evidently engages such key words as "one" and "distinct" and "equal," words that convey intelligibilities and relations that are in no other way available to us. Thus, the Three are distinct from one another, Father and Son and Spirit, but they are not distinct from the one divine essence; they are none of them distinct from the One Deity which each is and which each equally is. When we think about the way God establishes the knowledge of the Trinity in the Church, however, we may well ask whether the triune reality of God could have been conveyed to us without the incarnation, and without the very words of Jesus that address God as his Father, as someone distinct from and yet one with him (Jn 10:30). If we did not hear him speak of his Father, promise the Spirit, and more importantly, if we did not hear him address his Father, could we ever have known God is Triune? It is quite difficult to imagine some other way of introducing the mystery of the Trinity to us, some other way available even to God himself, granted that it is to us that this news is to be imparted, although it is not possible for us to say it is the only way.[13]

11. Robert Sokolowski, *Presence and Absence*, chap. 15; and Sokolowski, *The God of Faith and Reason: Foundations of Christian Theology* (Notre Dame, Ind.: University of Notre Dame Press, 1982), chap. 2.

12. Robert Sokolowski, "God the Father: The Human Expression of the Holy Trinity," *The Thomist* 74 (2010): 33–56.

13. For if the only motive of the incarnation is redemption, the permission of sin would be required for the revelation of the Trinity, which is not only unfitting but impossible.

Divine Testimony   The words of revelation that convey the reality of God and his plan are, in the end, his own words, his own testimony to us about himself. We should not let the description of revelation as imparting a "pattern" or design—originally something to be seen—obscure the fact that it is something to be heard. The words of prophetic revelation, even the Bible as a whole as we shall see later on, can be counted as "divine speaking"; and the knowledge we gain when we assent to what he has said is knowledge gained by testimony, divine testimony.

The role of human testimony as constituting the world we take as real is so important and omnipresent that without it, each man's world would become no larger than a very small neighborhood open to his own inspection, and in fact, it is to be wondered whether we would be able in any meaningful sense to speak of "men." It is a necessity both of our common epistemic situation, relying on testimony to constitute the world, and on the divine condescension, that the word of God meets us just as such, as testimony. Just as we accept a cabbie's considered judgment of where to find a good restaurant in a strange city, so we accept the prophet's testimony that he speaks for God, and so, we accept the divine testimony itself. There is nothing in the *structure* of the latter instance that removes us from the epistemically trustworthy stance of receiving testimony. Sometimes we accept a man's testimony that he speaks of what he has warrant to know for himself; sometimes we accept a man's testimony for another's speech, when he renders the other's testimony to us. Sometimes the credibility of testimony presents itself as an urgent issue before we accept it, and we address that in chapter 6.

Now, that hearing revelation is a matter of receiving the divine testimony as conveyed through prophet and apostle and preeminently by the incarnate Son of God himself is the traditional view of things. In the modern age, because of Immanuel Kant's declaration of the inability of human words to speak of God, and because of the more detailed knowledge of the historical character of revelation, it has sometimes been thought that we could no longer straightforwardly confess that God has spoken to us, and that we assent to what he himself declares. And there have accordingly been various attempts to find a pre-linguistic, experiential conduit of revelation. Such views, when taken strictly and when they strictly forbid an appeal to divine speech, cannot account for the Catholic tradition's sense that revelation imparts a knowledge truly divine, beyond our own compass, and that faith receives it.[14]

We will take up Kant in chapter 5 on the preambles of faith, where we deal with the analogical extent of human knowledge and language. The historical constitution of revelation, and therefore the historical vicissitudes of our ability to hear what God wishes to say to us and his ways of speaking to us, however, does nothing in the end to impugn the reality of divine speech, but rather, as we shall see, corroborates its credibility as a word really and truly addressed to us, historical beings as we are.[15] It alerts us, furthermore, to the ignorance into which sin has cast us, and also to the flexibility and extent of the divine condescension in speaking to us. This is something evidently recognized in Scripture: "In many and various ways God spoke to our ancestors in the past, but now ..." (Heb 1:1).

Deeds

Why must revelation take place through deeds, through the works of God and the answering works and actions of men?[16] The answer in general is obvious, perhaps, but is still usefully stated.

A General Answer   In the first place, God intends to *do* things relative to us, for us, in our favor. But he does these things respecting us as persons, and so, not without telling us what he is doing. Revelation—meaning simply the communication of news—is therefore certainly bound up with the deeds of God on our behalf that he undertakes for us, and wants us to know about.

In the second place, certain things cannot be communicated to a person without moral action targeting that person. Thus, one person cannot communicate full and perfect love for another unless he also undertakes

14. For the necessity of conceiving revelation as a matter of hearing the testimony of God, see Lamont, *Divine Faith*, chaps. 6 and 7; and Wahlberg, *Revelation as Testimony*, chaps. 3 and 4.

15. This distinguishes the revelation of the Bible from the alleged revelation contained in the Quran. The Quran presents itself as a pure speech of God within such a narrow frame of time that it cannot have the very thick relation to history that the Bible has.

16. See Gregory Vall, "Word and Event: A Reappraisal," *Nova et Vetera* (English) 13 (2015): 181–218.

to instantiate the *intentio benevolentiae* that love entails in the works of love. Our character, our moral identity, is both constituted and manifested by our relations with one another. God's "character" is not constituted, but it is manifested by his deeds.

In the third place, the addressee of God's revelation and the object of his care is the person in his fullness, and therefore the person as connected to other persons, familial, social, political. Revelation is, therefore, something public. No matter that we may think of it as first being formulated in the mind and intentionality of a lone prophet, its end is public; it is something for the community that is being saved.[17] This publicity of revelation also conduces to "works"—just as great deeds are the inscription in history of great ideas of great men, so even more for the ideas of God.

Again, beyond sharing his truth with us, God wants to share his love, as mentioned. Now, love makes the city, as St. Augustine taught, and without the city we are not fully men: we need the friendship of men to be happy men, and yet some of the conditions of friendship are political.[18] Therefore we may expect the love of God, his deeds on our behalf, who are social and political, to be writ large in history, even as is the destiny of nations and empires. We may expect revelation to entail the construction in history of the City of God.

So much, to speak generally. There are, additionally, two specific considerations to accompany the issues raised above about finding words to speak of the transcendent God and the triune God. There are special deeds, works, that correspond to the establishing of these things in the history of revelation.

Deeds Revealing the Transcendent God   To fix our reference in speech to the one transcendent God of creation who reveals his name to Moses, there corresponds the event of God's election of Israel, with attendant promises and gifts of land accomplished by God's mighty works. This

17. Ambroise Gardeil, OP, *Le donné révélé et la théologie*, 2nd ed. (Paris: Cerf, 1932), 41–57. The first edition was in 1909.

18. Aristotle, *Nicomachean Ethics*, trans. W. D. Ross, in *The Basic Works of Aristotle*, ed. Richard McKeon (New York: Random House, 1941), bk. 8, chap. 9.

event is not atomistic, but a series of events, a recurrent enactment of the promise across time. It is already articulated beforehand in the election of Abraham, continued in the extension of this election to his son and grandson, and finds a culmination in the election of Israel in its exodus from Egypt and at the giving of the law at Sinai and the conquest of Canaan.

The election of one man, and then of one nation, necessarily bespeaks the singularity of the object chosen over against all other objects at the same level. Abraham, just one, is chosen from among all the other men of his time. Israel, just one nation, is chosen from all the many nations. "The Lord did not set his love on you nor choose you because you were more numerous than other nations" (Dt 7:7). God's election of the one man, of the one nation, establishes the identity of the chosen. This is perhaps easiest to see with Israel; she is made the nation she is only via her election: "my father was a wandering Aramean and he went down to Egypt with a few people and lived there and became a great nation" (Dt 26:5). "I will say to those who are called 'not my people' 'you are my people'" (Hos 2:23). The election makes a non-people a people (see also 1 Pt 2:10). But this is true already of the patriarchs. Jacob becomes who he is through working out his mission, his election, over against Esau his brother and Laban his uncle. Within his deception of Isaac and Esau, his subsequent but more justified deception of Laban, and through his redemption in learning to care first for his wives and children more than himself—all of this a function of God's choosing him—he becomes the man he is. A similar point is obvious with respect to Joseph, and then also Moses (to stick with the most outstanding places where this dynamic of personal consolidation via God's election is evident).

But also—and this is the main point here—these elections just as plainly establish the identity of the One who chooses. It is no accident that God is the "the God of Abraham, Isaac, and Jacob": those historical connections, established by God's own deed and re-established by the answering reactions of patriarch and people, those connections are the very way in which the transcendent God is revealed in his transcendence to Israel.

The knowledge that God is creator, and therefore transcendent to the world, is mediated first through the identity he takes on in history: that

God is the creator of heaven and earth is, as it were, a conclusion drawn from the way he has acted and reacted with Abraham and Joseph, Moses and Israel. The conclusion is easily drawn. God promises Israel he will be her God and fulfill the covenant even over against all the other nations, and the gods of these nations. If his promise is trustworthy, he must be not only first among the gods, but the God of gods, the true God. And only if he is in charge of the rain and the land can he also guarantee the economic underpinnings of the nation and its vigorous history. God's historical actions in his election of Israel imply his transcendence as creator.

The election of Israel from among many nations is required for the revelation of the transcendent God to all the nations, to a humanity which had forgotten him. The Old Testament can give no satisfying account of this forgetfulness or of the worship of false gods, even in Wisdom 13:15–15:19 or Isaiah 44:9–20. But this is so not because of some speculative failure on Israel's part or because of the silence of God, but rather because of the unintelligibility of sin. The Book of Wisdom very much ascribes the forgetfulness of God to sin, and faced with its enormity and incomprehensibility, can find nothing more to say except to refer us to an inborn wickedness of man (12:11). Why do the nations need to find a blessing through Abraham? The formulation of the pre-history of the nation of Israel in Genesis 1–11 throws us back to the catastrophe of Genesis 3. The objective absurdity of sin prevents the speculative reconciliation of our ignorance of God with the good creation of a good Creator.[19]

Revelation of the Triune God in Deed   That revelation requires deeds and not only words finds a sort of final demonstration in the revelation of the Trinity. The deed that is the consummation of that revelation is the Paschal Mystery itself. The Trinity is manifest in this wise: the distinction of Father and Son is shown in God's abandonment of God on the cross (Mk 15:34). This is impossible without the incarnation, but also impos-

---

19. See the discussion of the origin of evil in St. Augustine's *On Free Choice of the Will*, trans. Thomas Williams (Indianapolis: Hackett, 1993), bk. 2, especially chap. 19. Nothing much more can be accomplished than Augustine accomplishes there. See also G. Mansini, "Error, Guilt, and the Knowledge of God: Questions about Robert Sokolowski's 'Christian Distinction,'" *Logos* 5 (2002): 116–36.

sible without the real distinction of persons, Father and Son. But at the same time, the unity of Father and Son—the Church will later say, unity of essence or nature—is likewise manifested in the fact of the perfection of Christ's offering, and in the acceptance of that offering by the Father signaled in the resurrection. Furthermore, the offering is made in the Spirit (Jn 19:30), and the risen Christ possesses the Spirit anew so as to give him to the Church (Jn 20:22; see Rom 8:11).

The revelation of the Triune character of God is one event with the concurrent revelation of the malice of sin and the mercy of God. The concurrence serves to highlight and to heighten the appreciation of the reality of the Trinity, the reality of sin, and the reality of divine mercy.[20]

Relation of Words and Deeds

The interaction of the deeds and the words is nicely expressed in *Dei Verbum*. "The works achieved by God in the history of salvation show forth and corroborate the doctrine and the realities signified by the words, and the words proclaim the works and illuminate the mystery contained in them" (no. 2). We have given some illustration of this above, but the relations are worth examining more slowly, because there are many.

First, the works of God "show forth" the *doctrine* and the *realities* signified by words. For instance, the gift of the manna in Exodus 16 enacts and so shows forth the reality of the steadfast love of God, a "doctrine" or teaching which is declared by Moses in song in the previous chapter.

Second, the works of God "corroborate" the *doctrine* and the *realities* signified by the words. The works corroborate *doctrine*, that is, show it to be trustworthy, as for instance the multiplication of the loaves does the Eucharistic teaching of Christ in John 6, while at the same time corroborating even the very realities signified by words. This last thing sounds strange, but is not, since our trust terminates in the realities of which the words of doctrine speak—Eucharistic presence is trustworthy.

Third, the words "proclaim" the *works* of God, as again in John 6 the discourse on the Bread of Heaven proclaims both the truth of the incarnation and the meaning of the Eucharistic sacrament.

20. See further G. Mansini, "Apologetics, Evil, and the New Testament," *Logos* 4 (2001): 152–68.

Fourth, the words "illuminate" the *mystery* contained in the works, as the discourse on the Bread of Heaven highlights the soteriological end of incarnation and Eucharist, and casts light on them by connecting them both to the type of manna in Exodus 16.

When we turn to the resurrection of Christ, we find an incomparable density of the interpenetration of word and work: the risen Christ, even as seen and heard, cannot even be apprehended as risen without the words he speaks to the disciples on the road to Emmaus, words that declare it and illumine its meaning, while at the same time the meaning of the cross is similarly declared in the terms of the law and the prophets. On the other hand, the sensuous and sacramental reality of the "work" of the Emmaus Eucharist corroborates the teaching about and the reality of the crucified and risen Christ. While the risen Lord announces the deed in Luke 24 on the road to Emmaus, in John 20, the deed of the resurrection itself corroborates a previously heard word: the Lord invites Thomas to explore his wounds, in demonstration of what the other disciples had already announced to him in his unbelief.[21]

The words are bloodless without events, and sustain no life; the events are mute without words, and declare no truth.

An Economy of Revelation across the Dual Testaments

Dei Verbum speaks of an "economy" of revelation, which is to say that the words and deeds form an intelligible pattern or form. Part of the pattern is simply the narrative unity that extends from Creation to Fall to redemption as inaugurated to redemption as executed to an anticipation of final glory. Even more, we should see that God *cannot* reveal himself as creator of the world and as provident Lord of creatures who exercise their freedom in time *except* through a narrative that extends from the beginning of creation and describes his engagement with Israel in time

---

21. Jean-Luc Marion, "'They Recognized Him; and He Became Invisible to Them,'" *Modern Theology* 18 (2002): 145–52. The French original appeared in 2001. See St. Thomas Aquinas, *Summa theologiae* III, q. 55, a. 5, c.; a. 6, c. and ad 1.

and anticipates the last trump.[22] Within this narrative unity, however, there will be correspondences of part to part, story to story, anticipations and fulfillments. And overall, the effect is to reveal God not simply in his transcendence, but in his personal engagement with those he is saving: the deeds and words of the narrative and the patterns therein are the created effects of the missions of the Spirit and the Word which climax in the incarnation and Pentecost, and the pattern as a whole reveals the Triune God.

Dual Testaments

The pattern can be perfectly discerned only once it is (almost) completed, which is to say, not until the words and events in the life of Christ who promises and then gives the Holy Spirit.[23] That there *is* a pattern is to be recognized already in the Old Testament. But *what* it is, is revealed only in the New Testament.[24] This bespeaks the unity of the testaments: the New Testament can be described simply as the written form of reading the Old in the light of Christ, or alternatively, the New is a reading of Christ, interpreting him, in terms of the Old Testament. In its written form, therefore, the pattern is beheld only according as the dual Testaments are seen together—so to speak, it is both lenses that produce the stereoscopic vision of revelation in its totality. This is easier to do reading the New Testament, since it is not composed without constant reference to the Old. It is harder to do, but just as necessary, reading the Old. That is to say, the pattern shows up in the Old Testament only when it is seen that Christ makes sense of all the events, all the institutions, all the promises and fulfillments, all the figures—prophets, priests, kings—in the Old Testament. The narrative unity of the pattern is one not just of action and

22. Christopher Seitz, *Figured Out: Typology and Providence in Christian Scripture* (Louisville, Ky.: Westminster John Knox Press, 2001), 139: "Only narrative is in a position to carry the weight of establishing theological truth when so much is at stake and where the issues are so complicated [as in the meaning of the divine name in Ex 3:14]. Propositions or religious experientialism fall short."

23. St. Irenaeus gives expression to this in *Against Heresies*, in *The Ante-Nicene Fathers*, vol. 1, ed. Alexander Roberts, James Donaldson, and Arthur Cleveland Coxe (New York: Cosimo Classics, 2007), bk. 4, chap. 26, no. 1.

24. See the study of Christopher Seitz, *The Goodly Fellowship of the Prophets: The Achievement of Association in Canon Formation* (Grand Rapids, Mich.: Baker Academic, 2009), esp. chap. 3.

re-action, move and countermove, but of type and antitype, promise and fulfilment.

What makes the Old Testament "old," in fact, is the novelty of Christ, a novelty never to be relegated to a dead past.[25] And just as basically, what gives the Old Testament its unity is the singleness with which everything in it—law and covenant, exodus and conquest, exile and return, and all the players therein—can be intelligibly related to Christ and his cross and resurrection and his sending of the Spirit onto the Church.[26]

Because God reveals himself to us in a historical economy, a narrative, and just because narrative cannot be replaced by any other genre of discourse or reduced to the form of a treatise, the narrative must always be revisited just as the thing it is, and just so, will spawn an infinity of treatises.

We will illustrate this pattern more at length in the next section of this chapter on Christ as the form of the pattern. But we need first to speak of its ground and the traditional way it has been considered in the Church.

Deeds within the Providence of God to Arrange

What makes the deeds and realities recounted in Old Testament history and prophecy part of the pattern of revelation as a whole? The possibility that the realities the Old Testament words immediately refer to also signify Christ finds its ground in the God whose providence is as wide as the history of the world he created and whose capacity to inspire Old Testament writers and redactors is as wide as his providence.[27] The wisdom of God is infinite, and enables his power to draw a design embedded in the peoples, figures, events, and institutions of Israel.

We can say, for instance, that it is because Christ exercises kingly prerogatives universal in scope, judging all men on the last day (Mt 25), that there were kings in Israel and Judah, the exercise of whose authority prompted reflection not only in 1 Samuel but also in Ezekiel and Daniel where a divine kingship is envisaged anew. We can say that it is because Christ establishes

25. Henri de Lubac, SJ, *The Sources of Revelation*, trans. Luke O'Neill (French, 1967; New York: Herder and Herder, 1968), chap. 3. This book was reprinted under the title *Scripture in the Tradition* (New York: Crossroad, 2000).

26. De Lubac, *The Sources of Revelation*, chap. 2.

27. St. Thomas Aquinas, *Summa theologiae* I, q. 1, a. 10.

a new and eternal covenant that there was a legendary covenant with Noah and temporal covenants with Abraham and Moses and David. We can say that because Christ is the beloved Son of God Israel was first his beloved son, and Abraham had also a beloved son, and Jacob had Joseph. And so on.

Since nothing is appreciated as final without the temporary, nothing definitive without the provisional, nothing perfectly fulfilled without approximations and sketches, these anticipations and foreshadowings of New Testament things are essential to our appreciation of them. We cannot see the New Testament things except against the foil of the Old Testament things.

There is a typological or figural reading of the Old Testament, therefore, a reading that picks out the pattern, the economy, inscribed in the events and personages and institutions of the history of salvation. Because the words signify things that are types of New Testament realities, Old Testament words mediate a meaning not always evident if our attention is restricted to the immediate context of their composition.[28] We return to this topic in the next chapter.

"Salvation History"

We have been saying that the pattern of revelation is a "history of salvation." This term, *Heilsgeschichte*, was coined in the nineteenth century and is associated with the Lutheran theologian J. C. von Hofmann and the University of Erlangen. It was intended to encompass not only the history of the communion of men with God, but the history of God himself, who makes himself Triune within the compass of sharing his life and truth with men. In this original and ambitious sense, it is not useful for Catholic theology, but we use it to mean, not the history of God, but the history only of the communion of the eternal and unchanging God with changing and temporal men. The following remarks may be helpful.

First, if "salvation history" is meant to encompass the whole of the pattern of revelation, then it must evidently include those meditations

---

28. The importance of allegory or typology is not much noted in Vatican II, *Dei Verbum*, although it is mentioned at no. 15. Pope Benedict XVI is more justly generous in acknowledging the importance of typology in the post-synodal apostolic exhortation, *The Word of God in the Life and Mission of the Church: Verbum Domini* (Frederick, Md.: The Word Among Us, 2010), nos. 37–41.

that take shape in the wisdom literature of the Old Testament. This literature springs from (as does the Book of Wisdom) or accompanies (as does Proverbs) the narrative of saving events recorded in the Old Testament.

Second, not all salvation has a history. Human salvation does, because human beings do not make themselves except in time, and human cultures, various attempts to perfect man, do not get themselves together except through and across history. So, salvation is historical for us, a transaction worked out between human freedom and the divine eternal freedom, which is creative freedom and has the initiative, and which encompasses in one moment all the temporal replies of man.

But there is also angelic salvation. Angels realize themselves in one moment, one decision, and not spread out over many acts of freedom. Therefore, angelic salvation is essentially non-historical, and becomes historical only by its association with the history of human salvation. The grace that gives charity to the nine choirs was not necessarily a Christological grace; but now, in fact, it is.[29] Again, the angelic warfare with the demons in the Book of Revelation (12:7) connotes angelic and demonic engagement in the human, temporal history of salvation.

Third, contrariwise, not all history is salvific. This is true in a kind of regional sense. The history of Rome was not salvific, if we read it with St. Augustine in the first books of *The City of God*. On the other hand, the history of Rome is encompassed by the history of salvation that stretches from Adam to Christ, from the first to the Second Adam. It is included in St. Paul's brief compression of the very dreary history of a fallen world without grace in the first chapters of Romans.

It may be objected here that all history must be salvific on the ground that God dispenses his grace in all times and seasons, even secretly and namelessly. Therefore, wherever there is a history of man, there is a history of grace and salvation. But this objection is not well founded. History is a public thing, a thing with names and events commonly recognized and carried forward by shared enterprises. Grace and salvation have a history only where God supplies the names and the words that rightly interpret events. Where he has not done so, we are incapable of supplying our own,

29. St. Thomas Aquinas, *Summa theologiae* III, q. 8, a. 4.

or saying how the history of India or China fits into the one plan we do know of, the plan whose key is Christ.

Last, we should remember also that not everyone thinks of history as Christians do. For the pagans, history is just one thing after another. It does not indicate any finality toward something not already inscribed in the rhythms of nature that indeed bring forth food and new offspring, but only to swallow them again in the penury of old age and the closure of the grave. The Roman historian Livy retold the legends according to which Jupiter would guarantee the safety and extent of the Roman Empire. But neither Jupiter nor the Romans are revealed to one another in this exchange of worship for empire. To recur to St. Augustine's account, once again, the history of Rome reveals only the passions and follies both of the Romans and the gods they worshipped.[30] If there is a structure to history, it is that of an eternal return of the same.

Contemporary thought about human destiny in the West still bears some faint glow of revelation about it. The history of salvation, the single meta-narrative of the West for over a thousand years, has made possible other grand narratives in the Enlightenment and post-Enlightenment West. There is the Marxist version of the coming redemption of man and man's labor immanent in the world and time, the end of man's alienation from man, the prospect of everlasting peace. More widespread, there is the expectation of infinite progress, where progress means more encompassing and more powerful technical means, greater freedom from the constraints of physics and biology, a more unrestrained social and political freedom to define one's own values and happiness. Increasingly, the meaning of this history is an advance to "more years," "more stuff," "more control" over the satisfactions, both bodily and emotional, of our own choosing, the engine of which progress is science and technology. Moreover, this "history" is embedded in a radically nonhistorical universe— that is, a universe that does not spring from freedom, is not the product of a divine choice, and does not conclude at a divinely chosen terminus. We return to a pre-Christian view of man, minus the classic appreciation of virtue. That the nihilism of this view of things recommends itself to so

---

30. St. Augustine, *The City of God*, trans. Marcus Dods (New York: Modern Library, 1950), esp. bks. 2 and 3.

many people is a great proof of our factual, fallen estate. Postmodern sensibilities may have made the myth of progress untenable to the cultured elite, but do nothing to address the nihilism of this view beyond insisting, in an ever louder voice, on the irreducibility of the "other" and his own values. In this regard, the "postmodern" is not at all unmodern.[31]

Christ the Design of Revelation

The patterned words and deeds of revelation, temporally distributed from the Old to the New Testaments, speak of Christ. The pattern of revelation in the Old Testament is a sort of drawing of Christ, anticipating the form of Christ. It gives us the form, more properly, of his mission, that is to say, of his *humanity* and the human exercise of his knowledge and love in order to redeem us and save us. The words of the Old Testament do not add up to, or cash out, the Word himself in his eternal and timeless splendor. There are no words for that. They add up to and foreshadow and cash out the Word *for us*, which is to say, the Word made flesh. And when the Word appears in the flesh, then he can be recognized for who he is.

The preparation and the outlining are altogether necessary because of the extravagance of the mystery. God cannot just tell us point blank that his Son is to become man and die for our sins. When stated bluntly, the mystery of the incarnation and the cross provoked derision in the ancient world. Who but ignorant slaves and uneducated women could credit the idea that the First Principle descends into the muck and mire of material existence, and does so out of love for man? Only those who do not really understand what they are saying could enunciate the proposition that God became man, and only those who profoundly misapprehend the chasm between divinity and humanity could think that God would die for man.

But how does one prepare to do such a deed and deliver such a message? In the way God did in fact prepare. The preparation of the gospel in the Old Testament itself cannot simply be a clear statement of Trinitarian

31. See Richard Bauckham's thoughtful remarks on the narrative unity of Scripture and the postmodernism of Jean-François Lyotard in "Reading Scripture as a Coherent Story," in *The Art of Reading Scripture*, ed. Ellen F. Davis and Richard B. Hays (Grand Rapids, Mich.: Eerdmans, 2003), 38–53.

reality, incarnation, and cross. The problem, then, simply returns before-hand. The preparation has to adumbrate something that cannot be recognized until the fulfillment turns our gaze to what makes the shadow, and until color and the third dimension of reality fill in the foreshadowed outline. Still, it is because of the foreshadowing, only because of the outline that the truth can really be communicated to us in such a fashion that we can apprehend it.

Two Patristic Statements of the Pattern

St. Irenaeus, in the *Demonstration of the Apostolic Preaching*, and St. Augustine, in his *First Catechetical Instruction*, give us models for discerning the pattern and its fulfillment in Christ.[32]

The *Demonstration* is divided into two parts. In the first, Irenaeus states the history of salvation from Adam and the fall to Christ's cross and resurrection within the framework of the Trinitarian Rule of Faith, and this is the "apostolic preaching," according to which one Father, one Lord, one Spirit address one humanity in one plan of salvation that stretches from creation to Christ to the Church. Part two shows the foreshadowing of the truths of part one in Old Testament theophanies and prophecies. The Old Testament demonstrates the apostolic preaching, both by explicating it and by grounding its truth in the all-encompassing providence and power of God to arrange the deeds and state in words a preparation for the declaration of the compassion of God that otherwise could not be heard. The preparation serves as a kind of sounding board that, once the gospel is enunciated in the dominical and apostolic preaching, prevents it from disappearing without echo into thin air.

The *First Catechetical Instruction* also tells the story from Adam to Christ, but demonstrates the credibility of the apostolic teaching with a different strategy. Augustine begins with a brief protreptic, which excludes honor, riches, and pleasure as stopping places for the human desire for happiness and rest, and locates that place, not in philosophical wisdom, but in God (chap. 16). How shall we possess this eternal blessed-

32. St. Irenaeus of Lyons, *On the Apostolic Preaching*, trans. John Behr (Crestwood, NY: St. Vladimir's Press, 1997); St. Augustine, *The First Catechetical Instruction* [*De Catechizandis Rudibus*], trans. Joseph P. Christopher (New York: Newman Press, 1946).

ness? Such a promise for human happiness can be no recent discovery, but was foreshadowed and foreknown from Adam. Then the argument proceeds by appeal to Old Testament types. "Not only the words of these holy men who in point of time preceded the Lord's birth, but also their lives, their wives, children, and acts were a prophecy of this time, wherein through faith in the Passion of Christ the Church is being gathered together from among the nations" (chap. 19, no. 33). And he proceeds from Adam through Noah to David and the prophets to the Lord Jesus, with due attention to the covenants that prefigured the everlasting covenant in Christ (chap. 22, no. 40).

Modern Statements of the Pattern

Multiplying Configurations   The more one looks, the more varied and distinct configurations appear; and it is very difficult to relate them all together, to spell out the intelligible connections in short compass. This leads one to think that, after all, there is nothing like reading the Book, again and again. There is a pattern of covenants leading up to the new and everlasting covenant, which has often been noted, and lots of things can be hung on the line of covenants from Noah to Christ. There is a pattern of finding the right form, the right kind of worship of God, that begins with the keeping of the Sabbath rest at the beginning of creation by the Lord himself, who subsequently enjoins this rest on Israel in the Ten Words, a rest in which Israel realizes her covenant partnership with God, sharing in his own fullness of repose contemplating the good creation fashioned by the good God. Planning for, building, rededicating the Temple all belong to this thread. It is continued in the New Testament, where true worshippers of God must worship him in Spirit and in Truth (Jn 4:24), where Jesus is this Truth (Jn 14:16), and where worshipping God in him is inaugurated in the Supper that fulfills all the previous sacrifices of the Old Testament, and where the Church is the new Temple of God (Mt 16:18; 1 Pt 2:5). Again, there is the thread of seeing God: Adam walks with God in the garden and so, perforce, sees him; but such intimacy of friend with friend is lost with the fall; the theophanies granted Abraham at Mamre or Moses in the third chapter of Exodus do not satisfy the desire to see God. Moses asks especially for this boon (Ex 34:18), and as a sort of assurance of the continuing presence of God with Israel on her path to the promised land. Moses speaks with God face to face (Ex 33:11), but until the Second Moses, no one sees the face of God until the face of Christ is seen (2 Cor 3:18), to see whom is to see the Father (Jn 14:9). Even so, there remains a promise to see God, in Paul, compared to which we see now only in a glass, darkly (1 Cor 13:12).

Aidan Nichols, OP   Aidan Nichols undertakes an exceptionally full and clear and accessible statement of the whole pattern in its most obvious, most predominant lines of Old Testament promise and New Testament fulfillment. He prefaces this demonstration with a criticism of modern neo-Marcionism, according to which the Old Testament cannot be Scripture for Christians. Here he follows Francis Watson's critique of F. Schleiermacher, A. von Harnack, and R. Bultmann.[33] He notes with Gerhard von Rad that the pattern of promise and fulfillment from Old to New Testaments is already to be found within the Old Testament itself. There are wheels within wheels, as in Ezekiel's vision. This is an important observation, because it means that we do not discover the pattern of promise and fulfillment only when the New fulfills the Old Testament—that would be much too late. We have to have already learned this pattern in simpler and more partial form in the Old Testament, in order to recognize both continuity and novelty when the New meets us. The over-all pattern Nichols discerns is one of a messianic promise "broadly conceived," so as to include within its scope the gift of Spirit, the restoration of paradise, the vindication of Mt. Zion, and the faithful remnant, the bride of the Messiah realized in the Church, the new Israel, the establishment of a new and everlasting covenant, the restoration of the Temple in an eschatological Temple, and the identification of the Messiah with the Suffering Servant.[34] The exegesis that most befits this schema of promise and fulfillment is of course typological.

---

33. Aidan Nichols, OP, *Lovely Like Jerusalem: The Fulfillment of the Old Testament in Christ and the Church* (San Francisco: Ignatius Press, 2007), 77–86.
34. See ibid., 87–89, for a summary statement.

Hans Urs von Balthasar and the Obedience of the Prophets   An especially
appropriate articulation of the pattern for a chapter on revelation is the
pattern extending from the prophets who speak the word of God and
point forward to an incarnate Word. There are two ways to think about
how Christ is to be discerned in Old Testament prophecy. We can think,
first, of the various prophetic sayings whose fulfillment is found in Christ,
a way already illustrated in the New Testament. So, for instance, "They
shall look on him whom they have pierced" in Zechariah 12:10 points forward to Calvary after Jesus' side is opened with a lance, just as "your king
comes to you ... humble and riding on an ass, on a colt the foal of an ass"
in Zechariah 9:9 points to Palm Sunday. Again, Jesus' silence at his trial
before the high priest (Mt 26:63) is taken to fulfill Isaiah 53:7, "he opened
not his mouth." This is the way developed not only in the New Testament
but more massively in patristic exegesis.

The second way looks to the prophets themselves, their mission and
what it takes them to execute it, as delimiting the mission of Jesus and
what it takes him to fulfill it. St. Augustine anticipates this way of taking
things, in the *First Catechetical Instruction*.[35] There is also a contemporary
development of it by Hans Urs von Balthasar.[36] In the first way, what the
prophets say, the content of their oracles, looks to Christ. In the second
way, the prophets themselves in their persons turn out to be figures of
Christ, especially in their obedience to the word of God.

Abraham the father of faith is also the father of obedience to God,
obeying the command to leave his father's house and journey to a promised land. Moses also is especially paradigmatic of prophetic obedience,
in his meekness before men and unflinching obedience to God, which
is exemplary as an obedience to God on behalf of the people. Moses is
ready to suffer for the sake of Israel, and suffer he does. He stands in the
Old Testament as a sort of archetype of the prophet, to be matched or
surpassed only by a second Moses (Dt 18:15).

Obedience cannot but be central to the prophetic office. *Obedire* is

---

35. St. Augustine, *First Catechetical Instruction*, 63.
36. Hans Urs von Balthasar, *The Glory of the Lord*, vol. 6, *Theology: The Old Covenant*, trans.
Brian McNeil and Erasmo Leiva-Merikakis (German, 1967; San Francisco: Ignatius Press, 1991),
pt. 2, "The Stair Way of Obedience."

originally *ob-audire*, and in this root sense a prophet who hears the word of God "obeys" him. But the obedience becomes more personal in the course of Old Testament prophecy, in the sense that it calls on more and more resources, makes a greater and greater claim on the personal response of the prophet.

So, for Hosea, obedience enters into his sexual conduct, and how he leads his life in a marriage in which his humiliation is the cost of maintaining it. A faithful man, faithful to the word of God, is bound to a faithless and profligate wife. Similarly, Isaiah's children enter into his service of the word of God: "I and the children whom the Lord has given me are signs and portents in Israel from the Lord of hosts" (Is 8:18). Jeremiah pays for his obedience to the word of God, for his fidelity to his mission, with his life. And before his death, his mission isolates him and earns him the enmity of king and people.

In these ways, the obedience of the prophet more and more defines who he is. Could there be a prophet who is nothing but his mission? Could there be a prophet for whom his mission is not the way to realize and perfect an already constituted person, but whose mission has no personal substrate but simply is the person?[37] He has been sent, like the prophets, but not chosen like the prophets.[38] Still, there is in the obedience of prophets a real anticipation of the Word made flesh. Christ's obedience to his mission is registered from his childhood—"Do you not know I must be about my Father's business?"—and culminates at Gethsemane—"not what I will, but what you will." From prophetic quotation of the Lord, we move to the personal words of the Lord delivered viva voce in the preaching of Christ. From the prophetic speaking of the word of God, we move to the very being of the Word of God. When Jesus

37. The mission of the Son into the world implies both his procession from his Father, as the one who sends, and the created term that makes him present to those to whom he is sent, which created term is the humanity he assumes from Mary; see St. Thomas Aquinas, *Summa theologiae* I, q. 43, a. 1. The humanity of Jesus, whose temporal course is the realization of the Word's mission, has no subsistence distinct from the Word.

38. Robert Sokolowski, *Eucharistic Presence: A Study in the Theology of Disclosure* (Washington, D.C.: The Catholic University of America Press, 1994), 125. A prophet is chosen; the person of the prophet is inducted into the divine plan by a mission that is extraneous to his being. But the Son is not chosen; he is begotten. There is no choice in God, and choice does not establish the distinction of persons *in divinis*.

quotes a prophet, he quotes himself. And from the obedience of a servant, we move to the obedience of a Son (Heb 5:8).

That the prophetic figures point to the incarnate Word cannot be foreseen prior to the incarnation itself. As with every set of figures and types, the unity of the Old Testament is outside of itself in a previously unimaginable point of convergence. But once the point of convergence is given, then the pattern as a whole is discernible; and we see that the corpus of Old Testament prophecy outlines the body, the humanity, of Christ in his obedience. Christ as man hears the word of God perfectly, because he is the Word: his obedience—hearing—in his humanity attests to his personal identity, as the Word of the Father. But this hearing of the word and obedience in act was already outlined in the prophetic speaking of the word, and in the prophets' obedience of their own lives. Christ's obedience to his Father fulfills their obedience to God; it undoes the dis-obedience of Adam by obeying the Law of Moses in all three categories, moral, judicial, and cultic, for the unity of the Testaments is clinched not only in broad outline but even in the details of the pattern.[39] It is an obedience that, when consummated on Calvary, manifests who he is, and so, the Trinity, and at the same time our redemption, but only by manifesting himself as the one who consummates what had before been outlined in the Old Testament.

The one who steps into the space prepared by the Old Testament is thus more than a prophet, more than John the Baptist. This is manifest from the very way he presents his message. He does not say "Thus says the Lord," but "I say," as in the Sermon on the Mount. He does not say by what authority he does what he does, for there is no authority prior to his. When he announces the gospel, and says that the time is at hand, he expects to be taken at his word, and requires that we take him at his word alone. If there were another word of someone else he could adduce as warrant for who he is, then he could not be who he is: there is no one by whom the Lord can swear but himself (Is 45:23; Heb 6:13–18). He has been sent (Mt 15:24; Lk 4:43), like the prophets, but with his own word since he is the Word.

39. St. Thomas Aquinas, *Summa theologiae* III, q. 47, a. 2; and see Matthew Levering, *Christ's Fulfillment of Torah and Temple* (Notre Dame, Ind.: University of Notre Dame Press, 201), 53, and 75.

Wisdom and the Word   The prophetic pattern invites us to look to Old Testament wisdom literature as well. Within the sapiential literature of the Old Testament, there are three great roles assigned to wisdom. She contains, first, the pattern of practical living by which one is virtuous and successful according to the first chapter of Proverbs, and she "cries aloud in the street" (Prv 1:20) for all who want life and prosperity to follow her. That is wisdom's first, more obvious, face. Second, however, she is the "craftsman" who labored with God in the creation of the world (8:30). In this light, wisdom was "brought forth" (8:24, 25) by God before the foundation of the world, and especially associated with the intelligibility of his work (see the "circle" and the "limit" and the "marking" of Proverbs 8:27, 29, 29 for the heavens, the sea, and the earth). It follows that that by which man lives wisely and prudently and happily is that by which the world was crafted in the first place: the happy life is in accord with the very way in which the world was first fashioned. God delights in wisdom and wisdom delights in the sons of men (30–31) to make them virtuous and wise.

Third, wisdom has a special relation to the people of Israel. In Sirach, wisdom is brought forth "from the mouth of the Most High" (Sir 24:3), an eternal reality (24:9), and told to make her dwelling in Israel; there she is to set up her tent, and Israel is her inheritance (24:8). So she is established in "the holy tabernacle," in Zion, in Jerusalem (24:10–11). This last, special relation to Israel is quite determinate: the wisdom who dwells in Israel is "the book of the covenant of the Most High God, the law which Moses commanded us" (24:23). This identification is made again in Baruch 4:1. If the virtuous and happy life of the Israelite is to live a life measured by that wisdom according to which God made the world, it must also be true that the Law of Moses governs Israel concordantly with that same wisdom.

In the Book of Wisdom, wisdom is an emanation of the glory of God (Wis 7:25) and an image of his goodness (7:26). She orders all earthly things well (8:1), and teaches the virtues (8:7). And she works throughout history, guarding and prospering the people of Israel. She delivered Adam from his sin (10:1), rescued Lot from Sodom (10:6), gave guidance to Jacob fleeing from his brother (10:10), saved Joseph (10:13–14), worked with Moses (11:1ff). The order and intelligibility of the history of Israel turns out to be concordant with the order and intelligibility according to which the world was made from the beginning. "For the universe defends the righteous" (16:17).

In the New Testament, there are many places that identify Jesus as Wisdom through identifying him as the one through whom God created the world. Thus, Colossians 1:16, John 1:3, and 1 Corinthians 8:6. Hebrews 1:3 rather clearly recalls Wisdom 7:26. Jesus himself makes the identification several times. The Sermon the Mount is a wisdom teaching (Mt 7:24), and a teaching with authority (7:29). Whose authority? In the face of the incredulity of his generation, he asserts that "Wisdom is justified by her deeds" (Mt 11:19). What wisdom? "Come to me all who labor and are heavy laden, and I will give you rest" (11:28), he says, repeating the call of Wisdom in Sirach 24:19 and promising the rest of Wisdom in Sirach 51:17. And the yoke the disciples are to take upon them in the next verse (Mt 11:29) sends us to the yoke of Wisdom in Sirach 51:26 (and see the yoke of the law in Jer 2:20 and 5:5). Learning from him, of him, is to learn a Wisdom whose authority is beyond that of scribe and Pharisee. In the same line, if the queen of the south came to hear the wisdom of Solomon, Jesus says that "something greater than Solomon is here" (Mt 12:42). What is greater in the line of wisdom in comparison to the man than whom no wiser can be imagined? Wisdom itself.

We have seen that Old Testament wisdom accompanied the people and saved them and was identified with the law that governed their lives. Consider then Luke 11:47–51 (see in parallel Mt 23:29–31, 34–36), where Jesus addresses the scribes (and Pharisees in Matthew).

for you build the tombs of the prophets whom your fathers killed [Matthew: "and adorn the monuments of the righteous"]. So you are witnesses and consent to the deeds of your fathers; for they killed them, and you build their tombs. Therefore also the Wisdom of God said, "I will send them prophets and apostles [Matthew: "I—Jesus—send you prophets and wise men and scribes"], some of whom they will kill and persecute" [Matthew: "crucify"], that the blood of all the prophets, shed from the foundation of the world, may be required of [Matthew: "may come upon"] this generation, from the blood of Abel the just to the blood of Zechariah, who perished between the altar and the sanctuary.

Yes, I tell you, it shall be required of [Matthew: "all this will come upon"] this generation.

From the story of Abel onward, with prophets and priests (and wise men and scribes—Matthew), the whole of the Scriptures are indicated, and in suffering persecution, Jesus fulfills them all. But there is a particular link to Wisdom and a stunning explanation of how incarnate Wisdom works in the world.

It is, to be sure, a pre-existent Wisdom. The recollection in Luke 11:49 of Jeremiah 7:25–26 ("I have persistently sent all my servants the prophets to them") makes Jeremiah's words already to be the words of Jesus. If the Wisdom of God is Jesus (see Matthew's version), already so identified because greater than Solomon (Lk 11:31 = Mt 12:42), then Jesus-Wisdom is represented as speaking in the Old Testament through the prophet. That is, the prophet's words were—are—really his words. But how in Jesus does Wisdom conclude a work he has presided over from the foundation of the world?

The recollection of Genesis 4:1–12 (the murder of Abel) and 2 Chronicles 24:19–22 (the murder of Zechariah) in Luke 11 together impart the unlovely truth that human history is most tellingly characterized as a history of violence in which righteous men and prophets are the privileged victims. And this is indicated too by the recollection of Genesis 9:5 in the "blood required," where of Noah and his descendants it is ordained that blood shed in violence must be paid for in like coin.[40] But now a deeper Wisdom enters into this history. Both the Matthean and the Lukan versions mean to say that, because the scribes and Pharisees will kill Jesus, "this generation" is liable for all past murder of every righteous man and every prophet. This could be true only if in some way the blood of Jesus is equivalent to all that prior river of blood, only if in some way all the righteous are somehow included in him, and the mission of every prophet is a part of his mission. Are the righteous then righteous by his righteousness? Have the prophets then spoken only his word, as the reminiscence of Jeremiah 7 declares?

The Matthean form says that "all this"—all this blood (the blood of

---

40. It is the same verb in both Luke and the LXX Genesis, *ekzêteô*.

prophets and just men); all this guilt—will "come upon" "this generation." Presumably, it comes upon them because they will kill Jesus (see the
parable of the Wicked Tenants, Mt 21:33–46, Mk 12:1–12, Lk 20:9–19).
But in saying that this blood "will be required" of this generation, Luke's
version means that the blood shed by "this generation" shall be matched
by shedding "this generation's" blood. That is what we gather by looking
back to Genesis 9:5–6. But where does that happen? We do not see such
judgment executed upon "this generation." It happens rather in the same
event in which "this generation" becomes liable for all the blood shed
since Abel, that is, in the death of Jesus. That is to say, the death of Jesus is
the culmination of guilt (Matthew)—the blood comes upon the generation that kills him. And at the same time, the blood is required of it, and
in fact paid, in the same event. And this is to say that Jesus' death is an
equivalent satisfaction for all the sins of all men since the foundation of
the world. The triumph of evil is at the same time its undoing.

In the Book of Wisdom, Wisdom arranges that the punishment of
the Egyptians is at the same time a blessing for Israel (Wis 11:5, 13). But in
the passage just analyzed, the death of Jesus is both the culmination of human malice and compensation for it. He fulfills the law spoken to Noah,
making an order of justice that could not have been anticipated before the
New Testament. The one by whom the world is made and made wholly
good with no thought of sin, that one becomes incarnate to re-create
things, and show himself a Second Adam, fulfilling a law given because of
sin in order to take sin away.

Of this stratagem of Wisdom, St. Paul will say that "it is not a wisdom
of this age or of the rulers of this age" (1 Cor 2:6), and that it is "a secret
and hidden wisdom of God" (2:7). It had, moreover, to remain secret and
hidden, for otherwise "the rulers of this age ... would not have crucified
the Lord of glory" (2:8). That they crucified him is the very way by which
the rulers were undone.

This stroke of Wisdom from within history, therefore, though we see
signs of it in the story of Israel and her guardian Wisdom, is something
altogether new. Still, the pattern across the Testaments is clear, such that
we cannot follow the Old Testament story of Wisdom to its end without
the New, nor appreciate the fullness and the novelty of the New without

the Old. Of course, there is a finality to the consummation of Christ, even in the terms of *Dei Verbum* with which we began this chapter. The relation of the wisdom of God to the deed of the cross, this installation of the wisdom of God in history by means of the cross, corresponds in the order of operation to the foundational order of being: as is this word of the wisdom of God to the cross, so is the Word of God to the event of the incarnation. In both orders, the deed/event enacts a divine intelligibility; in both orders a word/Word finds historical embodiment. There is no tighter relation of word and deed that *Dei Verbum* insists makes the economy of revelation.[41]

Christ the Agent of Revelation

Christ is not only the content of revelation but also its agent, the one who makes it happen. Could it in fact be merely about him if he were not its agent? Could there be a revelation about the Word of God if the Word does not himself declare it? Surely there could be no word of the cross—no intelligibility we could grasp of the cross—unless declared by the Word.

First, as we have read in Matthew 23, Jesus tells his disciples that he *has sent* the prophets who came before him and spoke through them. This is evidently a matter of his divinity. The Word speaks in their words. Second, he is the agent of revelation in his earthly career, in virtue of his humanity, for he does the things that fulfill the prophecies and answer to the types of the Old Testament. This is a matter of his own quite self-conscious agency, and this is important to remember, lest we imagine Jesus as a sort of imaginative construction of Christian theology, a product of others who read Scripture in order to figure him out, but without his own warrant and teaching for doing so. Third, just as in his divinity he sent the prophets before him, so once incarnate, he sends the apostles after him. Prophetic sending prepares for the mission of the Son; apostolic sending continues it.

These three aspects of his agency as revealer are brought together in Luke, who reports repeatedly and at some length how Jesus teaches the

<hr>

41. See Vall, "Word and Event," 183.

Church to read the Scriptures. As the first "Christian" exegete of the Old Testament, he teaches the apostolic Church how to read the Law and the Prophets and the Psalms so as to see him therein. This is the plain and exact message of Luke 24 where the risen Lord opens the eyes of the disciples on the road to Emmaus by opening the book to them. But it is also to be found in John and the Synoptics as we shall see in chapter 3. While he fulfills the prophecies and the types in his own incarnate person, therefore, he also *teaches* the disciples this very thing. He is not the *discovered* unity of the Old and New Testaments, a hypothesis worked out by Christian scribes. True it is that "every scribe who has been trained for the kingdom of heaven is like a master of a house who brings out of his treasure old things and new" (Mt 13:52). But it is he himself who first matches up the new with the old.

End of Revelation

We began this chapter by evoking the end of revelation as the manifestation of the Triune God and our call to communion with him. *Dei Verbum* contrasts this revelation in history via deeds and words with natural revelation, and this can help us better appreciate the end or goal of revelation. The constitution speaks of it, repeating the doctrine of *Dei Filius* from the First Vatican Council, itself grounded in Romans 1.[42]

By the natural light, the reason native to our species, we can come to know the one God from the things that have been made—so to speak, the things that have been made manifest the one God in his transcendent causality, and at the same time declare that he himself must be the end of all that he has made. Since he creates each and all and the whole and is eternal, he is provident and rules over all things, from the course of nations to the fall of the sparrow. Since such things are knowable by the natural light, they logically come before faith and as such are called the *praeambula fidei*. We return to them under that heading below.

42. The First Vatican Council's dogmatic constitution *Dei Filius* can be found in Tanner, *Decrees of the Ecumenical Councils*, vol. 2. The relevant section can also be found in *The Christian Faith in the Doctrinal Documents of the Catholic Church*, ed. J. Neuner, SJ, and J. Dupuis, SJ, 7th ed.(New York: Alba House, 2001), no. 113.

Should the knowledge of God that men can come to on the basis of the things that have been made also be characterized as a "word" spoken by God through or in these things, announcing his being and providence to us? Of old there used to be contrasted the "book of nature" and the "book of scripture." But they are not books in the same sense, and the "words" of the book of nature are not true words. These "words" evidently presuppose the creative word of God, who spoke such that they came to be. But they are more like traces of intelligent activity rather than witnesses testifying to a mind. For those words, words of God properly and truly, we must open the Bible.[43]

Even so, it is very helpful to fix and contrast a natural "word" and a supernatural word of God, just as it is helpful to fix and contrast the interior light of reason for our natural cognitive operations, which can in principle come to know God, and a supernatural light for faith, a light that is a gift given in addition to the natural light. Then too, there is man made in, as it were, the natural image of God, just according as finite and created intellect and freedom image the infinite wisdom and freedom of God. And there is a supernatural image of God, established once we know the Triune God by faith and love him in charity. These images correspond to the first Adam and second Adam, Christ, from both of whom we derive the conditions of our estate before God, from the first by nature and sin, and from the second by redemption and grace.

All these doublets therefore articulate a sort of "double gratuity."[44] It is one thing for us to be created, and enjoy the gift of a being that is distinct from God's being. It is another to enjoy sharing in his life as friends, being taken up into the Trinitarian relations, being conformed to Christ, becoming Temples of the Spirit. It is certainly true that God from before the foundation of the world eternally intends for us this supernatural end, friendship with him now and vision in heaven. But for the bestowal of this second gift, there must be a recipient able to receive it, and so there must be a first gift of created nature itself, necessarily ordered to its own created end, even if always in the mind of God further ordered to himself in his triune reality.

43. See St. Thomas, *Super Epistolam ad Hebraeos*, in *S. Thomae Aquinatis Super Epistolas S. Pauli Lectura*, vol. 2, ed. Raphaele Cai (Rome: Marietti, 1953), cap. 1, lect. 1, at 1:2 (no. 15).

44. For which see Pope Pius XII, *Humani generis* (1950), no. 26.

Because the incarnate Word discloses both the Triunity of God and completes the pattern of salvation, since he is himself the end of revelation, the goal that we share in by the Spirit of grace, there is no further word God has that he can speak to us. For this reason, revelation is said to be "closed" with the death of the last apostle. *Dei Verbum* expressly recognizes and teaches this (no. 4). That is, the passing of those who in their own life and experience knew the Lord means the absence of anybody who can give a *further* witness, or a *renewed* testimony, to what Jesus said and did, or provide an augmented description of his career. There is not anything more to be supplied. Anything more is reception of what has already been said, said fully, and therefore only commentary thereon.

There have been several attempts by Catholic theologians to speak of an ongoing revelation, or a continual revelation of God through the ages of the Church via post-apostolic prophecy or in the self-experience of Christian believers. But the Montanists of the second and subsequent centuries were excommunicated, and Joachim of Fiore was condemned by Pope Alexander IV in 1256. Modernism was condemned on just this score by Pius X in 1907. Where contemporary attempts to vindicate the idea of ongoing revelation on the ground of religious experience do not fall out and out into some form of Modernism, they merely confuse the categories. Revelation is closed. Better to speak that way and keep our heads clear for whatever else comes after the death of the last apostle, which, whatever it is, is not divine revelation. This question touches on the question of the "development of doctrine," and will be re-visited there.

The closure of revelation with the death of the last apostle is an immediate implication of the traditional understanding that the incarnate Word just is the fulfillment and meaning of the pattern of revelation disclosed in the dual Testaments in words and deeds. He is the form, the content of revelation, who cannot be grasped except in unity with his Father and Spirit in the work of redemption, and who is not so grasped except in the Church. The Word is not only the content, the spoken, but the speaker, who makes the many words of prophet and apostle also words of revelation. That the Word "speaks" is said without prejudice to that line of the creed according to which the Spirit speaks through the prophets. The personal difference between the two speakings will be taken up in the chapter on Scripture. If Christ is both form and agent, he is also the end of revelation: the Church, his beloved and who alone hears his voice and only him, hears him also as her head, for she is his body, and makes *una quaedam persona* with him, as St. Augustine taught. The whole Christ is therefore the end of revelation.

CHAPTER 2

TRADITION

There are four things that follow upon revelation, that keep revelation present and complete it—completion in a sense other than its completion at the death of the last apostle. Revelation is first communicated by the words and deeds that make salvation history and which culminate in the Paschal Mystery. "The things we have heard from our fathers," however, "we will not hide from their children, but tell them to the next generation, the children yet to be born" (Ps 78:3–4). This handing on of the deeds of the Lord and the words that illuminate them is Tradition. Tradition is prior to and encompasses Scripture, wherein the deeds and words accomplishing revelation are written down. On the other hand, Scripture gives a surety to Tradition that it would not otherwise have. But there are other things handed on with Scripture—most broadly conceived, these include the Church's Rule of Faith, her manner of life, her worship. These things provide the necessary framework for reading Scripture, and only they enable it to be read aright. According as these things—faith, the Christian virtues, worship—constitute the Church, the Church herself is "handed on." But considered as the community of salvation, she is also the subject of tradition, the one who "hands on." Just as she is the only adequate recipient of revelation, so she is also the agent who hands on what she has heard, generation to generation. Last, she can, if need be, determine newly articulated and normative interpretations of revelation, which are called "dogmas."

None of these four things—Tradition, Scripture, Church, Doctrine—exists without the others, and part of the task of understanding each of them is seeing how all stand together, and none can stand alone.[1] We begin with Tradition.

As is the soul to the body, so is tradition to a social body. Elemental material components may come and go, but the soul remains and maintains the body in its unity and identity. So also, some men may join and others take leave of some group or society, but its tradition maintains it in its unity and identity. Tradition is, in this way, a necessary stratagem for defeating death. It serves as a sort of memory that is not buried with the individuals composing the society. Earthly companies and societies and nations, however, can count on no more than a shared past and human customs and conventions as the principle of their traditions, except insofar as, sometimes, a nation or state's identity may be particularly indebted to the natural moral law.

So much is true also for the Church, but there is an important difference. There are easily identifiable customs, laws, beliefs, practices, writings, together with a shared past that make the Church look like any other earthly society. But also, there is a transcendent principle of the Church's Tradition, the Spirit of truth.[2]

Dei Verbum and Tradition

According to *Dei Verbum*, revelation is transmitted by both Tradition and Scripture. But they do not pull the load like two horses harnessed in

1. See Joseph Ratzinger, *Principles of Catholic Theology: Building Stones for a Fundamental Theology*, trans. Sister Mary Frances McCarthy, SND (German, 1982; San Francisco: Ignatius Press, 1987), esp. pt. 1, sec. 2, "Formal Principles of Catholicism," for the circumincession of Scripture, Tradition, and magisterium.

2. The indispensable treatment remains that of Yves Congar, OP, *Tradition and Traditions: An Historical Essay and a Theological Essay*, trans. Michael Naseby and Thomas Rainborough (French, 1960, 1963; New York: Macmillan, 1966).

tandem. Tradition is prior to Scripture in that the apostles handed on the gospel by their preaching, example, and ecclesial organization before ever the New Testament was composed.[3] They bequeathed to the Church the gospel (no. 7.1), an institutionalized Tradition in the form of an authoritative teaching authority located in the bishops (no. 7.2), and Scripture, both Old (no. 7.2) and New (nos. 7.1 and 8.1). Both Scripture and Tradition preserve the apostolic preaching (no. 8.1). Tradition turns out to be the more dynamic reality, since it is the continual handing on, generation to generation, of what was first received in such a way that, with the help of the Holy Spirit, there is progress in understanding the words passed on and the realities they signify (no. 8.2). Scripture is therefore itself one of the things handed on, and this is true not as a mere historical fact, but quite formally, since the canon, taken as the list of the things that count as Scripture, is made known to the Church only by the Tradition of the Church (no. 8.3). The Book cannot be recognized in its unity and integrity except by the light of Tradition. So, both are "bound closely together" (no. 9.1) and make up "one deposit of the Word of God" (no. 10.1).

Just because the Scriptures meet us so identifiably and accessibly, so compactly and yet so comprehensively, extending from the first creative word of God in Genesis to the second coming of Christ, they can easily be taken to contain all that we need to know as to what God has done for those whom he has loved and what he wants us to do in response. They present God's word "in an unalterable form," and are "the supreme rule of faith," the council says (no. 21.1). But they cannot function as this sufficient and supreme rule without Tradition (no. 21.1), for every reading of the Scriptures, whether at mass or seemingly alone in *lectio divina*, whether this reading be proposed in a sermon or written down in exegetical comment and excursus or in articles and questions of the *Summa theologiae*—*every* reading is an interpretation in the sense that it engages and depends on the subjectivity of the one who reads. The only adequately informed subject for reading Scripture is one informed by the Rule of Faith and the Christian virtues and Christian worship.[4] And for

3. Vatican II, *Dogmatic Constitution on Divine Revelation (Dei Verbum)*, in *Decrees of the Ecumenical Councils*, vol. 2, *Trent to Vatican II*, ed. Norman P. Tanner, SJ (London: Sheed and Ward, 1990), no. 7.1.

4. Congar, *Tradition and Traditions*, pt. 2, chap. 5.

an *authoritative* interpretation, moreover, one that surely connects us to the very intent of the God who reveals, there is required the magisterium, the authoritative teaching of the bishops, which is the other bequest of apostolic inheritance. By God's arrangement, the council says, Scripture, Tradition, and the Magisterium "are so connected and associated that one of them cannot stand without the others" (no. 10.3).

The Contents of Tradition, the *Tradita*

If we think of Tradition purely as an act of "handing on," a *paradosis*, then all the things handed on that make Christian life and thought will be included in its scope, all the *tradita* will be compassed within it.[5] According to Congar, we can take "Tradition" in the singular to mean the transmission of the whole gospel, the entire Christian mystery, delivered to us as it subsists in Scripture, sacrament, institution, and the interpretation of all these things throughout the ages.[6] So, there is a content, what is handed on, and a handing on—transmission in act. What then are the *tradita*, the things handed on, the content of Tradition? Seven things can be distinguished.

First, the apostolic Church hands on a witness to Jesus of Nazareth, his preaching, his work, and its culmination in the Paschal Mystery. "I delivered [*paredôka*] to you," Paul writes to the Corinthians, "what I also received" (1 Cor 15:3). The content of this already "traditioned" news is that Christ died for our sins, was buried, was raised on the third day, and appeared to Peter and the twelve (15:3–5). Paul can also speak to the Corinthians in the same formal terms of delivering what he received from the Lord relative to the Eucharist and its institution (1 Cor 11:23–25). And he witnesses to the authoritative traditions of the Church elsewhere (1 Cor 11:2; 1 Thes 2:15; 3:6). Equivalently, we find the same thing in 1 Peter 1:12, which speaks of the things "announced to you by those who preached the gospel to you"; and in 1 John, we read "that which was from the begin-

5. Ibid., pt. 1, chap. 1; Everett Ferguson, "*Paradosis* and *Traditio*: A Word Study," in *Tradition and the Rule of Faith in the Early Church: Essays in Honor of Joseph T. Lienhard, SJ*, ed. Ronnie J. Rombs and Alexander Y. Hwang (Washington, D.C.: The Catholic University of America Press, 2010), 3–30.

6. Congar, *Tradition and Traditions*, 287–88.

ning, which we have heard, which we have seen with our eyes, which we have looked upon and touched with our hands, concerning the Word of life ... we proclaim to you" (1 Jn 1:1–3a).

Second, however, the central witness to the passion and death and resurrection of Jesus is given only within the frame of the Old Testament categories that render the meaning of these events and guarantee their saving truth. The core of the gospel that Paul already receives and passes to the Corinthians is that Christ died for our sins "in accordance with the *Scriptures*," and was raised "in accordance with the *Scriptures*" (1 Cor 15:3–4). The Scriptures are so intimately wedded to the death and resurrection of Jesus in the apostolic witness that the twain cannot be put asunder. The divorce that the very first heresies try to declare between Jesus and the Old Testament will strengthen the Church's grasp on the indissolubility of the bond. The Old Testament was already authoritative for those who became Jesus' disciples and apostles. But now it is authoritative in a new way, since it is now newly and with a certain closure to be read for its Christological sense, the sense it was ordained to have from the time the prophet opened his mouth or the scribe set pen to parchment.

Third, as *Dei Verbum* already noted for us, reading the Old Testament in the light of Christ, or alternatively put, remembering Christ in the categories of and in light of the pattern of revelation already recorded there, the Church produces the New Testament; and this too is a bequest to the subsequent Church.[7]

Fourth, there is the Rule of Faith, in which the core apostolic witness to the life and death and resurrection of Jesus, the principle of the Christian reading of the Old Testament, is preceded by a confession of faith in his Father as the creator of all things, and followed by a confession of faith in his Spirit.[8] In Tertullian's version, the work of the Spirit is folded

---

7. Christopher Seitz, *The Goodly Fellowship of the Prophets: The Achievement of Association in Canon Formation* (Grand Rapids, Mich.: Baker Academic, 2009), 35–36, where he explains that the New Testament just is a function of the apostolic witness and the Christological reading of Law and Prophets; for a very neutral historical treatment, see Rowan Greer, "The Christian Bible and Its Interpretation," in Rowan Greer and James Kugel, *Early Biblical Interpretation*, ed. Wayne A. Meeks (Philadelphia: Westminster Press, 1986), esp. 128–36, in the section titled "Christian Transformations of the Hebrew Scriptures."

8. Congar, *Tradition and Traditions*, 26–30.

into the action of Christ: He sends the Spirit after his ascension, and before his return in glory.[9] Here is St. Irenaeus's version, late in the second century, from the *Adversus haereses*:

The Church, though dispersed throughout the whole world, even to the ends of the earth, has received from the apostles and their disciples this faith: [she believes] in one God, the Father Almighty, Maker of heaven, and earth, and the sea, and all things that are in them; and in one Christ Jesus, the Son of God, who became incarnate for our salvation; and in the Holy Spirit, who proclaimed through the prophets the dispensations of God, and the advents, and the birth from a virgin, and the passion, and the resurrection from the dead, and the ascension into heaven in the flesh of the beloved Christ Jesus, our Lord, and his [future] manifestation from heaven in the glory of the Father "to gather all things in one" (Eph 1:10), and to raise up anew all flesh of the whole human race, in order that to Christ Jesus, our Lord, and God, and Saviour, and King, according to the will of the invisible Father, "every knee should bow, of things in heaven, and things in earth, and things under the earth, and that every tongue should confess" (Phil 2:10, 11) to him, and that he should execute just judgment towards all; that he may send "spirits of wickedness" (Eph 6:12), and the angels who transgressed and became apostates, together with the ungodly, and unrighteous, and wicked, and profane among men, into everlasting fire; but may, in the exercise of his grace, confer immortality on the righteous, and holy, and those who have kept his commandments, and have persevered in his love, some from the beginning [of their Christian course], and others from [the date of] their repentance, and may surround them with everlasting glory.[10]

The Trinitarian form is more distinct than in Tertullian. The center is the gospel of the incarnation of the Son of God. It is preceded by a recollection of Genesis and its confession of the one Creator God who is Father of Christ, and it is followed by the confession of the Holy Spirit, who inspired the prophets to anticipate the saving event of Christ's birth, his passion and death and resurrection, and his return in glory. In this form, the New Testament's apostolic recollection of Christ's life and death is

9. Tertullian, *The Prescription against Heretics*, trans. Peter Holmes, in *The Ante-Nicene Fathers*, vol. 3, ed. A. Roberts and J. Donaldson (Grand Rapids, Mich.: Eerdmans, 1980), chap. 13.

10. St. Irenaeus, *Against Heresies*, in *The Ante-Nicene Fathers*, vol. 1, ed. Alexander Roberts, James Donaldson, and Arthur Cleveland Coxe (New York: Cosimo Classics, 2007), bk. I, chap. 10, no. 1.

said already to have been declared by Old Testament prophecy. The two Testaments have one voice.

If the Rule enunciates the principle by which the Old Testament is read by Christians, the reading of which produces the New Testament, then we have already been speaking of it in speaking of the first three *tradita* above. But it *does* become distinctly formulated in the second century and should be distinctly focused.

Moreover, the Rule should be counted among the most primitive *tradita*. Like the creed of which it is the ancestor, it follows the Trinitarian form of the Great Commission in Matthew 28:19 and the order of the baptismal questions. The Rule can seem rather to be a distillation of Scripture than a principle of interpretation (for the Old) and a principle of composition (for the New). Taken in its material form as we have it now, we can indeed think of it so. But formally, it is more primordial. It is prior to the New Testament or at least coeval with it, as explained above.[11] The Rule therefore also continues to function as the basic presupposition with which to read Scripture, Old and New. As St. Irenaeus put it, it serves as the "hypothesis" with which to read Scripture.[12] If we pick up *Macbeth* with the idea that we shall be reading a comedy of the marital life of the new Thane of Cawdor and his consort, we shall be disappointed. But we shall not be disappointed if we take the Rule to frame what we will find in the Old Testament.

To be sure, the parts of the Rule's expanded version of apostolic witness are readily discerned afterwards in the New Testament. The form of the

11. Christopher Seitz, "The Rule of Faith, Hermeneutics, and the Character of Christian Scripture," in his *The Character of Christian Scripture: The Significance of a Two-Testament Bible* (Grand Rapids, Mich.: Baker Academic, 2011), 198–99; he writes: "The rule of faith is the scripturally grounded articulation, based upon a proper perception of the hypothesis of Scripture, that Jesus Christ is one with the God who sent him and who is active in the Scriptures inherited, the Holy Spirit being the means of testifying to his active, if hidden, life in the 'Old Testament' and our apprehension of that" (198).

12. St. Irenaeus, *Against heresies*, bk. 1, chap. 9. On the Rule as the hypothesis of Scripture in Irenaeus, see John O'Keefe and R. Reno, *Sanctified Vision: An Introduction to Early Christian Interpretation of the Bible* (Baltimore: Johns Hopkins University Press, 2005), chap. 2, esp. 33–41; see also John Behr, *The Way to Nicaea* (Crestwood, N.Y.: St. Vladimir's Seminary Press, 2001), 29–32; also, Behr, *The Mystery of Christ: Life in Death* (Crestwood, N.Y.: St. Vladimir's Press, 2006), chap. 2. Rowan Greer is very good on Irenaeus and the interpretation of the Scriptures, too; see "The Christian Bible and Its Interpretation," 155–76.

Rule is Trinitarian, as noted, from Matthew 28. And the parts are easily recognized. The second part is the gospel itself, and it explains who the Son, Jesus of Nazareth is. Its first formulation is found in the announcement "the Lord is truly risen and has appeared to Peter."[13] His rising overcomes his death, and the appearance is unto the forgiveness of the sins of those who betrayed him, Peter pre-eminently, but only as standing in for all of us who find a like forgiveness as did he. This is the "gospel" of Matthew 28—the Kingdom is present, yes, but only in the crucified and risen body of Christ, the Son of God, whose forgiveness and good favor are now announced in the apostolic witness. This Christ, however, is Son, and Son of the God who made heaven and earth—he belongs to the divine reality even as St. Paul evidences from earliest Christian confession, as for instance in 1 Corinthians 6:8. The specification of God as Father, Father of Christ, is a presupposition of the second article of the Rule. The third article of the Rule also finds apostolic formulation, where, for instance, Paul appeals to the Spirit in which the Galatians first knew the gospel (Gal 3:2), and explains to them how it makes us call God our Father, too (4:6), or when he speaks of the Church as the pneumatological fullness of Christ (Eph 1:23).

Fifth, the apostolic Church hands on an authoritative interpretive office, the episcopacy, a part of apostolic office that can survive the death of the last apostle, and that interprets the written deposit of revelation in both Old and New Testaments. That is, insofar as is possible, the apostles hand on themselves that part of their mission and office that *can* be handed on.

How does this authoritative office perform its work? By imitating the way in which the New Testament itself is produced. That production was governed by reading the Old Testament according to apostolic witness to Christ. That witness removes the veil over Moses' face, over the face of the Old Testament, so that we see Christ therein (2 Cor 3:12ff.). Subsequent authoritative reading of Scripture, of both Testaments, continues to be governed by the Rule of Faith and subsequently by the ancient creeds.

Sixth, there is handed on the typical, but also defining and normative place to read the Scriptures and interpret them, and that is the Eucha-

13. The self-attestation of the risen Jesus passes over into the word of apostolic witness; see Heinrich Schlier, "Kerygma und Sophia," in *Die Zeit der Kirche: Exegetische Aufsätze und Vorträge*, 4th ed. (Freiburg: Herder, 1966), 1:215–16.

rist. The Eucharist is defining, normative, in this sense, that no interpretation of Scripture is true if it cannot be read congruently with Breaking the Bread, doing the "this" that the Lord enjoined Christians to do on the night before he died. No a-Eucharistic or anti-Eucharistic reading of Scripture can be true.

The Eucharist holds this place in the interpretation of Scripture, not just because some pieces of the New Testament were almost certainly composed to be read just within that context,[14] but because the Eucharist makes present the action and the reality about which the Scriptures speak. The action of the Mass is the action of the economy of salvation as a whole, culminating in the Paschal Mystery, whose central act, the Lord's sacrifice at Calvary, the Mass represents in making present the Priest and Victim of that sacrifice. The Eucharist insures that, no matter our distance in secular time and space, we are speaking of no distant thing when we read the Scriptures. Rather, the witness of the Scriptures renders present the supreme Witness to the mercy of God, whose testimony is true of its own self, the Witness who is present in his human substance and reality wherever two or three gather in his name to celebrate Mass.[15]

Seventh, and last, there is also a form of life, especially, a form of charity, by which Christians live, and it, too, is a normative principle of correctly reading the Scriptures. This principle works in close conjunction with the previous principle, since the *res* of the Sacrament of the Altar, the ultimate reality it is ordained to produce, is nothing else but the expansion of the sacramentalized Body of Christ into the Mystical Body, re-charging the charity of this Body with the charity of the Head. So St. Augustine must therefore be right—no interpretation of Scripture is right if it makes charity cold, and all interpretations are right if they are in accord with it.[16] The Eucharist makes present the very reality that the Old Testament speaks of typologically, the Church of Christ, and the reality whose fulfilment both

14. Denis Farkasfalvy, OCist, *Inspiration and Interpretation: A Theological Introduction to Sacred Scripture* (Washington, D.C.: The Catholic University of America Press, 2010), chap. 4, "The Eucharistic Provenance of the Christian Bible."

15. It is enough to mention just the Eucharist, since all the other sacraments find their end and norm therein.

16. St. Augustine, *Teaching Christianity: De Doctrina Christiana*, trans. Edmund Hill, OP (Hyde Park: New City Press, 1996), bk. 3, 10/14–15/23.

Testaments speak of in hope, the Lord's return. Between these two senses of Scripture, however, there is needed the moral understanding of Scripture, which makes charity real, and which is exercised not simply in the Eucharistic assembly, but wherever Christians live and work. The form of charity that is to enliven all Christian existence is therefore fittingly picked out as a seventh thing passed on to the Church by the apostolic generation.

Tradition hands on Scripture and apostolic witness and its record in the New Testament. But the Testaments speak of the other things Tradition passes on, for it speaks of the elements of the Rule of Faith, of apostolic office, of the Eucharist, of grace and charity and the other sacraments that actualize them. In this respect, there is a sort of circumincession of Scripture and Tradition.

The end of revelation, *Dei Verbum* says, is to draw near to the Father in Christ through the Spirit (no. 2). This closeness to God is a closeness befitting our personal dignity, and so a closeness in knowledge and love, a knowledge of God as Trinitarian, a love of God in the power of his own love. It is a closeness God aims to establish generation to generation until the Lord comes. The object of Tradition, therefore, is to hand on the means of this closeness to God, namely, the word of God and the sacraments of grace and charity.[17]

Agents of Tradition

We have inventoried the contents of Tradition. In doing so, we were trying to think about the apostolic witness, the Testaments, the Rule of Faith, in their relation to each other and so have been thinking of the original agent of Tradition as the apostles and apostolic Church. But we must consider the agent of Tradition more fully.

Christ as Agent of Tradition

Christ himself, more justly than the apostles, should be thought of as the original historical agent of ecclesial tradition, and this is part and parcel

17. See Andrew Meszaros's paraphrase of Congar in "The Regressive Method of Ambrose Gardeil and the Role of *Phronesis* and *Scientia* in Positive and Speculative Theologies," *Ephemerides Theologicae Lovaniensis* 89, no. 4 (2013): 320, relying on Congar, *Tradition and Traditions*, 237–38.

of his founding of the Church. He hands on to the Church a way to pray, teaching us to call God "Father" every day. The Eucharist comes from his hands with the command to "do this," just as the double commandment of charity comes from his lips. Insofar as the New Law of charity is the grace of the Holy Spirit, then that, too, is his bequest to the Church: "Receive the Holy Spirit; whose sins you forgive they are forgiven" (Jn 20:23). Last, he hands on as well a structured Church, with a structure indicative both of the eschatological fulfillment of Israel (the Twelve) and the universal extent of the Church (the missioning of the 70 or 72).[18]

The Scriptures, too, pass to the Church from his hands. This is true of both Testaments. The Old is handed on to the Church, not directly from the synagogue, but from Christ, that is, with instructions on how to read it (Lk 4; and 24). It is not read by Christians therefore without the knowledge that the law, the prophets, the psalms speak of Christ. The New is written in the same spirit, under the direction of the same Spirit of interpretation. In this light, there is to be discerned once again a Rule of Faith that precedes the New Testament, and it is the Lord's Rule.

All these things pass to the Church so that she, too, may hand them on.

The Spirit and the Church

Evidently, when the apostolic Church hands on what she has received of revelation, she does so in the power and with the authority of the Spirit.[19] And subsequent generations of the Church do the same. The Lord's promise that the Spirit will help us recall all the things he has said to the first disciples (Jn 14:26) has always been understood as a promise fulfilled in every generation of the Church. The Holy Spirit, as it were, transcending every age, presides over the bequest each generation of the Church makes to the next.

This presiding of the Spirit is variously realized. First and fundamentally, every Christian parent is in principle competent to pass on the Scriptures and how to read them according to the Rule of Faith, together with the prayers and the form of charity, to his or her children. When a

18. On which, see Joseph Ratzinger, *Called to Communion: Understanding the Church Today*, trans. Adrian Walker (German, 1991; San Francisco: Ignatius Press, 1996), 24–25.

19. See especially Congar, *Tradition and Traditions*, pt. 2, chap. 3, "The Subject of Tradition."

mother teaches her children the Our Father, there is an act of Tradition. The more formal and official acts of Tradition that take place under the direction of bishop and priest, deacon and catechist, are, we might say, at the service of the act of Tradition that every Christian makes, if not always in words, at least by the example his or her life. Apart from these many countless acts of manifesting the truth of the gospel, it is hard to see how any more official acts of tradition and witness could maintain the deposit of revelation in a living way in the world.

All these things call into being the *sensus fidei* shared by all the faithful, an adequate norm of the interpretation of revelation, which does not gainsay the truth that the more official and formal and magisterial acts of traditioning have their own unsubstitutable role and purpose, since the two work in tandem.

Taking both Christ and the Spirit together, then, the divine missions establish the Church, which is commissioned to transmit the things, word and sacrament, which make for fellowship with God. The divine missions are the first cause, the first exercise of "handing on." They establish the Church as the proximate subject of the acts of handing on until the Lord comes.[20]

20. See Meszaros, "Regressive Method," 320, summarizing Congar, *Tradition and Traditions*, 265.

CHAPTER 3

SCRIPTURE

It is hard to imagine a long transmission and therefore a long ecclesial tradition of the word of God without writing, and so without the Writings, the Scriptures.[1] Revelation consists in words and deeds. Deeds, or facts, are difficult to fix in permanent form without writing, and difficult to arrange in some ordered sequence without writing.[2] As for the New Testament, the necessity of recording in some stable form both eyewitness testimony to the events of Jesus' life, as well as an accurate remembrance of his words, plays an important role here, as we shall see in more detail in chapter 6.

In chapter 1, it was maintained that we cannot fix the mind's reference to absent things and especially to the transcendent God without words, and it is also true that we cannot fix our reference to deeds without the written word. Once past, they are in themselves absent, though they may

1. For a brief but very satisfying theological introduction to Scripture, see Hans Urs von Balthasar, "Holy Scripture," trans. Jeremy Holmes, *Nova et Vetera* (English) 5 (2007): 707–24.

2. See Jan Vansina, *Oral Tradition as History* (Madison, Wis.: University of Wisconsin Press, 1985), 173–85.

maintain a presence in their effects. "The very notion of a historical fact depends on the possibility of writing," Robert Sokolowski observes, and so does the arrangement of facts in time, in a steady, reliable, temporally ordered sequence.[3] And evidently, we cannot really have just one historical fact without its relation to many such facts. They come in ordered manifolds without which we do not possess any of them. Without written records of facts, "what happened" is liable to dissolve into a sort of insubstantial hearsay, soon forgotten, unless, because of its importance, some sequence of actions is remembered within a tradition of oral discourse. The reliability of such traditions for the preservation of both words and deeds can be high.[4] But by the nature of the case, this reliability is enhanced, is kicked up to another level, when oral traditions work with written records. Such was the case for the early Christian preservation of the memory of Jesus. We can imagine that a wholly oral tradition might have served for many years. But it is difficult to imagine it surviving the tumultuous history of the breakdown of the Western Empire and the invasions of the Mediterranean basin and of Europe and the Near East, not to mention the challenges of disparate missionary endeavors, without copyist and monk. The utility of written records for the preservation of Christian identity, however, was immediately perceived, for one of the ways by which the Empire oppressed and persecuted Christians was to burn their books. Destroying the written Christian record was just as important for inducing oblivion as was silencing the Christian confession by death.

The invention of writing, therefore, something previous to the cultivation of philosophy and the maintenance of the peace of the Roman *imperium* as long as it lasted, can thus be seen to serve as a necessary *preparatio evangelii*. The gospel could not have been launched in the world with the success it has had without writing.

But of course the Scriptures do not read themselves. The Church reads them. And they are read rightly, according to the intentions of their

3. Robert Sokolowski, *Eucharistic Presence: A Study in the Theology of Disclosure* (Washington, D.C.: The Catholic University of America Press, 1994), 140.

4. For words, see Birger Gerhardsson, *The Reliability of the Gospel Tradition* (Peabody, Mass.: Hendrickson Publishers, 2001), 9–14; see the careful conclusion of Vansina, "Oral Tradition Assessed," in Vansina, *Oral Tradition*, 186–201.

authors and Author, only in the way the Church reads them, as giving access to Christ. It is this interpretative experience of them that first meets us and is the ground on which the questions of canonicity, inspiration, and inerrancy are fittingly addressed.[5]

Hermeneutics: How the Church Reads the Scriptures

According to the Tradition of the Church, the Church reads Scripture according to Scripture, and therefore according to both its literal and figural senses.[6] We have necessarily anticipated this in chapter 1 since we cannot speak of the pattern of revelation without noting the figural, Christological form of Scripture.

The Foundation of the Literal Sense according to Scripture

At the beginning of one of his expositions of Genesis, St. Augustine gives a short division of the kinds of things we find in Scripture.

In all the sacred books, we should consider the eternal truths that are taught, the facts that are narrated, the future events that are predicted, and the precepts or counsels that are given.

Then he asks:

In the case of a narrative of events, the question arises as to whether everything must be taken according to the figurative sense only, or whether it must be expounded and defended also as a faithful record of what happened.[7]

He says that no Christian will deny that a narrative should be interpreted figurally, and cites 1 Corinthians 10:11 and Ephesians 5:31 for his warrant. But he does not directly answer the question as to whether that is the only sense to be expounded. He takes it for granted that the text must be ex-

5. See Denis Farkasfalvy, OCist, *Inspiration and Interpretation: A Theological Introduction to Sacred Scripture* (Washington, D.C.: The Catholic University of America Press, 2010), 11–12.

6. See James Kugel and Rowan Greer, *Early Biblical Interpretation*, ed. Wayne A. Meeks (Philadelphia: Westminster Press, 1986), for the origins of Jewish and Christian "interpretation" of Scripture. For the patristic tradition, see Michael Graves, *The Inspiration and Interpretation of Scripture: What the Early Church Can Teach Us* (Grand Rapids, Mich.: Eerdmans, 2014.)

7. St. Augustine, *The Literal Meaning of Genesis*, vol. 1, trans. John Hammond Taylor, SJ (New York: Paulist Press, 1982), bk. I, chap. 1.

pounded also literally. Perhaps he expects that whoever takes up a book titled *De genesi ad litteram* will share this view. Still, what answer could be given to the direct question? The answer is apparent from the character of the Gospels, two of which expressly undertake to deliver eyewitness reports of the life of Jesus. The Gospels are evidently concerned to be read literally. But then this concern for the straightforward narrative sense of what the evangelists report of Jesus bleeds into a concern for the narrative truth of all the other stories picked up or alluded to in the Gospels, from Genesis to Exodus, to Samuel and Kings. So much we should expect from the character of revelation through words and deeds as expounded in chapter 1.

How is the narrative sense to be expounded? To be sure, with the aid of modern historical studies, and *Dei Verbum* addresses their utility in discovering the literal sense of all the books and pieces of the Bible.[8] The literal sense of Scripture is not available to one who approaches the Bible without faith, however, and the constitution says this, too. A right understanding of Scripture, it teaches, demands: (1) a reading in the light of the Spirit who inspired it; (2) attention to the content of the whole of the Bible in interpreting any single passage; (3) attention likewise to the Church and her Tradition of reading (no. 11). And over all this interpretive task presides the knowledge of faith.

All these things are required to get to the *literal* meaning of the Bible. And that implies, by contrast, that the literal meaning of the Bible is not rendered up to one who reads without faith. This is worth insisting upon, because of the common supposition that the literal sense of Scripture is something available to anyone who reads it. It is not. The supposition that it is so available is a dictate of the rationalist and Enlightenment context in which historical criticism of the Bible arose. This does not mean that such a saying as "Jesus went up to Jerusalem" (Jn 2:13) requires faith to understand it. But we must beware of too facile a distinction between sense and reference, where a reader may think he knows the sense of a passage while thinking it must be false since it has no reference. "The Holy Spirit will teach you all things" (Jn 14:26) will be false if there is no Spirit. Will

8. Vatican II, *Dogmatic Constitution on Divine Revelation (Dei Verbum)*, in *Decrees of the Ecumenical Councils*, vol. 2, *Trent to Vatican II*, ed. Norman P. Tanner, SJ (London: Sheed and Ward, 1990), no. 11.

the saying also be understood? The necessity of faith for determining the literal sense of Scripture is closely united with the very most fundamental view of revelation and of what revelation is about, Christ. If this is not believed, if the referent is not the Christ of the Church's faith, then the New Testament dissolves into the many incompatible senses of modern post-Christian exegesis and historical reconstruction. We have neither the truth nor the meaning of the text.

There is another way to get at this point. God, we say, following *Dei Verbum*, speaks to us in human words. If the human words are treated exclusively as human words, therefore, we will not hear them rightly. In the same way, neither should we think that we understand the humanity of Jesus on its own, apart from its union with his divinity, apart from its subsistence in the divine Word. The common presupposition for approaching the literal sense of Scripture, in other words, is a sort of hermeneutical Nestorianism: the Son of God and the Son of man are two distinct persons, and we can, in principle, have one without the other. But if that is false, there can be no presupposition that we can have the literal sense of Scripture without granting the possibility of its truth and where that truth is properly theological and supernatural.

Dei Verbum insists that the whole of Scripture must be read in order to understand any part of it (no. 12.3). Beyond being basic hermeneutical good sense, and understanding theologically that Scripture is one necessarily coherent declaration of God the parts of which must be mutually illuminating, this follows from chapter 1, where the one pattern of revelation is constituted from all the books of the Bible. The pattern is a pattern of the whole and not of any single part, though doubtless some parts are more obviously expressive of the form of Christ. Scripture itself attends to this very issue. In Deuteronomy, there is warning neither to add to nor take away any words from the Law (Dt 4:2)—it is a whole. The Book of Revelation closes with a solemn warning against tampering with the text (Rev 22:18–19). This injunction is rightly taken to cover the whole of the Bible which Revelation concludes.[9]

9. See on this issue Richard Bauckham, "Reading Scripture as a Coherent Story," in *The Art of Reading Scripture*, ed. Ellen F. Davis and Richard B. Hays (Grand Rapids, Mich.: Eerdmans, 2003), 38–53, with reference to Jean-François Lyotard and metanarrative.

The Foundation of the Figural Sense of Scripture

The Church reads the Scriptures as she was taught to read them by Christ. She reads them as finding the great pattern across the Testaments of the revelation of God contained therein, the pattern whose intelligibility is Christ.[10]

Could things have been different? In the *Philosophical Fragments*, Søren Kierkegaard asks us to consider whether it would have been enough for Jesus' contemporaries to have left us with the bare notification of their belief that God became man, lived and taught among us, and then died.[11] Kierkegaard wanted to extricate Christian faith from purported philosophical and historical demonstrations of it. But evidently, the Incarnation, the Triune God, cannot in that way be manifested to us, and they cannot be manifested as *for us*—the Trinity as our destiny and the Incarnation as the way to it—in so exiguous a way as a bare announcement. We argued in chapter 1 for the necessity of preparation before God could declare to us the truth of the incarnation of his Son.

In chapter 1, we also tried to explain why revelation must be in words *and* deeds. Revelation establishes communion of life and love with God and man. But human life and love are incarnate, and therefore even divine life and love, if it is to be shared with us, has to be sealed in public covenant, celebrated in visible sacrifice and meal, and in the Old Testament, maintained by the land that sustains life and by the conquest of the land. But covenant and conquest are not works of a day, and are appreciated only if anticipated, promised, and then let to grow and develop.[12] They are appreciated more acutely when the covenant faithfulness of Israel decays, and the land is lost. Positively, they show themselves by the preparation that slowly installs them in history, and by the time and thought

---

10. This is not necessarily to gainsay the continuing legitimacy of an alternative Jewish exegesis of the Old Testament; see Farkasfalvy, *Inspiration and Interpretation*, 191–93, with reference to the statement of the Pontifical Biblical Commission of 2002, *The Jewish People and Their Sacred Scriptures in the Christian Bible* (Boston: Pauline Books and Media, 2003) which speaks, at no. 22, of such legitimacy.

11. Søren Kierkegaard, *Philosophical Fragments*, ed. and trans. Howard V. Hong and Edna H. Hong (Princeton, N.J.: Princeton University Press, 1985), 104.

12. As Francis Martin says in "Election, Covenant and Law," *Nova et Vetera* (English) 4 (2006), "the spiritual sense of Scripture is based, not on a theory of text, but on a theology of history" (867).

and action it takes to work out the entailments of covenant life with God in a common life.[13] Common life requires law, and common life with God requires worship; and these are large things, and many faceted. All these things together, and including the human agencies of patriarch and prophet, priest and king, are as big and many faceted as the Old Testament itself. Nor can they make satisfying narrative sense without a description of our first estate and our fall therefrom, the story of how man proceeded from a good God to alienation and misery.[14] Only with that "pre-history" can the historical call of Abraham stand out for what it is, and only so do we have some explanation of the otherwise inexplicable infidelities of Abraham and his heirs, infidelities which educate them about the fidelity of God. The contemplation of the new thing God does with Israel, in Jacob's descendants, in the family's expansion into a promised nation, in the equipment of that nation according to covenant promise with law and land, king and prophet, is a long work, stretched out over centuries, and only in its exuberance adequate to show the majesty of a provident God who plans and rules from eternity.

The only thing missing from the Old Testament is a fitting conclusion. That conclusion is found in Christ. But then contrariwise, that conclusion does not make any sense on its own without the things that lead up to it. So, as Sokolowski observes, "Christian things ... could not have come to light simply and directly by themselves." They come as a fulfillment, as something that was prepared for; and their need to be profiled against the Old Testament is "a presentational necessity."[15] If the conclusion of the Old Testament is found in Christ, then like every conclusion, it provides a light in which what prepares for it is differently appreciated than without it. From Christ, there must in the nature of narrative truth be light cast back on what went before, and a corresponding reflecting light from prior Old Testament events which gives the categories in

13. See Sokolowski, *Eucharistic Presence*, 152–53, on the required breadth of the Old Testament to see the implications, results, requirements, scope of the Covenant, and to see the changes it works in what is possible in the actions and lives of men.

14. St. Thomas Aquinas, *Summa Contra Gentiles, Book Four: Salvation*, trans. Charles J. O'Neil (Notre Dame, Ind.: University of Notre Dame, 1975), chap. 55, no. 12, says that man had to be left long to himself and his frailty in order to know his need for grace.

15. Sokolowski, *Eucharistic Presence*, 144–45.

which to speak of Christ himself. Things will appear differently than they first did in the Old Testament.

This difference of appearance is not a special exegetical trick or procedure borrowed from the rabbis or from secular allegorical hermeneutics. By which I do not mean that knowledge of Rabbinic exegetical practice is not relevant to interpreting, say, Matthew. It is, however, secondary. Such practice is a means to an end. But the end is given in the reality and teaching of Christ. Thus, there is no secret and recondite hermeneutical key to the Christian interpretation of Scripture. Nor did the first Christians have to "test" whether the Christological reading worked, now for the prophets, then for the narratives of the Pentateuch, next for the Psalms to find out the extent of the transformation of the prior writings. In a flash, at a trumpet crash, the whole Old Testament and the things therein changed aspect. It is a difference of "presentational form," a phenomenologist might say.

So, the *realities* the Old Testament speaks of will appear differently. They will stand out, as the very things they are in their historical form and actuality, as harbingers of the New. And that is to say that the *text* of the Old Testament will have more than one meaning. It will have the ordinary meaning of any text, informing us about that to which it is referring. So when Nathan speaks to David, we understand how David's life is being shaped by the word of God delivered through the prophet. But while Solomon is David's son according to the flesh, so is Christ. And therefore, in addition to the original and ordinary and historical sense of the text, there will be another sense that it has, since the realities it originally has to do with find their finality in Christ. There will be, as the Church recognized from the beginning as she was taught to do so by Christ, a spiritual or mystical or typical or figural sense to the text. She will see the eternal Son of David in Christ and the Temple he builds in the Church. Because of his transcendence to history by his eternity and to the things that have been made by his creative power, the words of God that spoke originally of past things can, through these things, speak also of present and future and even eternal things.

The New Testament on Reading the Old Testament

That Scripture comes in dual Testaments is thus no accident, but a kind of necessity for communicating Christ to us, if we think how something so large should be conveyed to material, bodily, and sexual, social, political, historically conditioned creatures such as ourselves. The duality is, perhaps more obvious the first time we pick up the Book. But it is also obvious that the two parts make one whole, and the very organization of the Bible indicates this. Here, Matthew's position in the Bible is strategic. The Old Testament in its Christian arrangement ends with Zechariah and Malachi. The Lord says through Malachi, "Behold, I send my messenger to prepare the way before me" (Mal 3:1), and again, "Behold I will send you Elijah the prophet before the great and terrible day of the Lord comes" (Mal 4:5). We hardly open Matthew, when John the Baptist is presented in chapter 3, "preparing the way" (also recalling Is 40:3) and subsequently identified as the Elijah who was to come (Mt 11:14). Then further along, the one whom Zechariah described as "humble and riding on an ass" (Zec 9:9) shows up on Palm Sunday at Matthew 21:2. The parts of the Bible, the Testaments, come to us in a way such that their assembly is obvious—we do not need a schematic. The plugs of Matthew evidently fit into the sockets of Zechariah and Malachi—we know how the thing is supposed to work.[16] Matthew is much more crammed with connections to the Old Testament than the few citations just mentioned, of course. The explicit claims to fulfillment are markers for the larger claim Matthew makes, namely that the whole pattern of Israel's story is recapitulated and comes to fulfillment in Jesus, who keeps the old law perfectly and gives a law more perfect than that of Moses, who makes a final covenant, and who establishes a more astonishing divine presence, his own, within the covenanted people of God.[17]

All the Gospels address this issue of the connection of Christ to the Old Testament, Mark tacitly, the others expressly. In John's Gospel, the Jews search the Scriptures, and Jesus says to them, "because you think

16. See Leroy Huizenga, "The Matthean Christ, Center of Salvation History," *Letter and Spirit* 9 (2014): 11–29.

17. See Richard Hays, *Reading Backwards: Figural Christology and the Fourfold Gospel Witness* (Waco, Tex.: Baylor University Press, 2014), chap. 3.

that in them you have eternal life; and it is they that bear witness to me" (Jn 5:39). The Jews stop with Scripture, but should move on to what they refer to, Christ. The Jews seek an intra-textual salvation: "although the precepts of the Law are life-giving," St. Thomas says, "they nonetheless do not have life in themselves," and the Lord is saying that they are life-giving "only insofar as they lead to me, Christ."[18] The Scriptures, read transitively, so to speak, contain just this access to Jesus as the Son, knowing whom is to have life. "Moses wrote of me" (Jn 5:46), Jesus says, so that if we believe the witness of Moses, we will believe Jesus is the Son. But it was not only Moses who anticipated Jesus. "Abraham rejoiced to see my day; he saw it and was glad" (Jn 8:56). Abraham rejoiced at the promise of a son to be born of Sarah (Gn 17:17), and therefore Isaac stands forth as a harbinger of a greater Son of a greater promise.[19] This is an invitation to think not only of the joy of Jesus' birth, which John does not recount, but which Luke does (Lk 2:10), but also of the sacrifice of Isaac, which John does not allude to but which St. Paul does (Rom 8:32). To Abraham and Moses, the fourth evangelist adds Isaiah, who "saw his glory and spoke of him" (Jn 12:41). Isaiah sees the glory of the Lord at his call (Is 6:9–10), this glory, the glory of one who is "exalted and lifted up" (52:13), is the glory of the servant who was "despised and rejected by men" (53:3), who bore our sorrows (53:4), "was wounded for our transgressions" (53:5). The name of the Father is glorified (Jn 12:28) when the Son glorifies his Father by his obedience unto death, the lifting up from the earth (12:32–33), because his human obedience reveals his filial identity, and manifests him as the Father's name.

In chapter 1, we traced some of the connections of Old Testament wisdom to Jesus in Matthew and Luke. This is well developed in John, too, as we might expect, both from the mouth of Jesus and the pen of the evangelist. Jesus presents himself as the Bread of Life in chapter 6, the Bread come down from heaven. What sustained Israel in the wilderness, the manna rained down from heaven (Ex 16:4), is now a sign of a greater sustenance, the Bread of an eternal Life. But the narrative of Exodus 16

18. St. Thomas Aquinas, *Super Evangelium Sancti Ioannis Lectura*, ed. Raphael Cai, OP (Rome: Marietti, 1952), 5:39 (my translation).

19. See St. Irenaeus, *Against Heresies*, bk. 4, chap. 7, no. 1.

connects us to the meditation on God's providence in Wisdom 16:20ff., where God nourishes the life of the people in the desert. In Sirach 24:21 and Proverbs 9:5, wisdom itself is the bread that sustains life before God. Wisdom pitches her tent in Jacob according to Sirach 24:8, just as the Word among us in John 1:14. This constellation of texts is remarkable, as it leads us to connect food for ordinary life with the food for moral and religious rectitude, the connections all linked together in Christ. These connections spread out also to the water of wisdom in both Testaments.

The unity of the Testaments, or rather of Christ and the Old Testament, is quite thematic in Luke. There is a sort of climax in Luke 24, where the risen Lord supplies the categories, Old Testament categories, for making sense of the appearance of his risen body to the disciples. But this is not a single shot. It has already been prepared for by the Lord's reading of himself into the scroll of the prophet Isaiah at Nazareth in Luke 4 (cf. Is 61:1). And we see the implementation of this teaching in the preaching of the Church in Acts. Thus, when the Ethiopian eunuch reads of the Servant in Isaiah 53, and wonders to Philip about whom the prophet is speaking, Philip repeats the identification already made by Jesus in Luke 24. The Church, that is, faithfully rehearses the interpretation of the Scriptures just as it was taught by Jesus.

St. Paul is confident that what was written in the Law of Moses was written for our sake—for the sake of Christians (1 Cor 9:10). He gives Christian exegetes a compressed lesson in how to read in Galatians. Hagar and Sarah are two covenants. But this is an allegory. Hagar is Mt. Sinai, bearing children unto the slavery of the law, but Sarah stands for the Jerusalem which is above, and if we are in Christ, we are then children of Abraham not according to the flesh—like the people who remain in the old covenant—but are children of the promise, according to the Spirit. So we are free from the law. That is the conclusion that concerns Paul. But there are many leads to take up from Galatians: the Church as fruitful mother (Gal 4:26), the law of charity perfecting the Law of Moses, the distinction of the covenants themselves, which point to and reflect one another. Moreover, Paul crowns his reading of Genesis 21 with a quotation from Isaiah 54: "Rejoice, O barren one who does not bear; break forth and shout, you who are not in travail; for the children of the desolate one are many more than the children of her that is married." This is remarkable, for we see that, simply as regards exegetical practice, Paul is doing nothing not already announced in the Old Testament. Isaiah finds that the return of the exiles to a Jerusalem stripped of her children by the great captivity is already pre-formed in the gift of a child to a barren Sarah (Is 54). Isaiah finds a pattern in Exodus and creation itself for what God was doing in the return of the exiles to the Promised Land (Is 43). Paul, too, can find the greater pattern whose last link is Christ. Henri de Lubac explains:

All the words of Scripture refer finally to the unique Word: that is where the unity of the Book comes from. It is that in particular that constitutes the indissoluble unity of the two testaments. Just as the two cherubim of pure gold with spread wings that, inside the Abode of the Lord, faced one another at the two ends of the propitiatory, their gaze turned toward Him, so the Old and New Testaments, both one and the other, equally regard Jesus, and it is the same testimony that their voices alternately render to him, whose contrast is founded in harmony: "Jesus Christ, at whom the two Testaments gaze, the Old as what it awaits, the New as its model, both as their center."[20]

He is quoting Pascal.[21] But the two cherubim as the two Testaments facing one another because facing Christ—that's Gregory the Great, from his sixth homily on Ezekiel.

If we bear in mind what de Lubac has just said together with how the New Testament reads the Old, then we shall say that the literal sense of the Old Testament is *for* its figural sense: that is, the Old Testament is principally for figuring out the great pattern of the economy of salvation whose form is Christ. This will be important for thinking about both inspiration and inerrancy.

St. Thomas on Figural Reading

The figural reading of Scripture is witnessed in the New Testament, since the New Testament as a whole can be called the figural reading of the Old, a reading practiced by the Fathers of the Church and defended by

---

20. Henri de Lubac, SJ, *La Révélation divine*, 3rd ed. (Paris: Cerf, 1983), 161.
21. See Blaise Pascal, *Pensées*, trans. W. F. Trotter (New York: Modern Library, 1941), no. 739 (Lafuma 388).

the magisterium.[22] There is a classic expression of it in St. Thomas's seventh *Quodlibet*, where the traditional four senses are concisely explained:

Sacred Scripture displays the truth it hands on in two ways: by words and by the figures of things. The display which is by words constitutes the historical or literal sense; whence everything that is rightly construed from the very meaning of the words belongs to the literal sense. But the spiritual sense … is found or consists in this, that certain things are expressed by the figure of other things, because visible things are usually figures of invisible things, as Dionysius says. Hence the sense taken from figures is called the spiritual sense. The truth that Sacred Scripture hands on through the figures of things, however, is ordered to two things: namely to right belief and to right action. If it is ordered to right action, then there is the moral sense, which is also called the tropological sense. But if it is ordered to right belief, we have to distinguish things according to the order of what is believed. For as Dionysius holds (*Celestial Hierarchy*, c. 4), the position of the Church is midway between that of the synagogue and that of the Church triumphant. Therefore, the Old Testament was a figure of the New, but the Old and the New together are figures of celestial things. The spiritual sense, therefore, as ordered to right belief, can be founded in that mode of figuration by which the Old Testament figures the New; and this is the allegorical or the typical sense, according to which those things that happened in the Old Testament are interpreted as about Christ and the Church; or it can be founded in that mode of figuration by which the New and the Old together signify the Church triumphant; and this is the anagogical sense.[23]

22. For the Fathers, see especially John Cassian, *The Conferences*, trans. Boniface Ramsey, OP (New York: Newman Press, 1997), Conference 8, no. 3, and Conference 14, no. 8. For the magisterium, see Leo XIII, *Providentissimus Deus*, no. 15; Pius XII, *Divino Afflante Spiritu*, no. 26 (J. Neuner, SJ, and Jacques Dupuis, SJ, *The Christian Faith in the Doctrinal Documents of the Catholic Church*, 7th ed. [New York: Alba House, 2001], no. 235); Vatican II, *Dei Verbum*, nos. 15–16.

23. St. Thomas Aquinas, *Quaestiones Quodlibetales*, ed. Raymund Spiazzi, OP, 8th ed., revised (Rome: Marietti, 1949), quod. 7, a. 2, c.: "sacra Scriptura veritatem quam tradit, dupliciter manifestat: per verba, et per rerum figuras. Manifestatio autem quae est per verba, facit sensum historicum sive litteralem; unde totum id ad sensum litteralem pertinent quod ex ipsa verborum significatione recte accipitur. Sed sensus spiritualis, ut dictum est, accipitur vel consistit in hoc quod quaedam res per figuram aliarum rerum exprimuntur, quia visibilia solent esse figurae invisibilium, ut Dionysius dicit. Inde est quod sensus iste qui ex figuris accipitur, spiritualis vocatur. Veritas autem quam sacra Scriptura per figuras tradit, ad duo ordinatur: scilicet ad recte credendum, et ad recte operandum. Si ad recte operandum; sic est sensus moralis, qui alio nomine tropologicus dicitur. Si autem ad recte credendum, oportet distinguere secundum ordinem credibilium; ut enim Dionysius dicit, iv cap. *Caelestis hierarchia*, status Ecclesiae medius est inter statum Synagogae, et statum Ecclesiae triumphantis. Vetus ergo testamentum figura fuit novi: vetus simul et novum figura sunt caelestium.

The Canon of Scripture

The canon of Scripture is the list of books in which the Church has cognitive access to Christ. They are the books whose literal and spiritual senses give us revealed and certain access to Christ. So, the canon includes the books that contain the apostolic witness delivered with apostolic authority, and that is the New Testament. The canon also contains those books of the Jewish Law and Prophets and Writings which, read in light of the apostolic witness, speak of Christ prophetically, refer to those realities that prefigure him, and develop the categories in which Christ understands himself and the apostolic Church explains him; and those books are the Old Testament. The canon is the list of books that measure up to the Rule (*kanôn*) of Faith.

The Tridentine Decree

In this way, beginning with the content of revelation, it is easy to state why a book is on the list. It is more complicated to say how we know this. The

---

Sensus ergo spiritualis, ordinatus ad recte credendum, potest fundari in illo modo figurationis quo vetus testamentum figurat novum: et sic est allegoricus sensus vel typicus, secundum quod ea quae in veteri testamento contigerunt, exponuntur de Christo et Ecclesia; vel potest fundari in illo modo figurationis quo novum simul et vetus significant Eccesiam triumphantem; et sic est sensus anagogicus." I give my translation in the text. The reply to the fifth objection is helpful, too; I render it as follows: "these four senses are not attributed to Sacred Scripture such that they are to be spelled out for every part of it. Sometimes there are four, sometimes three, sometimes two, and sometimes only one. In Sacred Scripture, temporally later things are especially signified by earlier things; and therefore sometimes in Sacred Scripture something is said about a temporally prior thing according to the literal sense that can be spiritually understood about something later, but not the reverse. Now among all the things that Sacred Scripture narrates, those that belong to the Old Testament are first; and therefore those things which according to the literal sense look to the deeds of the Old Testament can be explained in four senses. But in the second place, there are those things that belong to the state of the present Church, in which those things that pertain to the head are prior, relative to the things that belong also to the members; for the true body of Christ, and the things that were done in it, are figures of the mystical body of Christ, and of the things that are done in her—as we ought to take what is exemplary for living in Christ himself. Also, future glory is shown to us in Christ before its time; whence those things that are said literally of Christ the head can be explained relative to his mystical body allegorically, and morally, by referring to our acts which ought to be formed according to his pattern, and anagogically, insofar as in Christ the way of glory is shown to us. But when something is said of the Church according to the literal sense, it cannot be explained allegorically, unless perhaps those things that are said of the primitive Church be explained as dealing with the future state of the now present Church; still, they can be explained morally, and anagogically. But those things that are said morally according to the literal sense are not rightly explained except allegorically. Those things that according to the literal sense belong to the state of glory can be explained rightly in no other sense; for they are not figures of other things, but all other things figure them."

most accessible but relatively late magisterial determination of the canon of Scripture, at the Council of Trent, was made in the midst of Protestant efforts to curtail the canon then acknowledged and in use by the Church. Luther questioned the canonical status of certain New Testament books that he thought doctrinally suspect or of no doctrinal weight (Hebrews, James, Jude, and Revelation), although he never excluded them. With regard to the Old Testament, Protestants recognized the Masoretic list of books—the list of Rabbinic Judaism—and distrusted the additions or so-called deutero-canonical books found in the Septuagint (Maccabees, Sirach, Wisdom, Esther, etc.).

Since the very sources of Church teaching and the theological elaboration of it were therefore in question in the sixteenth century, Trent's first decree was of a suitably fundamental theological nature (Session 4, April 8, 1546). The council recognized the gospel of Christ as "the source of all saving truths and norms of conduct." It asserted that "this truth and rule are contained in the written books and unwritten traditions." It next received and venerated "all the books of the Old and the New Testament" since the one God is "the author of both," together with the "all the traditions concerning faith and practice," whether they proceeded from the mouth of Christ or by the dictation of the Spirit.[24] And there followed the list of the forty-six and twenty-seven books of the Old and New Testaments. Putting Trent and Vatican II together, we can say that these are the books which record in written form the pattern or economy of revelation established by the words and deeds of the history of salvation.[25] Moreover, it is only these books that do so; the Church recognizes no other texts as inspired so to do.[26]

The confession that God is the author of these books, repeated in *Dei Verbum* (no. 11), does not, however, indicate the ground by which the

24. The translation of Trent is from Neuner and Dupuis, *The Christian Faith*, no. 210. Trent repeats the list of the Decree for the Copts of the General Council of Florence of 1442 (Neuner and Dupuis, *The Christian Faith*, no. 208), while the First Vatican Council confirms the teaching of Trent in *Dei Filius*, chap. 2 (Neuner and Dupuis, *The Christian Faith*, no. 216). The decrees of the Council of Trent can also be found in Tanner, *Decrees of the Ecumenical Councils*, vol. 2, and the decrees of the Council of Florence in vol. 1.

25. Vatican II, *Dei Verbum*, no. 2.

26. See the Congregation for the Doctrine of the Faith, *Dominus Iesus, Declaration on the Unity and Salvific Universality of Jesus Christ and the Church* (2000), no. 8.

Council of Trent recognized the canon, for which recognition the fathers of Trent adduced the simple fact that these books are accustomed to be read as holy and canonical in the Catholic Church.[27] Catholic Christians therefore know the canon on the authority of the Council of Trent. Whence, however, this customary reception? How did the Church originally know what to receive and what not?

Self-Declaring Books?

If we look at the books themselves, it can be seen that some books of the Bible declare themselves to be what they are. The Gospel according to Mark declares that it is the gospel (1:1), and therefore wraps itself in the mantle of the first words of Jesus that it records in 1:15, which fulfill Isaiah 52:7 and 61:1, already recognized as inspired texts (cf. the Lord in the synagogue at Nazareth at Lk 4:16–21). The end of Matthew's Gospel makes a similar self-advertisement. The Lord Jesus commissions the eleven disciples to make further disciples, which amounts to repeating the teaching and commandments of Jesus already recorded in the Gospel; and he promises to remain with them to the end of the age. The continued presence of the risen Jesus guarantees the authenticity of the apostolic preaching and so of Matthew's Gospel itself.[28] In the Old Testament, the Book of Jeremiah, like Mark, similarly declares upfront that it contains the words of Jeremiah, to whom the word of the Lord came (Jer 1:1–2). But other biblical texts do not do this. And some texts that do do this, like the gnostic texts that proffer further words of Jesus, quoted at length, were not accepted as canonical.

The Canonical Principle

If the label, even if present, is not convincing all by itself, perhaps the proof is in the performance, the performance of reading it: those books are canonical that give access to Christ, just as we have said. The trouble, how-

27. Nor does the decree of Pope Damasus in 382 contain any explanation of how the Church knows what books belong to the canon, nor do other early authoritative statements, such as the letter of Innocent I to the bishop of Toulouse in 405 or the North African councils of Hippo in 393 or of Carthage in 397 and 419.

28. See Farkasfalvy, *Inspiration and Interpretation*, 33–34, on the end of Matthew's Gospel: "The conclusion of the Gospel of Matthew is an appendix of 'self-authentication.'"

ever, is that, apart from the canonical books and whatever other magisterial or ecclesial teaching we have that will itself be measured by the books, we ourselves have no cognitive access to Christ. Our cognitive possession of Christ is strictly dependent on the books themselves. We said above that the New Testament was composed when the Rule of Faith intersected with the Old Testament. That same rule of composition is also the principle of the formation of the canon—that is, of taking reflex possession of what has been written under its informing sway.[29] It is a principle that finds expression in the New Testament, for as the Letter to the Ephesians has it, "the household of God," the Church, is "built upon the foundation of the apostles and prophets, Christ Jesus himself being the cornerstone" (Eph 2:20).[30] That is, Christ joins the prophets who foretold and the apostles who remembered; the one whom the apostles refer to by name is the meaning of the prophets. Here in embryo are the dual Testaments, more clearly recognized in the second century by Irenaeus.[31]

The problem for us, however, is that we do not now possess the apostolic witness and the Rule of Faith independently of the New Testament itself. Our position is not the same as the position of the apostolic Church, but is dependent on the apostolic Church; our cognitive access to Christ is wholly dependent on the faith of the first Christians. By the same token, their access to Christ was structured differently from ours. They were in the positon of reading gospels and letters while still in the possession of reliable and in principle verifiable oral traditions originating

29. See Farkasfalvy, *Inspiration and Interpretation*, 91, 93, on the principle of canonicity: the Church "recognized as constitutive of its beliefs both the apostolic traditions and the Scriptures coming from Judaism, which were regarded as holy and normative by Jesus and his disciples. In coming to this self-understanding, the Church realized that the Spirit who inspired the Jewish Scriptures was identical with the Spirit of Christ, who gave the Apostles their post-resurrectional faith and the courage (*parresia*) to understand and proclaim Christ as the one central event giving ultimate meaning to the whole divine plan of salvation" (91); the canonical principle functioned "as an a priori principle to facilitate the formation of the New Testament canon" (93). For the simultaneous and mutually conditioning work of the Rule of Faith and the Scriptures, Old and New, see C. Seitz, "The Rule of Faith, Hermeneutics, and the Character of Christian Scripture," in Seitz, *The Character of Christian Scripture: The Significance of a Two-Testament Bible* (Grand Rapids, Mich.: Baker Academic, 2011), 191–203.

30. See Farkasfalvy *Inspiration and Interpretation*, 92, on this passage with Eph 3:5, Lk 11:49, Rom 1:1–2, 1 Pt 1:10 and 12, and 2 Pt 3:2.

31. Farkasfalvy, *Inspiration and Interpretation*, 114; and see his "Theology of Scripture in St. Irenaeus," *Revue Bénédictine* 78 (1968): 328–29.

with the Lord and similarly verifiable reports of eyewitness testimony to his life. Just so, it was possible for them to read a new book as containing authoritative apostolic witness without having first of all to have captured that fact as such in a judgment of canonicity. If there is a distinction between finding a book that contains the word of God, and the express articulation of that fact, "this book is inspired of God and is the word of God," as a necessarily prior warrant for finding the word of God in it,[32] they could be on the first side of that distinction without any need to refer to some prior canonical judgment or make a judgment of their own. The passage of time, however, would make such a judgment, such an express capture of canonical status, altogether necessary for the Church to remain in the truth of the gospel. Sooner or later, therefore, there had to be express and common assurance that, because the apostolic Church found this or that book truly expressive of remembered apostolic witness, giving it access to Jesus as the Christ of the God of Abraham and Moses, then we, too, can be confident it will do the same for us.

Opinions differ as to when we can see an expression of such common assurance as to canonicity, for in the nature of things, such expressions can be more or less complete and explicit, and one can set the bar for clarity where one wishes. For some, a firm canonical judgment is not discernible until the first half of the fourth century, with Eusebius of Caesarea (d. 339/340).[33] This is too exigent. Some common assessment of the status of the Gospels and Acts was surely in place by the mid-second century, if we are to judge by what Irenaeus makes overt and confident appeal to in the latter part of that century as authoritative texts. The canon of the New Testament is therefore substantially in place certainly by the end of the second century.[34] Moreover, the Apostolic Fathers cite the words of the

32. See Karl Rahner, SJ, "Inspiration in the Bible," trans. Charles H. Henkey, in Rahner, *Inquiries* (New York: Herder and Herder, 1964), 70–1.

33. See Lee Martin McDonald's massive *The Biblical Canon: Its Origin, Transmission and Authority* (Peabody, Mass.: Hendrickson Publishers, 2007), 308: "Eusebius … set forth the first clearly identifiable listing or catalogue of NT Scriptures."

34. Greer, "The Christian Interpretation of the Bible," 110. For a mid-second century agreement on the Gospels, see Farkasfalvy, *Inspiration and Interpretation*, 103. According to Joseph Lienhard, the consolidation of the canon transpires from before Irenaeus to the first part of the third century, and at about 400 we have a "fixed" canon of twenty-seven books (*The Bible, the Church, and Authority: The Canon of the Christian Bible in History and Theology* [Collegeville, Minn.:

Lord quoted in the Synoptics as authoritative, just because they are his words. But Irenaeus takes the Gospels themselves, in their literary integrity, as authoritative.[35] For Irenaeus, canonicity is absorbed within the more original fact of apostolicity. It is more original because it is something that first presents itself to the early Church before any meditation on the conditions of preserving it in writing, and this is just how we should expect things to fall out when the idea of inspiration has yet to be applied in a thoroughgoing way to the apostolic writings.[36]

A Self-Closing Canon in an Apostolic Church

There are indications of a concern for canonical judgment, and even canonical closure, in the New Testament itself. We saw this above where Ephesians speaks of the prophets and apostles as the foundations of the Church. A sort of outline of a canon shows up in 2 Peter: "You should remember the predictions of the holy prophets and the commandments of the Lord and Savior through your apostles" (2 Pt 3:2), a rough table of contents for the Old Testament, Gospels, and Letters. Moreover, it makes sense that 2 Peter would suggest this outline, since, by announcing Peter's imminent death, it is also concerned to indicate that the time of receiving new letters with apostolic authority is over. It makes the same move as does 2 Timothy, which announces the departure of the Apostle, his finishing the race (2 Tm 3:6–7). Moreover, 2 Peter witnesses to the fact that Paul's letters are already received as "Scripture" in 3:16, where at the same time it claims for itself and 1 Peter a like status, since they are to regulate the reading of Paul. Second Peter is no later than 125 AD, and so is making judgments well within the afterglow of the Church's memory of the apostles.[37]

The Gospels themselves fell within that same glow of the Church's memory of the apostles. This is most apparent with Mark, composed ac-

---

Liturgical Press, 1995], 27–28). See also Bruce Metzger, *The Canon of the New Testament: Its Origin, Development, and Significance* (Oxford: Clarendon Press, 1987), 257–66.

35. Lienhard, *The Bible, the Church, and Authority*, 31–34; Greer, "The Christian Interpretation of the Bible," 115, who observes that it is first Irenaeus for whom the second Testament is the "New Testament."

36. See Farkasfalvy, "Theology of Scripture in St. Irenaeus," 333.

37. For this paragraph, see Farkasfalvy, *Inspiration and Interpretation*, 44 and note 35.

cording to common opinion from 66 to 70 AD in Rome. Why did it survive over against its revised form in Matthew (to take the ordinary view of modern critics on the priority of Mark to Matthew), whose addition of the citations and footnotes Mark supposed we could see without help, makes of Matthew a much more user-friendly account? It survived because of its apostolic, which is to say, Petrine, authority. Likewise, Luke is associated with Paul. And John, however we determine the authorship, is in surprising alliance with Mark. We will revisit this in chapter 6.

This concern for closure within the New Testament is dogmatically important: the recognition that something is in the canon—that is to say, that it is an authoritative witness to the revelation consummated in Christ—is itself a deliverance *within* the revealed word. This is a dogmatic point: *That the word of God has been fully spoken and that this can be recognized is a fact *also* revealed.*

The long and the short of this is that the acceptance of the canon is bound up with our reception of the teaching and forms of the apostolic Church as a whole. As with the reflexive possession by the Church of the other *tradita*, it is a matter of "coming to consciousness" of what is already *there*. We read as Scripture what the apostolic Church read as Scripture. We read the Old Testament as did the apostolic Church, reading it against the Rule of Faith in the light of the resurrection (Lk 24), "examining the Scriptures" to see if indeed "it was necessary for the Christ to suffer and to rise from the dead" (Acts 17:3, 11). We read also the initial records of apostolic witness, namely the apostolic letters, and the narrative syntheses of apostolic witness written in the last third of the century, the Gospels. We trust the first Christians' discernment of apostolic witness in a written form, the witness by which they in the first place became Christians by assenting to it with the assent of faith. Our acceptance of the canon is on the same basis and comes with the same warrant as our acceptance of a continuing apostolic office in the episcopacy, of the Rule of Faith, of the Eucharist and its shape, and of the commandments of charity. Our recognition of all these things is a function of our confidence in the Tradition of the Church.[38]

38. See Vatican II, *Dei Verbum*, no. 8, for the canon.

Now the apostolicity of the Church, and therefore also of what it took to be authoritative witness to Christ, is a matter of faith, a *theologoumenon*, and not simply a matter of history done with no presuppositions.[39] We do not discern the continuity of apostolic witness from the twelve to the writers of the Gospels to the subsequent Church apart from faith. There is enough evidence to make such continuity plausible. This is important, and the appeal to evidence, even if not coercive, maintains the continuity between reason and faith. But the apostolicity of the Church, and therefore of the apostolic witness as contained in the New Testament, are articles of faith rooted in the fundamental faith that the word of God has been spoken once and for all by the Word Incarnate and therefore cannot pass away. History necessarily bears on the intelligent assent in faith to such truths. But they are not just dumb deliverances of a positivistic history, and this includes even the apostolic character of the New Testament itself. There is a difference between the apostolicity of the Church as a mark of the Church—discernible with good human faith—and apostolicity as a property of the Church, something that flows from its essence as the Body of Christ and the People of God, apprehended by divine and Catholic faith.

The fact that Second Peter and the Second Letter to Timothy anticipate the closure of the time when the Church may expect further apostolically inspired missives is important not just for the history of the assembly of the canon of Scripture, but also theologically. In so doing, these letters anticipate our own epistemic situation. That is, they are both confident that the churches in Cappadocia and Ephesus will continue with undiminished faith in Christ and in fidelity to apostolic tradition even when there are no longer any apostles or even apostolic men to consult. Second Peter is quite explicit about this, since it is written "to those who have obtained a faith *of equal standing* with ours" (2 Pt 1:1). Faith does not depend on having seen and heard the Lord, or on having heard the gospel from eyewitnesses who did. The word of apostolic witness, the word of the written Gospels themselves, bridges the gaps in space and time with no detriment to what is grasped of Christ and his work or saving faith in it. This fact is affirmed, moreover, with dominical authority: in the Lord's

39. Farkasfalvy, *Inspiration and Interpretation*, 48.

saying to Thomas that they who have not seen but believe are blessed (Jn 20:21) as well as in the Great Commission at the end of Matthew. We have already said something about this capacity of human words to accomplish such transcendence of space and time, a capacity only they possess, and will return to it when we speak of the *praeambula fidei* in chapter 5, and when we contrast words and experience.[40]

Marcionism and Gnosticism

Two heretical movements of the second century moved the Church to take a more reflexive grasp of the canon. Marcion of Sinope did not recognize the God of Abraham and Moses as the Father of Jesus, and wanted to jettison the Old Testament, together with most of the New, except for the letters of Paul and the Gospel according to Luke. The perception that the Testaments are divided as between a god of justice and a God of mercy, as between a strict and arbitrary and often unreasonable disciplinarian and a compassionate Father remains a contemporary issue for evangelization and catechesis. There are strategies to meet these concerns in reading the Old Testament, and they are contained in making overall sense of what *Dei Verbum* and the Fathers of the Church call the economy of salvation, an economy established in deeds and words. First, the economy is, as Irenaeus held, an economy of the education of *fallen* man, an education inculcated and demonstrated in the Lord's dealings with Israel. The justice of God may appear very rough to us in such things as the slaying of the entire households of Korah, Dathan, and Abiram because of their revolt against Moses (Nm 16) or in the slaughter of the Amalakites (1 Sm 15). We do not share assumptions common in the ancient world about the corporate nature of human identity and responsibility. Seeing that punishment and reward are to be meted out to each alone on the basis of the merit of his own actions is an achievement within God's moral education of Israel (Ezek 18), but not presupposed to it, and not something that can be legislated in an instant at the dawn of her history. Second, the victories of the Lord of Hosts, as inflated and as bloody as they are in

40. For the New Testament's anticipation of bringing the gospel to those who can only hear of it, see Robert Sokolowski, *The God of Faith and Reason: Foundations of Christian Theology* (Notre Dame, Ind.: University of Notre Dame Press, 1982), 121.

body count, were read for their spiritual, tropological (moral) sense by the Fathers. "He shall seize and shall dash your children on the rock," the psalmist says, hoping that Babylon will be punished (Ps 137:9). But the Fathers dash the desires that spring from a sinful heart against the rock who is Christ. These challenges should be met head on in catechesis, else we do nothing but pay lip service to the truth that revelation occurs in and as history, making of history some tale in which everything is said adequately and clearly from the beginning, and in which there is nothing frightful, nothing appalling, nothing sinful to record. We will return to this when discussing inerrancy.

The second heretical movement of the second century was Gnosticism. While the response to Marcion was to insist on keeping the Old Testament fully a part of the Scriptures, the response to Gnosticism was to exclude its purported additions to the canon's New Testament half. These additions included texts that alleged a more secret teaching of wisdom intended by the Lord Christ for those who are moved by some spirit that despises the flesh. Like Marcion's wisdom, it was a wisdom that owed nothing to the Old Testament, which he, too, understood to speak of a god who is not the high god, transcendent to the material world indeed, a world he did not even make. In this respect, Marcionism and Gnosticism are both anti-material, anti-incarnational, anti-historical. The Gnostics proposed to find true wisdom in gospels purporting to be from the Lord Christ, discourses which, like Marcion, detached Jesus from the Old Testament, and detached him as well from the narrative of his own life, stretching from his birth to his Baptism, to the cross and to resurrection. In this way, the truth of the gospel could be boiled down to some few propositions about the higher wisdom and disdain for the flesh. The disdain could as easily be displayed in profligacy as asceticism, and the "wisdom" at issue need no longer find display in the bodiliness of the world or provide guidance for how to manage the moral narrative of our own embodied lives. St. Irenaeus, in responding to the strange picture of Jesus constructed by Valentinus and Basilides, defended both the canon of the Scriptures as the Church already possessed it, with no secret additions to be countenanced, and the Rule of Faith as the interpretive key to that canon.

Does Gnosticism have as contemporary an echo as does Marcionism? It does, in the ever renewed attempts to find some god within ourselves and within our own experience, so that the self can legislate for itself, and experience may be untutored by either Testament. The echo most clearly sounds in the multitude of modern and largely invented spiritualities, from cultivation of nature-pantheism to the resurgence of what is supposed to be some more ancient paganism, and many of which urge a sexual discipline that is indistinguishable from profligacy.

The question of the canon of Scripture involved in the Church's rejection of both Marcionism and Gnosticism says something important about the nature of revelation as a whole: both rejections in their own way tie revelation to history. Rejecting Marcionism is a matter of keeping the necessary foil against which to recognize Christ, and this foil is very much a matter of history, the pattern of words and deeds of the economy of revelation. Rejecting Gnosticism is also a matter of insisting on history, not the historicity of the Old Testament foil, but the historical character of Christ's life and career as testified to by eye witnesses.

The Inspiration of Scripture

Why Inspiration Is Necessary

The necessity of inspiration follows directly from the reason why a book is included in the canon: if some book gives us or contributes to giving us certain access to Christ according as he is the principal agent of the economy of salvation and according as he reveals the Trinity, and since the truths stating such matters are above the capacity of reason to know naturally, either by way of perceiving their truth or by way even of conceiving their possibility, then such a book must proceed from the breath of God, from the inspiration of the Holy Spirit.[41] This is an illation of proportionality: if the book gives us knowledge of what is above us, it must have a cause proportionate to that knowledge; that is to say, its author must be

---

41. On inspiration and inerrancy, see the recent production of the Pontifical Biblical Commission, *The Inspiration and Truth of Sacred Scripture*, trans. Thomas Esposito and Stephen Gregg (Collegeville, Minn.: Liturgical Press, 2014).

moved, both cognitively and volitionally, by the Holy Spirit. This motion of the Holy Spirit in the hagiographer is "inspiration."[42]

Inspiration means that, cognitively, the human author must be moved both to formulate the supernatural truth and assent to it; volitionally, the human author is supposed to love this truth, including what it is about (God and his economy), the one who makes it true (God), and those to whom it is addressed (the community of salvation, actual or potential). "Formulation of the truth" includes formulating it in various ways: in narrative, legislation, and doxology; in parable and in theological assertion and argument. These categories are themselves large. Narration, for instance, may be historical, as either witnessed, or reported from witnesses, or reconstructed. And narration may be invented. Theological assertion may be about God, man before God, Christ, the Church, the sacraments, and so on.[43]

Inspiration in the Bible

We would be led to assert the reality of the inspiration of prophet and apostolic preacher, of scribe and hagiographer on the strength of the above argument, even if there were not express assertions of inspiration in Scripture itself. The call narratives of Moses and of such prophets as Isaiah and Jeremiah, for instance, are assertions that God will give them the words they are to speak. Prophetic oracles regularly announce the prophet's experience that "the word of the Lord came to me." Second Peter 1:21 speaks of the inspiration of *prophets*: "men moved by the Holy Spirit spoke from God." This is sometimes called "subjective inspiration." Second Timothy 3:15–16 speaks of the *texts* of Scripture as inspired: "all scripture is inspired by God," and this is "objective inspiration."

42. For the Fathers and medievals, the category of "inspired writing" is broader than the category of "Scriptural-canonical book"; conciliar and patristic texts could be "inspired," although St. Thomas tended to make the categories coextensive; see Yves Congar, *Tradition and Traditions: An Historical Essay and a Theological Essay*, trans. Michael Naseby and Thomas Rainborough (New York: Macmillan, 1966), 119ff., and for St. Thomas, 93.

43. Pierre Benoît's distinction between revelation as God's direction of a speculative judgment in prophet or apostle and inspiration as God's direction of the practical judgments attendant upon expressing speculative judgments is relevant; see his *Aspects of Biblical Inspiration*, trans. J. Murphy-O'Connor, OP, and S. K. Ashe, OP (Chicago: Priory Press, 1965), 121–22.

Can one hold the *text* to be inspired without implying that its human author is inspired? Can we have objective inspiration without subjective inspiration? If we could, that would solve some puzzles of interpretation.[44] But this seems difficult to reconcile with *Dei Verbum*, according to which God uses human authors, so acting in them and through them—inspiring them—that they wrote "all the things and only the things he willed" (no. 11). As we will see, however, it is not always easy to pick out the "subject" of subjective inspiration.

Since the texts of Scripture are composed of words, and since it is evident at Matthew 19:4–5 that Christ takes such texts as Genesis 2:24 as a word spoken by God, then it follows that we may speak of "verbal inspiration." This too seems also to follow from *Dei Verbum*, number 11: "All that the inspired authors, or sacred writers, affirm, should be regarded as affirmed by the Holy Spirit."

The Double Authorship of the Bible

If the hagiographer or prophet or apostle speaks in Scripture, and if God speaks in Scripture, the very same words, how are these speakings related to one another? And if the human writer is an author of the text, is God also to be styled an author of the text? Because the books are written under the inspiration of the Holy Spirit, *Dei Verbum* concludes that "they have God as their author" (no. 11).[45] But what God authored is also authored by men. God "chose and employed [*adhibuit*]" men for the writing of these books, men who "made full use [*utentes*] of their powers and faculties," and so are "true authors," consigning to writing just what and no more than what "God acting [*agente*] in and through them" wanted them to write (*Dei Verbum*, no. 11). God is an "author," therefore, but the hagiographers are "*true* authors."

Dei Verbum's way of speaking, where God is an "author" but the hagiographers are "*true* authors" is an invitation here to take "author" analogi-

44. John R. T. Lamont, *Divine Faith* (Aldershot, UK: Ashgate, 2004), 155–56.

45. Previous magisterial declarations of divine authorship and inspiration can be found in the Decree for the Copts of the Council of Florence (Neuner and Dupuis, *The Christian Faith*, no. 208), Trent (Neuner and Dupuis, *The Christian Faith*, no. 210), the First Vatican Council (Neuner and Dupuis, *The Christian Faith*, no. 216), and the letter of Leo XIII, *Providentissimus Deus* of 1893 (Neuner and Dupuis, *The Christian Faith*, nos. 226–27).

cally.[46] God and the hagiographer are not joint authors. God does not put pen to paper; the human authors do. They do so using all their human faculties and powers of conceiving and articulating and expressing what they want to say. Just so, they are true authors. Modern theologians, lest we be misled into supposing God is understood as a "literary author" of the Bible, like to distinguish God and the human writer as instigator and author, or as producer and author, as *Urheber* and *Verfasser*.[47] The Latin *auctor* is susceptible of both meanings, and this calls for thinking out the relations between God and Jeremiah, God and St. Matthew. In this way, we will not make the mistake of supposing God wrote a letter to Philemon.[48]

The analogical sense of God's authorship keeps us also from supposing that what the human author asserts, which *Dei Verbum* tells us at number 11 is asserted by the Holy Spirit, is asserted in the same way as the human author asserts it. This is important for understanding both sense and inerrancy.

The Human Author as Instrument of God

God "employs" the "true human authors," or we might say applies them to their work, and "acts in and through them," according to *Dei Verbum*. The language of "employing" or "applying" is congenial to the Thomist account of prophecy, according to which God would make of the prophet or hagiographer his instrument.[49] The distinction of principal agent-instrumental agent is one of four analogies that Louis Alonso-Schökel notes in his landmark study, *The Inspired Word*. The Holy Spirit is said in tradition also to "dictate" the Scriptures. The human writer is likened also, third, to a messenger. And just as a human author of fiction may express himself through the characters he fashions, so God may express himself in the same way; and this has the important feature that the liter-

---

46. Farkasfalvy, *Inspiration and Interpretation*, 214–15. *Verbum Domini*, no. 19, however, switches the attribution, surely more faithfully respecting the *primus analogans* of the analogy: "one recognizes the full importance of the human author who wrote the inspired texts and, at the same time, God himself as the true author [*verus auctor*]." Benedict XVI, *The Word of God in the Life and Mission of the Church: Verbum Domini* (Frederick, Md.: The Word Among Us, 2010).

47. Rahner, *Inspiration in the Bible*, 13–14.

48. Farkasfalvy, *Inspiration and Interpretation*, 213ff.

49. For which see Benoît, *Aspects of Biblical Inspiration*.

ary character does not always assert the very things the author believes are true.[50]

If we take the dictation or messenger model strictly, then it turns out that the hagiographer is not really an author, but only a secretary or a servant. *Dei Verbum* excludes that understanding by holding that the hagiographers are "true authors." There is a diametrically opposite error, according to which God's inspiration is nothing but the Church's assurance subsequent to the entirely human production of the book that it does not contain any error. This view evacuates God of any authorial role, and calls on no special will or operation by which what is recorded is what he directly wills and nothing but that. This view of inspiration as "subsequent approbation" was maintained in the sixteenth century by Sixtus of Siena and was condemned at the First Vatican Council. The very similar view of "negative assistance" was likewise condemned at that council, for if the words of the book are really God's words, then he does more than intervene in order to save the book from error. This is another reason for saying that there can be no objective inspiration without subjective inspiration; some human subject or subjects produce the text, and inspiration must first touch them.

In fact, the "dictation" or the "messenger" models are not really alternatives to the "instrument" model. A secretary who takes dictation is after all still nothing but an instrument of the one who dictates. He lends his ears and hands to the author. A messenger lends his legs, and he is an instrument, too. Alonso-Schökel illustrates the instrument analogy from the Fathers of the Church, where the instrument is a flute (Athenagoras), a pen (Jerome), or a hand, the paradigmatic human instrument (Augustine).[51] So, all these ways think of God using an instrument. The decisive issues are how to think about God's causing of created causes, and what the capacities of the instrument are. If we follow *Dei Verbum*, these capacities will include all the powers of the human instrument, meaning

50. Louis Alonso-Schökel, *The Inspired Word: Scripture in the Light of Language and Literature*, trans. Francis Martin (Spanish, 1966; New York: Herder and Herder, 1965): instrument, 58ff.; dictation, 66ff.; messenger, 73; and an author's created characters, 73ff. The last analogy may help with understanding Ecclesiastes, if we take the Preacher not only as the human author's creation, but as God's.

51. Alonso-Schökel, *The Inspired Word*, 59–60.

especially that his mind and will will be "used" by God. And only in that way, then, will it be true to say that the human instrument is a "true author." As to God's causality, it enables (by creation), sustains (by preservation), and moves (as both agent and end) the created agent to do precisely the things the agent does according to its nature.[52] But this is true also for Euclid's production of his geometry. If the text in question in some way conveys some more-than-natural truth which is God's personal word, then a more personal directing of the human mind to things above and beyond its natural scope is required; a higher end will require a more-than-natural divine movement.

When we think about the relation of the revealing God to the human author through whom he is accomplishing his revelation in written form, we can get mixed up either about the sovereign freedom of God to accomplish what he will through this human agent, or about the freedom and integrity of that agent. But it is not as if the inspiration of the books of the Bible is the only place where we have to think out what such a dependent, causal relation of the human agent to God does and does not imply. Every ordinary exercise of human agency is created and sustained by God in its every moment, but without prejudice to the natural properties of this exercise, one of which is freedom. God's causality is sovereign, and its sovereignty includes its transcendence to worldly categories, just as it includes its transcendence to the world itself. So, St. Thomas says, God arranges not only for all events, but also for both the necessity of necessary events, and the contingency of contingent events, including the event of human choice.[53] God's causality does not impede our agency but enables it, and according as we cooperate with him by obeying the natural law, our freedom becomes more free, more of what it wants to be as made in the image of God's freedom.

Things do not change in the supernatural order. When we make the assent of faith, we are not doing something contrary to reason, and God, who gives us the light of faith, is not deforming our mind or coercing our will. Rather, he is enabling our mind to be more of what it is as mind, more truthful, and precisely by embracing the most important truths,

52. For a short treatment, see St. Thomas Aquinas, *Summa theologiae* I, qq. 103–5.
53. St. Thomas Aquinas, *Summa theologiae* I, q. 19, a. 8.

truths about God and Christ and human destiny, truths that are above it, and by embracing them on the ground that the Truth has revealed them. This makes mind more mindful.

Now, inspiration is, as it were, an augmented case in comparison with faith, a greater supernatural empowerment of our mind and will compared to the empowerment enjoyed in faith and charity. The greater activity of the hagiographer in actively composing is undergirded by a greater divine activity than in the more simple act of faith, which is rather more receptive by comparison. But just as the divine activity of providing the light of faith, which gives us a greater share in the *Prima Lux* of which the natural light of the mind is a share befitting human nature, does not diminish human mind or freedom but lifts it up into a larger arena of operation, such that we think the thoughts of God's secret counsel for the salvation of man and rejoice in the freedom to cooperate with infinite Love, so also neither does the light of inspiration diminish or impede the mental capacity or freedom of the hagiographer whose task it is first to think and formulate those divine thoughts. When St. Paul expresses outrage at how swiftly the Galatians abandon the gospel, he does so with his own counsel and freedom, but his astonishment speaks a word of God, a word God himself desires and stands by as revealing his own mind to us about the non-negotiable character of the gospel. Again, when Paul writes a letter to Philemon, and freely, we may decline to say that God has written to Philemon. But there is a word of God being spoken that God wants to be heard, first by Philemon, but also by us, about the equality of Christians. And in both cases, inspiration does not diminish Paul, but makes him more himself.

Dialogical Inspiration

The emphasis of Vatican II on the freedom and personal engagement of the human author of Scripture can be indicated in another and very consequential way. This way was proposed by Joseph Ratzinger at the time of the council, but it did not find its way into the text.[54] It surfaced when Cardinal Josef Frings asked Ratzinger to comment on the draft schema

54. A partial expression can be found in Benedict XVI, *Verbum Domini*, nos. 22 and 24.

De fontibus revelationis.[55] Ratzinger noted its appeal to St. Augustine and his teaching that the Lord *dictated* to the evangelists whatever he wanted us to know about his deeds and words.[56]

Ratzinger observed that the dictation image is something Augustine borrowed from Philo of Alexandria. With Philo, it was associated with a sort of complete overpowering of the human instrument in ecstasy, and so very definitely subverted any view according to which the human writer exercised his own reason and will.[57] Ratzinger suggests instead that an account of the inspiration of the Christian Scripture should be guided by what Scripture shows us, namely that Scripture itself is "the result of God's historical dialogue with human beings."[58] Dialogue connotes the responsibility and freedom of both partners. What would a dialogical view of inspiration look like?

Two steps lead us to this view. First, Jesus says at Matthew 19:4–5 that "he [God] who made them from the beginning made them male and female, and said, 'For this reason a man shall leave his father and mother and be joined to his wife.'" "For this reason," etc. is Genesis 2:24, where the words are not represented as being spoken by God, but are the words of the writer of Genesis. But the Lord takes it that even the words God is not evidently represented as speaking are nonetheless God's word; *Dei Verbum* repeats this traditional view according to which the Scriptures "contain and are the word of God" (no. 24). But second, recall the dialogues between God and some human being, dialogues which are then included *within* Scripture itself. God calls Samuel in 1 Samuel 3:10, "Samuel! Samuel!" And Samuel answers God: "Speak, for thy servant hears." Is Samuel's answer to God also part of God's word, God-speaking-to-us? Yes, it is. Samuel shows us an exemplary promptness and obedience before God, and the inspired writer of Samuel includes that in what he contributes to the written word of God. Not all responses of men are

55. See Jared Wicks, SJ, "Six Texts by Prof. Joseph Ratzinger as *Peritus* before and during Vatican Council II," *Gregorianum* 89 (2008): 233–311; see text 4: "On the Schema on the Sources of Revelation: Address to the German-Speaking Bishops, October 10, 1962."

56. The citation is to St. Augustine's *De Consensu Evangelistarum* 1, 35 (PL 34, 1070).

57. See Aidan Nichols, OP, *The Shape of Catholic Theology* (Collegeville, Minn.: Liturgical Press, 1991), 114.

58. Wicks, "Six Texts," 279.

exemplary in the sense of things to be imitated. Other responses are included in Scripture, but as warnings to us. The word of God includes the description of Saul's disobedience to the word of God spoken by Samuel in 1 Samuel 15. The conversations and mutual relations between God and some human being, considered as whole exchanges, become the "word of God." The conversation between God and Job at the end of Job is entirely the word of God, including Job's expressions of humility and unworthiness before the transcendence of God.

But now—a third step—we expand our time frame. Some of these conversations and enacted relations between God and man are very large and take place over many years. The Book of Isaiah records a long conversation between the Kingdom of Judah and God that extends from the time of King Uzziah to the return of the exiles from Babylon. Just as in a human conversation, re-action responds to action. What God speaks to us in the words and deeds that Isaiah (and those who take up his mantle) records or alludes to depends on what the kings said and how the people understood and accepted their exile as punishment for faithlessness. It is not only the human response that is conditioned by God's prior word. God's word and action are also conditioned by the human word, the human condition, they in turn respond to. And this great conversation between God and Judah presupposes prior and subsequent ones of equal magnitude and complexity.

In this way, a dialogical view of inspiration emerges, a complement to the dialogical course of the words and deeds in which the economy of revelation is constituted in history, as was seen in chapter 1. Inspiration bears on the very writing down of the words of Scripture, of course. And sometimes what is written down is itself a dialogue, short or long as the case may be. But also, the hagiographer himself can play a role in the dialogical unfolding of the word of God, as Isaiah and the other prophets did, as did also, to take another instance, the Chronicler in his re-touching of the history recorded in Kings. The Chronicler speaks another, subsequent, but also inspired, word about the kingdoms of Judah and Israel, one formed in the context of different theological concerns and themes. The word of God, through the hagiographers themselves, comments on the word of God and furthers its articulation.

Taking note of the dialogue between God and Israel, and describing inspiration itself as dialogical, does not insert God into time and make him subject to change. It inserts the word of God into history and makes it subject to changes dictated by the free response of saint and sinner, holy and sinful communities. Whatever good there is in the universe, of nature or grace, is willed by God in the same act by which he wills his own goodness, for all such goods are likenesses of the divine essence, nor does this remove the contingency of those likenesses of divinity that are created free acts.[59] Nor does the fact that all good things, including all good and free decisions and responsive actions of men, are willed by God in the one act by which he wills his own infinite goodness mean that the only source of the drama to which the dialogue gives rise is sin, the culpable refusal of man's response to God, which is not willed by God but only foreseen. For within the good responses to God's word and his invitation, there can be responses of varying degrees of generosity; and therefore the shape of dialogue and the narrative and the economy really depend on human freedom, and not just sinful human freedom. This is important to point out, lest in thinking about the shape of the dialogue, the narrative, the pattern as a whole, we think that sin somehow contributes to make things more dramatic, more beautiful, better, more interesting than they would otherwise be. While this or that aspect of the goodness of the universe may in fact depend on God's response to sin, the goodness and splendor of the universe does not so depend on the absolute evil of sin such that things are better with sin than without.

What is the advantage of viewing things dialogically, in contrast to the dictation view? In the first place, it takes account of the properly personal character of the hagiographers themselves, and closes off any sort of ecstatic or mechanical view of the human composition of the holy books.[60] Second, it integrates the work of the hagiographer into the very pattern of revelation itself, the pattern unfolded by the words and deeds

59. For the three clauses of this sentence, see St. Thomas Aquinas, *Summa Contra Gentiles, Book One: God*, trans. Anton Pegis (Notre Dame, Ind.: University of Notre Dame Press, 1975), chaps. 76, 75, and 85.

60. St. Thomas Aquinas, *Summa Contra Gentiles: Book Three: Providence, Part II*, trans. Vernon J. Bourke (Notre Dame, Ind.: University of Notre Dame, 1975), chap. 154, *ad fin.*, teaches that prophecy is not ecstatic.

of salvation history.[61] As the case may be, one inspired writer may be more active in the history itself than another. Some are more strictly recorders of prior dialogue exhibited in word and deed. Others more obviously contribute to the dialogical construction of the economy of revelation. Third, it more manifestly inserts revelation and inspiration into that context where we see that the personal reality of God is communicated to prophet, to hagiographer, to Israel, and to us. Dialogue is an exchange of information and news. But also, it is a manifestation of mutual respect, of mutual trust, and of mutual love. In this regard, it is proper to speak of revelation, and inspiration, as events of personal encounter and exchange that, by engaging the mind, also engage the will. Fourth, it conduces to making us realize that any single word of God must be interpreted in the context of the whole, where other parts suggest other points of view, other concerns, even re-directions of the sense of things (as with Chronicles relative to Kings). Fifth, it lets the individual prophets and hagiographers assume their own fully contextualized place as speaking from and to the People of God as a whole. The role of the People of God as a whole is thereby indicated in the composition of the books of Scripture.[62] And this prepares us to see the role that the People of God will have, especially via the magisterium, in the interpretation of Scripture.[63]

Last, it brings us to a very wonderful appreciation of the climax of revelation in Christ. How can we know him without following all the conversations he had with his disciples and his opponents, and all the moral transactions between them? He is revealed in what he says, in how he responds, in how he reacts, and in how people react to him. But also, while he certainly speaks from and for God his Father, he also speaks from and for us, and as a representative of unsurpassable authority. He is both "Son of God" and "the Son of man." Therefore, he instances a sort of God-man dialogue than which no greater can be conceived when, at Gethsemane, he speaks to his Father and listens to him. Just here, a dialogue between Father and Son in the Spirit reveals to us the Trinitarian relations, and the

---

61. Vatican II, *Dei Verbum*, no. 2.
62. Pope Benedict XVI, *Jesus of Nazareth: From the Baptism in the Jordan to the Transfiguration*, trans. Adrian J. Walker (New York: Doubleday, 2007), xx–xxi.
63. Lamont, *Divine Faith*, 176.

way we are ourselves to be taken up into those relations, by imitating and sharing in the obedience of the incarnate Son.

The writers of the New Testament should also be thought of in this dialogical way. The ultimate and final word of God is spoken in the Word made flesh, true. But the Church answers that word, repeats it, in the Spirit inspired books of the New Testament. God the Father speaks to us by the incarnate Word. And the Bride inspired by the Spirit hears this Word, recapitulates it in the New Testament, and says "Maranatha; Come, Lord Jesus" (Rv 22:17, 20).

Individuals or the Community?

Just as we have made the Church the perfect reader of the Scriptures who knows how to read according to the economy of revelation and with the Rule of Faith as the key to unlock them, and just as we impute to the apostolic and post-apostolic Church the ability to recognize the canon of Scripture and most crucially the canon of the New Testament, so the dialogical character of inspiration just outlined, where the people as a whole figure as a partner in the conversation, seems to make the subject of inspiration first Israel and subsequently the Church of the apostolic age. We thus make the earliest communities in which the writings of the New Testament were composed the only adequate agent of the very composition of these writings.[64] How is that to be understood?

According to some historical hypotheses as to the production of the gospels, there is first a period of anonymous oral tradition, with constant modifications in the re-telling; second, there is a subsequent stage of written collections of sayings or stories; and third, from the hand of some further compiler, the process culminates in a whole text, although perhaps still to be edited by some other writer. In this way, the "authors" of the received text of the gospel grow into a small platoon.[65] This way of thinking about inspiration is expanded in the dialogic view, which would merely

64. See Rahner, *Inspiration in the Bible*, Conclusions, 2, (d).
65. See John L. McKenzie, SJ, "The Social Character of Inspiration," *Catholic Biblical Quarterly* 24 (1962): 115–24; for the Old Testament, see Dennis J. McCarthy, SJ, "Personality, Society, and Inspiration," *Theological Studies* 64 (1963): 553–76; also, Nichols, *The Shape of Catholic Theology*, 127–29; and more recently, Robert Fastiggi, "Communal or Social Inspiration: A Catholic Critique," *Letter and Spirit* 6 (2010): 247–63.

note the communal or social context in which all such partial composers or writers of the final record have their existence. On the other hand, when Alonso-Schökel discussed the "social character of inspiration," he observed that "there is no such thing as a literary work produced by 'everybody.'"[66]

Moreover, it goes very contrary to the description and self-expression of certain prophetic books to think that the voice of, say, Jeremiah, is irrecoverably lost between layers and layers of tradition. And for the gospels, we must beware of depersonalizing the texts, and so of mitigating the authority of personal witness which they bear about them.[67] More pointedly, the witness of the gospels is of its nature bound to the claim of a responsible reportage of *eyewitness* testimony, as will be argued subsequently in chapter 6. What we must do, therefore, is insert the unique literary voice and the eyewitness within the community to which and sometimes for which they speak. There are arias that make no sense unless sustained by the whole opera, we might say. Still, the aria is a solo performance. What we must do, therefore, is recognize gradations of inspiration, participations in the inspiring work of the Holy Spirit according to how precisely one is describing the economy of salvation, and how close one is to the ultimate form of that pattern, the life of Christ.[68]

Notwithstanding the irrecusably personal voice of some biblical writings, the "community" hypothesis has its advantages. For Karl Rahner, it solves at a stroke the question of how the Church constituted the canon of the New Testament. The community as a whole that is the one "mind" producing the New Testament must have also the wherewithal, the authority of the Holy Spirit, to recognize these books as canonical. Joseph Ratzinger also sees advantages to the "community" hypothesis. It is a "collective subject," the People of God, that is "the deeper 'author' of the Scriptures", which means, equivalently, that the individual author "does not speak as a private, self-contained subject."[69] The "deeper value" of his

---

66. Alsonso-Schökel, *The Inspired Word*, 224.

67. See Gerhardsson, *The Reliability of the Gospel Tradition*, 74.

68. St. Thomas, in his inaugural sermons, notes gradations in prophecy, where the major prophets are more immediately related to the mystery of Christ than the others; see *Thomas Aquinas: Selected Writings*, ed. and trans. Ralph McInerny (New York: Penguin Books, 1998), 10. See Congar, *Tradition and Traditions*, 90, for gradations in inspiration.

69. Benedict XVI, *Jesus of Nazareth*, xxi, xx.

words, the value according to which they intend Christ and the Church, can then be apprehended as within the purview, certainly of the community for which the individual speaks, and even of the individual himself. If we take the community across time, then the words of Scripture, the words of the Old Testament, and expressly in their Christological and ecclesiological import, become, as it were and in a quite surprising way the literal sense of the Scriptures. The literal sense has at this point absorbed any distinct spiritual sense of Scripture.[70]

Human Authors and the Senses of Scripture

The last observation brings to the fore the long delayed but pressing issue of the authorial intention of the human authors of Sacred Scripture. It can be objected that since the writers of the New Testament were completely uninterested in the human authorial intention of the Old Testament works they used, so can we be similarly indifferent to it.[71] However this inattention may be possible for a hagiographer, it does not seem to give us a similar warrant for ignoring the contexts of texts, and we supposed as much in speaking of the literal sense above. We are not in the same place as a hagiographer where we may use prior words, inspired words, for further inspired projects. For its part, *Dei Verbum* very clearly tells us of the necessity in our own reading of Scripture to pay attention to what the human authors, "true authors," had in mind (no. 12).

So, when we discern the literal meaning of what the human author wanted to convey, then we have attained also at the same time to what God meant to say to those who first heard or read the prophecies and praise, the stories and histories and sapiential reflections on them that compose the Old Testament, and to what he means to say to those who hear these things now. That is how we took things above. That is how St. Thomas takes things.[72] This is the literal and properly "theological" sense of Scripture.

But can what God literally meant and what the human author literal-

70. Aaron Pidel, SJ, "Joseph Ratzinger on Biblical Inerrancy," *Nova et Vetera* (English) 12 (2014), 316–18.

71. Peter Enns, *Inspiration and Incarnation: Evangelicals and the Problem of the Old Testament* (Grand Rapids, Mich.: Baker Academic, 2005), 116, as cited by Matthew Levering, *Mary's Bodily Assumption* (Notre Dame, Ind.: University of Notre Dame Press, 2015), 96–97.

72. St. Thomas Aquinas, *Summa theologiae* I, q. 1, a. 10, c.

ly meant diverge? When Peter said and Luke wrote that "there is no other name under heaven by which we can be saved," then we suppose that what they meant, God also meant and still means for us who read Acts 4:12. But other times, it seems that some distinction is called for. It may be that what Qoheleth meant to say about the fragility and vanity of human life, and the uncertainty of what there is to hope for after death is not quite what God means us to hear now when we read Ecclesiastes within the entire context, not only of the Old, but especially of the New Testament (cf. 1 Cor 15:19). Perhaps we should say that, absent God's word, absent his determination of human destiny, then on that condition life is vain, and that that is what God means to say in Ecclesiastes. That Qoheleth (or perhaps some author distinct from Qoheleth if we take him as a literary figure) means to say this is another question. It is not evident that Qoheleth expressly knows the condition that renders life vain. Does Alonso-Schökel help us out here? Can we understand Qoheleth to be a literary creation? When we read that man's happiness consists of bodily pleasures at 5:17, St. Thomas takes the author (for him, Solomon) to be speaking not in his own and therefore not in God's voice, but only as a spokesman for Epicureanism.[73] This question leads to the topic of the inerrancy of Scripture.

When we consider the figural senses of Scripture, they are evidently intended by God, who alone arranges the course of history so that things can signify as well as words. What is the relation of the allegorical and anagogical senses to the human authors? Must they not know Christ in order to intend them?[74] This question evokes a dilemma. If the spiritual senses are intended, then the Old Testament prophet or hagiographer seems to have had to step out of his time and place, and there is imputed to him a distinct knowledge of the economy of salvation that seems to

73. St. Thomas Aquinas, *Summa Contra Gentiles, Book Three, Part I*, trans. Vernon J. Bourke (Notre Dame, Ind.: University of Notre Dame, 1975), chap. 27, *ad fin*.

74. Denis Farkasfalvy, "How to Renew the Theology of Biblical Inspiration?" *Nova et Vetera* (English) 4 (2006), says that *Dei Verbum* leaves us with the false impression that "the human being's consciousness sets limits to the divine meaning. Whatever the [human] author does not intend consciously cannot be truly in any form or shape a part of the authentic meaning of the text" (239). He is right, but it remains only an impression; the false conclusion would follow necessarily only if the text said that God intends *only* what the human author intends. It does not say that, and, as is often noted, adverts to the need to interpret the part in terms of the whole.

contradict his historical context, his historical limitation, and indeed, his supposed first order business in declaring a word of God suited to God's contemporary dealings with Israel and the nations. On the other hand, if it is not intended, and the human author composes a writing whose full or Christological sense completely escapes him, then, while this possibility can indeed be suggested by the idea that the human author is an instrumental cause, it nevertheless reduces him to a sort of inanimate or at least unknowing agent, accomplishing through his proper work something he knows nothing of, because it has been taken up and given a sense beyond his ken by God. Doubtless there is a sense in which whatever we do in our own agency is rendered up to a providence whose purposes we do not discern in detail. But here, God would seem to use a human being in a manner that little befits the full personal reality of human agents.

We have just seen Ratzinger's solution to this dilemma, whereby the individual authors stand forth only as representing a larger subject, the People of God, with a greater intentionality, operating within a larger horizon of meaning than any one individual. But there is a solution also in the terms in which St. Thomas explains the senses of Scripture. The dilemma, as such, should be refused in just the way it is proposed. It focuses too narrowly on the sense of the words themselves. It is rather the *things* the Old Testament writer refers to—the worship, the kings, the events, and so on—that bear a sense that anticipates the New Testament. The "principal author" does not have, as it were, to manipulate the human author's mind and intentionality in order to produce a sense that bears on the New Testament, subverting his own intention of the inspired truth that he does see and understand so that, unbeknownst to him, it serves double duty. That the human author understands the spiritual senses in some large sense, senses more than the immediately intended word, is the position and the weakness of the position of those who argued for a "*sensus plenior*," according to which the deeper meaning God intends is somewhat but not clearly and fully understood by the human author.[75] But for St. Thomas, and even though he himself admits the possibility of imputing the figural or spiritual sense to the intention of the Old Testa-

75. Raymond Brown, "Hermeneutics," in *The Jerome Biblical Commentary* (Englewood Cliffs, N.J.: Prentice-Hall, 1968), no. 57.

ment author,[76] there is in general no need for him to worry about that.[77] Rather, the super-temporal providence of God that arranges all things wisely and sweetly can also arrange that the things that the Old Testament person speaks have their own meaning as anticipating something in the New Testament.[78] For St. Thomas, it is the realities of the economy to which the original text refers that are the bearers of further meaning informing us of Christ and the Church. The intention of the human author could then strictly fall out of consideration. For Ratzinger, the text produced by those who speak to and for the People of God, and the text thereafter heard by the People of God in its entire temporal breadth, can have a further meaning than that occasioned by its composition.[79]

Word and Spirit in Inspiration

St. Irenaeus attributes the inspiration of Scripture to Father or Son or Spirit. But Christ remains the content of Scripture, and the apostles carry out their witness to the revelation of the Word because of the presence and power of the Spirit.[80] This invites us to consider the relation of the Scriptures to the Trinitarian Persons more nearly.

Since the Father alone "speaks" within the Trinity, and speaks his co-equal and co-eternal Word, then it makes sense to think of the Father as speaking the words of the Old Testament in which the Word made flesh is prefigured and predicted. This is how Hebrews takes it (Heb 1:1). And for the same teaching, see St. Stephen's speech in Acts 7:56. All the words of the Old Testament, which add up to the adumbration of the Incar-

76. St. Thomas Aquinas, *Quodlibet* VII, q. 6, a. 1, ad 5.

77. He worries about it when he can think of no meaning for some Old Testament word except an allegorical sense. So, for instance, he thinks Psalm 22 can really have only a spiritual, Christological sense. If that is the only sense it can have, how could it be composed apart from the psalmist's knowing it? See Gregory Vall, "Psalm 22: *Vox Christi* or Israelite Temple Liturgy?" *The Thomist* 66 (2002): 175–200.

78. See also Sokolowski, *Eucharistic Presence*, 148–50.

79. Jared Staudt, "Aquinas and the Exegesis of Benedict XVI," *Nova et Vetera* (English) 12 (2014): 331–63, reports what William Wright says on the difference between Thomas and Ratzinger, "Patristic Biblical Hermeneutics in Joseph Ratzinger's *Jesus of Nazareth*," *Letter and Spirit* 7 (2011): 191–207. Staudt ("Aquinas," 360) thinks Aquinas and Benedict stand closer together on the text as bearing a richer meaning than does Wright ("Patristic Biblical Hermeneutics," 205), and after all, we might observe that the realities that are the foundation of the spiritual senses are mediated to us only by the words we now have.

80. Farkasfalvy, "Theology of Scripture in St. Irenaeus," 323–26.

nate Word, will be the speaking of the Father. Of course, insofar as we are thinking of created words formulated by prophet or apostle or even of the Lord Jesus, these are products of a divine efficient causality common to the three Persons. But this by no means settles the question of which person these commonly created words manifest as the person *speaking* them. So, we do not slip into tritheism in maintaining that the Father speaks the words of the Old Testament, words that amount as a whole to speaking his incarnate Son. This is nothing more except to repeat the patristic analogy between the written word and the Incarnation: they are both manifestations of the Word made flesh.[81] They are not the manifestation of the Word alone; it is rather the Word *made flesh* that is the keystone of the arch formed by the Testaments, and both Testaments show us the humanity of the Word.[82]

In the New Testament, the incarnate Word speaks human words, and these words can be quoted, and when they are quoted in the Gospels then the voice of the Word is made present once again. What of the other words of the New Testament? If they are the words of the Bride, who has first heard and is repeating back to the One who first addressed her, then we may want to say they are all the locution of the Spirit and the Bride who say "Come" (Rv 22:17). Although the Holy Spirit does not "speak" *in divinis*, since speaking is proper to the Father, the Spirit of the Lord is associated with prophecy in the Old Testament (Is 61:1; Ezek 11:1, 5; Dn 5:11; Jl 2:28–29); and we want to say that the Spirit is the Spirit of the inspiration of Scripture and, just as the Creed has it, that "he has spoken *through* the prophets." The Spirit who inspired the Old Testament that Jesus took as speaking of him (Jn 5:46) is the same Spirit who enables the apostolic witness and assures its trustworthy record in the New Testament.[83]

81. Farkasfalvy, *Inspiration and Interpretation*, 219–20, also 133–34; see Mary Healy, "Inspiration and Incarnation: The Christological Analogy and the Hermeneutics of Faith," *Letter and Spirit* 2 (2006): 27–41.

82. Benedict XVI, *Verbum Domini*, no. 29, quoting St. Bonaventure. See Origen in Hans Urs von Balthasar, *Origen: Spirit and Fire, A Thematic Anthology of His Writings*, trans.Robert J. Daly, SJ (German, 1938, 1956; Washington, D.C.: The Catholic University of America Press, 1984), nos. 200, 201; and Henri de Lubac, SJ, *History and Spirit: The Understanding of Scripture According to Origen*, trans. Anne Englund Nash (French 1950; San Francisco: Ignatius Press, 2007), chap. 8, "The Incorporations of the Logos."

83. Farkasfalvy, *Inspiration and Interpretation*, 91. Generally, the Holy Spirit presides over the events in which the Word is made present. Just as the Holy Spirit elicited Mary's faithful

St. Thomas distinguishes the roles of Word and Spirit relative to Scripture as follows. Every true created word, whether known by nature or received in faith, is a participation of the Word of the Father—just insofar as it is true, it must imitate subsistent Truth, the eternal Truth of the Father expressed before the foundation of the world. That is to say, the content of Scripture is always a manifestation of the Word, and this is all the more true according as Scripture is ordered entirely and exclusively to manifesting the Word made flesh.[84]

This means that the words of Jesus, of the incarnate Word, are both his and his Father's, as Thomas explains in his commentary on John.

When he speaks of his own words, he uses the plural, "my words"; but where he speaks of the word of the Father, he speaks in the singular, saying "And the word which you have heard, is not mine"; because by "Word of the Father," he wants himself to be understood, who is the Father's unique Word. Whence neither does he say he is his own, but the Father's, because neither is he his own Image, nor his own Son, but the Father's. But all the words in our hearts are from the unique Word of the Father.[85]

The words are his because pronounced by him, but originally they are the Father's, who primordially speaks the Word himself.[86]

The role of the Holy Spirit, on the other hand, is to lead men to the

---

conception of the word of the angel's message in her mind and presided over her conception of the Word in her womb, so he effects the consecration of the gifts at the priest's invocation (see Benedict XVI, *Verbum Domini*, no. 16).

84. See Gilles Emery, OP, "Trinity and Truth: The Son as Truth and the Spirit of Truth in St. Thomas Aquinas," in Emery, *Trinity, Church, and the Human Person: Thomistic Essays* (Naples, Fla.: Sapientia Press, 2007), 106.

85. St. Thomas Aquinas, *Super Evangelium Sancti Ioannis Lectura*, no. 1951: "cum loquitur Dominus de sermonibus suis, pluraliter dicit, 'Sermones meos'; ubi autem loquitur de sermone Patris, loquitur in singulari, dicens 'Et sermonem quem audistis, non est meus'; quia per Verbum Patris seipsum intelligi voluit, qui est unicum Verbum eius. Unde nec suum se esse dicit, sed Patris, quia nec sua imago est, nec suus Filius, sed Patris. Sermones autem omnes in cordibus nostris sunt ab unico Verbo Patris." St. Thomas tells us that he is here reporting St. Augustine's observation.

86. St. Thomas Aquinas, *Super Evangelium Sancti Ioannis Lectura*, no. 1950: "that is, [the word you have heard me speak] is not mine as from myself, but it is mine as from another, namely from the Father who sent me.... The word which you heard, pronounced by me, a man, is indeed mine, insofar as I pronounce it, and it is not mine insofar as it is mine from another [idest, non est mihi a meipso, sed est mihi ab alio, scilicet a Patre qui me misit.... sermonem, sive sermo, 'quem audistis,' a me homine prolatum, est quidem meus, inquantum ipsum pronuntio, et non est meus, inquantum est mihi ab alio]." Thomas directs us to John 7:16.

reception of the truth, natural or supernatural, and most evidently when the truth concerns the incarnation of Truth. This he does, according to St. Thomas, because the Spirit is the mutual love of Father and Son, and the love that is poured into our hearts by the Holy Spirit is naturally attributed to him, even though it is the efficient product of all three Persons.[87] So, apropos of John 14:17, Thomas says:

the Holy Spirit leads to the knowledge of the truth, because he proceeds from the Truth, who says, "I am the way, and the truth, and the life" (14:6). In us, love of the truth arises when we have conceived and considered truth. So also in God, Love proceeds from conceived Truth, which is the Son. And just as Love proceeds from the Truth, so Love leads to knowledge of the truth: "He [The Holy Spirit] will glorify me because he will receive from me and declare it to you" [16:14]. And therefore Ambrose says that any truth, no matter who speaks it, is from the Holy Spirit. "No one can say 'Jesus is Lord' except by the Holy Spirit" (1 Cor 12:3); "When the Paraclete comes, whom I shall send to you from the Father, even the Spirit of truth ..." [15:26]. It is a characteristic of the Holy Spirit to reveal the truth because it is love which impels one to reveal his secrets: "I have called you friends, for all that I have heard from my Father I have made known to you" (15:15); "He showed it," the truth, "to his friend" [Jb 36:33].[88]

Knowing the truth, we are assimilated to the Truth and in that way the Word teaches all men all things—something St. Thomas would know from the *De Magistro* of St. Augustine. But the Holy Spirit teaches as making us receptive to this truth because of love. At John 14:26, Jesus says the Holy Spirit will teach us. St. Thomas explains that he does so as making us able to receive the teaching of the Son.

Next he treats of the effect of the Holy Spirit, saying, "He will teach you all things." For just as the effect of the mission of the Son was to lead to the Father, so the effect of the mission of the Holy Spirit is to lead the faithful to the Son. The Son, however, since he is begotten wisdom itself is the truth itself; above, 15:6—"I am the way, the truth, and the life." And therefore the effect of a mis-

---

87. Emery, "Trinity and Truth," 106–7.

88. St. Thomas Aquinas, *Super Evangelium Sancti Ioannis Lectura*, no. 1916; I give here the Larcher translation, in St. Thomas Aquinas, *Commentary on the Gospel of John, Chapters 13–21*, trans. Fabian Larcher, OP, and James Weisheipl, OP (Washington, D.C.: The Catholic University of American Press, 2010), at 14:17.

sion of this kind is to make men sharers in the divine wisdom, and knowers of the truth. Therefore the Son gives us doctrine, since he is the Word; but the Holy Spirit makes us able to receive [*capaces*] his teaching.[89]

The Son gives doctrine, as being the subsistent truth and wisdom of which doctrine is a participation. The Holy Spirit gives it as making us able to hear it. As to the Father: "Since someone's teaching is nothing else than his word, and since the Son of God is his Word, it therefore follows that the teaching of the Father is the Son himself."[90] The Father gives doctrine as speaking the Word, and works in the work and mission of Word and Spirit—through his hands, as Irenaeus would put it. There is, then, an articulation according to the Persons, all three, for the teaching of the one God.[91] But the Holy Spirit does not speak from the outside and in a bodily way, St. Thomas says at 16:13, "but interiorly in the mind by illuminating it [*illuminando*]."[92]

A Religion of the Word, but Not of the Book

The high doctrine of inspiration embraced by the Church makes of the words of the Bible the words of the Holy Spirit, the words of God. It is

---

89. St. Thomas Aquinas, *Super Evangelium Sancti Ioannis Lectura*, no. 1958: "Consequenter agit de effectu Spiritus sancti; dicens, 'Ille vos docebit omina.' Nam, sicut effectus missionis Filii fuit ducere ad Patrem, ita effectus missionis Spiritus sancti est ducere fideles ad Filium. Filius, autem, cum sit ipsa sapientia genita, est ipsa veritas; supra 14:6: 'Ego sum via, veritas et vita.' Et ideo effectus missionis huismodi est ut faciat homines participes divinae sapientiae, et cognitores veritatis. Filius ergo tradit nobis doctrinam, cum sit Verbum; sed Spiritus sanctus doctrinae eius nos capaces facit." Remember that, as Gilles Emery says in his *Trinity in Aquinas* (Ypsilanti, Mich.: Sapientia Press, 2003), "all natural human knowledge is a participation in the Word" (288); see for instance St. Thomas's *Lectura* at 1:26, no. 246; and at 8:55, no. 1284. St. Thomas makes the same point in the *Summa Contra Gentiles, Book Four: Salvation*, trans. Charles J. O'Neil (Notre Dame, Ind.: University of Notre Dame, 1975), chap. 13, no. 11.

90. St. Thomas Aquinas, *Super Evangelium Sancti Ioannis Lectura*, at 7:16, no. 1037: "cum doctrina uniuscuiusque nihil aliud sit quam verbum eius, Filius autem Dei sit Verbum eius: sequitur ergo quod doctrina Patris sit ipse Filius."

91. See Emery, "The Personal Mode of Trinitarian Action in St. Thomas Aquinas," 115–53, in Emery, *Trinity, Church, and The Human Person*, esp. 129–38, on how for St. Thomas the three Persons can act in one action according to their personal mode.

92. See Benoît, *Aspects of Biblical Inspiration*, 84–85: "what is revelation but the Word made manifest, and inspiration but the movement of the Holy Spirit? ... By his Word, God manifests his Being, his ideas, his desires, and his plans for his creatures. By his Spirit, he infuses the energy and dynamism by which his Word is fulfilled.... In revealing his intentions to his spokesmen, God breathes into them his Spirit and places his Word on their lips."

not quite true to say that the Bible "contains" the word of God, meaning that we have to deduce from the human words there some further, divine word, or wait for some further actualization of the text to make it the word of God. Of course, as Ratzinger insists, a word is not a word until it is heard, and revelation is not revelation until someone apprehends it.[93] But it is a mistake so to pile up the conditions of hearing that we cannot point to the Book and say, "There is the word of God." It is therefore hard to agree with Raymond Brown in his mature reflections on the character of Scripture and its interpretation when he says categorically that "God does not speak."[94] If he does not speak, the Bible is not nor can it even contain a word of God. Brown says God does not speak because, if the biblical word were God's own, it would be unconditioned and exhaustive.[95] Furthermore, redaction criticism shows that prophets formulate their own words and do not receive them from God.[96] And the Bible as a whole contains errors.[97] To these objections one can reply that a divine word spoken in human words need not be exhaustive or historically unconditioned, nor does it preclude that God uses the prophet's and redactor's own powers of formulating it. We take up inerrancy shortly. Brown's denial has the consequence that philological and historical and critical studies of Scripture are completely unfettered by any theological principle; exegesis is an exclusively human work that proceeds by reason alone; it is extra-theological. And this, according to Michael Waldstein, is Brown's principle concern.[98] Such an alienation of the work of the determination of the literal sense of Scripture from theology would be a startling innovation in Catholic theology.

---

93. Joseph Ratzinger, *Principles of Catholic Theology: Building Stones for a Fundamental Theology*, trans. Sister Mary Frances McCarthy, SND (San Francisco: Ignatius Press, 1987), 147; see also his *Milestones: Memoirs, 1927–1977* (San Francisco: Ignatius Press, 1998), 108–9. This view seems to be within hailing distance of the emphasis on revelation as event in Karl Barth and Rudolf Bultmann. See the discussion of Barth in Mats Wahlberg, *Revelation as Testimony: A Philosophical-Theological Study* (Grand Rapids, Mich.: Eerdmans, 2014), 85–89.

94. Raymond Brown, SS, *The Critical Meaning of the Bible* (New York: Paulist Press, 1981), 1.

95. Ibid., 4 and no. 8.

96. Ibid., 9.

97. Ibid., 17–18.

98. Michael Waldstein, "*Analogia Verbi*: The Truth of Scripture in Rudolf Bultmann and Raymond Brown," *Letter and Spirit* 6 (2010): 114–15.

On the other hand, the high view of inspiration embraced by the Church should not be taken to commit us to a kind of "textualism," according to which our attention, as it were, stops with the words there in the Bible, and we begin to treat the Bible the way Muslims treat the Koran. What prevents this is the fourfold gospel itself. Precisely because there are four versions of it, we are invited to proceed to the reality that the words mediate, and not find our attention hijacked to a sort of Kabbalism or gematria of the text.[99] The words, as expressing propositions immediately or by implication, terminate in the reality referred to, as St. Thomas noted, and we are supposed to be more interested in the realities than in their mediation.[100]

An obsessive attention to the mediation of the realities rather than to the realities mediated is forbidden also by the evident fact of the translatability of the Bible and the realization that the transmission of the teaching of faith and the intricacies of theological argument are borne up just as much by the Hebrew and Greek as by the Latin or English, the Swahili or Quechuan. When the Lord God confused the tongues at Babel, the original language in which he spoke to Adam and Eve was lost; and the Hebrew in which this confusion is recorded becomes just one more among the many languages of man. Its privilege is historical, not theological.[101]

Pope Benedict XVI makes this same point when he says that Christianity is a religion of the Word but not of the Book.[102] And again:

Moslems believe that the Koran was directly dictated by God. It is not mediated by any history; no human intermediary was needed; it is a message direct from God. The Bible, on the other hand, is quite different. It is mediated to us by a history, and even as a book it extends over a period of more than a thousand years.... It becomes clear that God did not just dictate these words but rather that they bear the impression of a history that he has been guiding; they have come into being as witness to that history.[103]

99. Sokolowski, *Eucharistic Presence*, 143.

100. St. Thomas Aquinas, *Summa theologiae* II-II, q. 1, a. 2, ad 2.

101. Paul Mankowski, SJ, "Language, Truth, and *Logos*," in *The Oxford Handbook of Christology*, ed. Francesca Aran Murphy (Oxford: Oxford University Press, 2015), 15–16.

102. Benedict XVI, *Verbum Domini*, no. 7.

103. Joseph Ratzinger, *God and the World: Believing and Living in Our Time* (San Francisco: Ignatius Press, 2002), 151–52.

The Inerrancy of Scripture

Why Inerrancy Is Asserted and Its Scope

Because God is its author, Scripture is said to be "inerrant." Inerrancy has been thought of as a property following from the inspired character of Scripture. Just as, speaking of revelation, we say that God cannot be deceived or deceive,[104] so also the writings in which he expresses himself can have no mistakes in them.[105]

Inerrancy has perhaps been the most vexed issue in the theological consideration of the Bible for Catholics in the last 150 years, an issue closely governed by how inspiration is conceived. If "whatever the inspired authors ... affirm, is affirmed by the Holy Spirit," however, as *Dei Verbum* has it (no. 11), then the implication is that biblical inerrancy is unbounded, and the council itself draws the conclusion: "we must acknowledge that the books of Scripture teach firmly, faithfully and without error the truth that God, for the sake of our salvation, wished the biblical text to contain." When we uncover "the meaning the biblical writers actually had in mind," then "that will also be what God chose to manifest through their words" (no. 12).

There have been attempts, however, to make the sentence affirming inerrancy bear only on the truths that concern our salvation.[106] But this is quite contrary to the history of the conciliar text, which went from affirming that only "saving truths" were inerrant to affirming the Church's traditional doctrine of "unrestricted inerrancy."[107] The council does not say that "the truth that God wished the text to contain" is a truth bearing directly on our salvation. The truth in question is *"for the sake of our*

---

104. Vatican I, *Dei Filius*, in Tanner, *Decrees of the Ecumenical Councils*, vol. 2, chap. 3.

105. The inerrancy of Scripture became a major magisterial issue with Leo XIII's *Povidentissimus Deus* of 1893 (Neuner and Dupuis, *The Christian Faith*, nos. 226–27), whose teaching was repeated by Benedict XV in 1920 in *Spiritus Paracletus* (Neuner and Dupuis, *The Christian Faith*, nos. 230–31), and by Pius XII in 1950 in *Humani Generis* (Neuner and Dupuis, *The Christian Faith*, no. 238).

106. Farkasfalvy, *Inspiration and Interpretation*, 186, cites R. Brown; Brian Harrison, "Restricted Inerrancy and the 'Hermeneutics of Discontinuity,'" *Letter and Spirit* 6 (2010): 225–46, discusses Brown and R. A. F. MacKenzie; see also Avery Dulles, SJ, "Vatican II on the Interpretation of Scripture," *Letter and Spirit* 2 (2006): 18–19.

107. Farkasfalvy, *Inspiration and Interpretation*, 186; Harrison, "Restricted Inerrancy," 233–36.

salvation," and indicates the end of the truths Scripture contains. But many kind of truths, especially historical truths, bear on "our salvation."

The inerrancy or unqualified truth of Scripture is itself a properly theological truth. That is, it is a truth that follows from what we hold in faith about the Scriptures, especially the priority of the divine to the human authorship of the Scriptures captured in the idea of inspiration. In the face of that view of Scripture, when we encounter texts that seem to say something false, then we have puzzles but not evidence that Scripture is not inerrant. The truth of the inerrancy of Scripture follows from the very content of the revelation Scripture communicates to us. For Scripture as a whole and considered in its unity gives us unfailing and certain access to the revelation of God and so an unfailing and certain access to Christ and the Trinity, to a knowledge of our final end, and to a knowledge of how to attain to it. This access is principally conveyed, as chapter 1 has it, through the entire pattern of the deeds and words that constitute the economy of salvation. This access cannot be mistaken; it therefore follows that the Scripture that records the pattern does not give us *another* god or another Christ (cf. 2 Cor 11:4), and in this respect is "inerrant." Or to put it another way, insofar as Scripture renders the Word made flesh for us in its many words, then of course it must have the absolute truth of the Truth of God himself. In this respect, the inerrancy of Scripture is correlative to the impeccability of Christ. The questions raised by the message and the strategies by which the individual hagiographers contribute to that end are necessary, but secondary.

Questions Provoked by the Claim to Inerrancy

The questions raised may be (a) metaphysical, (b) moral and legal, (c) historical.

Metaphysical Problems   In the Book of Exodus, God hardens Pharaoh's heart so that he opposes what he is instructed to do through the mouth of Moses, God's prophet (Ex 4:21). Has God incited Pharaoh to act immorally, such that God is here presented not only as the author but as the first cause of sin? That would be a big stretch. For one thing, it is not clear that all of Pharaoh's opposition to Moses is immoral. The king is, according to his lights, trying to take care of his kingdom. But granting that, his opposition is immoral in that he unjustly oppresses Israel (Ex 1:10–14), presumes to take innocent life in having the male children of Israel slain (Ex 1:15–16), and sinfully opposes what he can and ought to recognize as the hand of God afflicting Egypt (Ex 8:19). "Hardens" is a verb in the active voice. But not all active voice verbs really name a positive action. God may harden a heart by not giving grace to hear, grace to change. In that case, he is not the cause of sin. But why should God withhold his grace? So that he may get glory over Pharaoh by leading Israel out of Egypt notwithstanding the great king's opposition. This manifestation of God's faithfulness and power to Israel is part of the point of the narrative, and insofar as it reports the events accurately, of the events. Pharaoh, and precisely in his own freely chosen immorality, is used by God. On the other hand, the story does not concern itself with Pharaoh's ultimate salvation.[108]

Again, God's relation to evil is not always expressly articulated according to what he positively wills and what he permits (cf. Is 45:7; Am 3:6).[109] But such passages should be controlled by passages that declare his innocence (Dt 32:4; Hab 1:13).[110]

Suppose that the figure of Qoheleth discharges the mind of the writer of Ecclesiastes, and that what Qoheleth asserts is what the writer asserts, and that what the writer asserts is asserted by the Holy Spirit. Human life is therefore vain, and there is nothing to hope for after death (Eccl 1:2, 17, 4:3; 3:19–22, 9:5). Qoheleth asserts what the ungodly man of the Book of Wisdom asserts, and which the same book denies (Wis 2:1–3; 2:23; 3:4). Should we say that what is answered within the confines of one book, the Book of Wisdom, is answered within the boundaries of the Bible as a whole? This lets us say, conservatively, that the Holy Spirit merely "uses" but does not "affirm" the teachings of Qoheleth, and we can suppose that the human author of Ecclesiastes does not affirm them either. Such a distinction between use and affirmation or teaching was proposed and found approval at Vatican II.[111] Or should we rather say that Qoheleth

---

108. See Thomas Joseph White, OP, *Exodus* (Grand Rapids, Mich.: Brazos Press, 2016), 25–31, on the figure of Pharaoh, and 59–70, on hardening of hearts.

109. See St. Thomas Aquinas, *Summa Contra Gentiles, Book Three: Providence, Part I*, chap. 71.

110. St. Thomas Aquinas, *Summa Contra Gentiles, Book One: God*, chap. 95.

111. For this intervention of Cardinal Raúl Silva Henríquez, see Brian Harrison, "Restricted Inerrancy and the 'Hermeneutic of Discontinuity,'" 244–45.

fits into the entire pattern of revelation as the enquirer he is—the questions he asks are just exactly the questions God wishes us to ask, just so as to appreciate God's answers, even if the answers are not received and repeated by Qoheleth himself. As said above in discussing inspiration, we are to understand that human life as we know it now is indeed vain and empty apart from the promise of Christ and his fulfilment of it by grace (cf. Rom 8:20), and that whatever life there be after death is not that participation in Life such as God wishes for us. And those things, we may imagine, the Holy Spirit can very well wish to assert and have us hear.

Moral and Legal Problems   It has been observed that some of the Old Testament legislation is evidently intended by the human author to be an everlasting enactment.[112] So it is at Exodus 12:14 for the Passover. Was then the hagiographer mistaken, or did God repent of his legislation? But if Passover is a type of the Last Supper, then we can say not only that it is still kept, but that the original intention that Passover be celebrated perpetually is likewise fulfilled. This insight is at least as old as St. Augustine.

Samuel tells Saul in 1 Samuel 15 that obedience is better than sacrifice (1 Sm 15:22), and this important teaching has played an enormous role in Christian and religious moral life. The obedience in question, however, was to put the defeated Amalakites to the ban (15:3). For St. Thomas, all men are liable to natural death because of original sin, and therefore God can command the death of anyone without injustice.[113] But for many, the text of 1 Samuel means that God orders the immoral slaying at least of women and children innocent of waging war against God's holy people.[114] One can point out in reply that the Lord's command forbids individual Israelites from seeking to profit from the results of national and politically necessary policy. One can remind moderns of the corporate identity of people in the ancient world, so that all are saved or perish together, and that the imputation of dignity and rights to individuals is a work by no means complete, even today. One can remember that the moral education of Israel and the Church by God is not the work of a day

---

112. Aaron Pidel, "Joseph Ratzinger on Biblical Inerrancy," 314–15.
113. St. Thomas Aquinas, *Summa theologiae* I-II, q. 94, a. 5, ad 2.
114. See Benedict XVI, *Verbum Domini*, no. 42.

or season. All these factors that try to distinguish the slaying of the Amalakites from genocide as contemporarily conceived, moreover, amount in the end to identifying things that would not be true had Adam and Eve not sinned. Divine providence works within a world conditioned by a violence and brutality that was not willed by God from the beginning. This sort of apology for what Samuel ordered, what God commanded, is a sort of judgment on what the moral market would bear a thousand years before Christ.[115]

Historical Problems   The access Scripture gives us to God and Christ and the economy of salvation does not consist exclusively in some deliverance of a set of metaphysical and moral truths, but occurs within a history of salvation. The metaphysical truths are often enough implications of the story, as God's creation is not only directly taught but is an implication of his ability to give an absolutely trustworthy guarantee to history. And the moral truths are, often enough, transcriptions of the divine benevolence, faithfulness, mercy, and kindness that his actions are informed by. The history is public, even as Christ is incarnate and the Church visible. The actions of Christ and his disciples and his opponents were not things done "in a corner," as Paul reminded Festus (Acts 26:26).

However, the inclusion of truths of history within an inerrant Scripture does not imply that everything constituting the economy of salvation is described with an unvarying historical exactitude; rather, the descriptions Scripture offers us admit of inventions, verisimilitudinous guesses according to the lights of the human authors, fictional elaborations of narrative truth, and minor slips that have nothing to do with the point of the assertion.

For inventions, guesses, and elaborations, see for instance the descriptions of military strategies, engagement, outcomes in Joshua and Judges. For a minor slip, it was Ahimelech, not Abiathar, who gave David the Bread of the Presence to eat in 1 Samuel 21 (cf. Mk 2:23–28).

Beyond the plasticity of historical narrative, there are also out-and-

115. See Matthew Ramage, "Violence Is Incompatible with the Nature of God: Benedict, Aquinas, and Method C Exegesis of the 'Dark' Passages of the Bible," *Nova et Vetera* 13 (2015): 273–95.

out Old Testament fictions, like the Books of Jonah and Judith. Granted these fictions, which recension of Esther do we take as normative? (All of them—they are like drafts of a novel within which we more easily discern the point of the tale.) The Book of Tobit is fiction, but the providence of God which it so beautifully teaches is not.

And narrative is, it seems—and as the Lord God knew and intended it to be, and which is the reason he uses it and must use it to reveal himself—infinitely rich. This is true of *ordinary* human narrative—which does not imply there are no bounds to interpretation. And it is certainly true of biblical narrative, and that is part of the divine plan of how to speak to us.

Thus, certain statements about how things stand between us and God or about what God has done in his Christ, statements that emerge from the narrative and found, say, in St. Paul or in some speech in Acts (or statements on the lips of Jesus himself), brook no opposition or qualification. But they emerge from a narrative, a history; and the New Testament insists not only on the theological import of the life and death and resurrection of Jesus, but also the historical character of the events apropos of which these statements are made.

But then there are what seem to be reports of historical events, and sometimes with what purport to be careful description thereof, that are harder to judge. If we think the story of Jonah is a parable, we cannot similarly remove any historical reference to, say, the Exodus of Israel from Egypt. The parabolic status of Jonah makes no difference to how it conveys meaning to us either in the context of the Old Testament alone, or within the discourse of Jesus and the text of the gospel when we read of "the sign of Jonah." But the stories of the Exodus or of the kingdoms of Judah and Israel or of the Babylonian exile cannot similarly be construed as what we today would call fiction.

The problem is complicated by the fact that, internal to Scripture, one piece quotes, alludes to, alters, and directly comments on another piece. When Isaiah 43 and Psalm 77 recall Exodus 14, where God cleaves the waters and makes a path through the sea, we can note how the passages connect the saving power of God in history to his creative power when his Spirit breathed over the waters, and recall that one of the first works of creative order is the division of water and land, water and water. And one could say at this point that the meaning of all the pieces together consists in their mutual chorus, and that, once we have the chorus, it does not matter whether anyone walked dry shod through the sea.

But this can go only to a certain point. Something in authentic continuity with the nation of Israel was released from the iron furnace of Egypt, and unless that is true, the intentionality not only of many texts but also of the worship of God at Passover escapes from earthly reality in such a way that the texts and the worship become difficult to defend as truthful acts.

Ratzinger's Solution to These Problems

As we have just seen, one solution to texts that seem erroneous is to maintain that the author's genre allows him wide latitude for the invention of detail and background story. Another is to deny that the human author intended to make any assertion in the seemingly erroneous text. He was merely supposing and using some common estimation in his milieu but was not embracing that estimation itself. This second solution solves, but it seems more like adding another epicycle to the Ptolemaic planetary system to account for yet one more pesky fact of observation. It seems arbitrary, where what is required is to re-think things entirely in the interest of simplicity of explanation.

Joseph Ratzinger has proposed a better and more elegant solution in tune with his supposition that we are to see the author of Scripture as the entire community of the People of God. The individual writer surrenders his authorial role to the greater community, as we have seen. It thus turns out that the whole People ends up having authorial responsibility for the whole of Scripture.[116] And at that point, the possibilities for thinking about "intention" widen enormously. They widen so much so that Ratzinger need make no appeal to what any individual author intends and can speak only of what the *text* intends, the text as understood by that same People. If the People are the adequate human authorial authority of the text, then the heirs of that People maintain that authority diachronically;

116. Ratzinger, *Jesus of Nazareth*, xx–xxi.

and then it transpires that in a certain sense we consult the same author now when we inquire of the text as to what it says as would be done in the nineteenth or twelfth or second century. We consult the same author, that is, if we inquire what the Church hears now. At this point, then, the intention of any single text can be measured against the intention of the whole Book as heard by the Church. Perhaps the single text positively corroborates the meaning of the whole Book—the single economy of Christ. Perhaps it instances a dissenting, but then still clarifying voice, a response to which is found elsewhere in the Book.

Revelation, for Ratzinger, is not just the Scriptures themselves, but the Scriptures when they are heard, in the event of the Church's hearing of them, and where the single thing meant is the form of Christ. The discussion of inerrancy, in other words, returns us full circle to the issue of hermeneutics with which we began this fundamental theological consideration of Scripture.

Conclusion: A Ratzingerian Recapitulation

First, there is the content or meaning of Scripture. What Scripture, the word of God, communicates to us is the pattern of revelation, which is to say Christ, who is the revelation of the Father in the Spirit, who is also the realization of salvation, since through the Spirit he incorporates in his Body the People of God, returning all things to Trinitarian reality.

Second, there is the canon of Scripture. Scripture as a whole communicates this to us. The parts of Scripture, the individual books, belong to it only as contributing to this communication. The canon of Scripture is the list of books that contribute to the one, whole, pattern, the one manifestation of Christ. This contribution is as various as the kinds of things the books contain: poetry, praise, law, legend; historical reconstruction, surmise, and invention; historical report; legislation; sapiential meditation on law and history; prophetic anticipation of immanent and transcendent divine fulfilment of history. The canon is known to us in that it is the list of books used by the Church, and according to which the Church had access to Christ as guaranteed by the measure of the apostolic witness whose memory lasted into the second century.

Third, there is inspiration. Since the truth and utility of the individual books and pieces, even of the individual propositions, where such are salient and most in play, function unto their end only as indicating and describing and integrated into the whole pattern, it is rather the People of God as a whole, who discerns the pattern and hears the one Word, that should be thought of as the adequate and so inspired "author" relative to the whole Book and not each individual prophet or scribe or sage, individually moved by God as they doubtless were. As it were, the individual prophets and hagiographers surrender their individuality, their authorial propriety, to the whole people, who give expression to the whole pattern in their thoughts and praise and meditations and theologizings, for whose sake the whole pattern is in the end elaborated, so that the People of God may know whence they came, why and how they are saved, and to whom they will return. This means that it is only the Church that hears revelation, since only the Church hears the whole, and so can tell what each piece means within its integral and proper context. Just as St. Paul said, referring to testing Christ in the wilderness and the people's grumbling, "these things happened unto them by way of example; and they were written down for *our* admonition, upon whom the end of the ages are come" (1 Cor 10:11). Even claims to eyewitness testimony, yielding reports of what the Lord Jesus said and did, as ineliminable as they are, are also surrendered to a greater whole.

Fourth, there is inerrancy. Considered formally and so as contributing to the expression of the entire pattern, the parts in their own ways are therefore divinely ordained to this expression and as such "true" just as the whole pattern is true and truly renders the one economy of salvation in Christ. This is the positive statement of what negatively is called inerrancy. The truth in question therefore is not a truth as bearing first of all on the truth or falsity of every proposition, every declarative sentence, where such can be found and listed for consideration, but truth as really contributing to the whole pattern. This does not restrict the truth in question to matters bearing exclusively on salvation, since what was done for the sake of our salvation was done in the world and publically and historically. Still, taken singly, some declarative sentence or other considered in itself, and apart from its contribution to the whole, and even some book in its surface meaning (e.g., Ecclesiastes), may be historically false, or morally unacceptable, or metaphysically misleading. The topic of inerrancy, in other words, returns us to the question of content, to the hermeneutical postulate that parts are made sense of in the whole, reminds us that the whole is not constituted until the last word of the New Testament is composed and recognized as canonical, and that making sense of the parts may mean understanding them typologically.

In a word: revelation occurs when the one to whom it is given beholds the lifting of the veil: thus, it occurs when the deposit of revelation, Scripture, is heard as the whole it is (in which whole alone, as a whole, the form of Christ is inscribed) by the Church; and no part is heard except in function of the whole to which it belongs.[117]

117. For this recapitulation, see especially Pidel, "Joseph Ratzinger on Biblical Inerrancy."

CHAPTER 4

CHURCH AND DOGMA

Revelation occurs only if the one addressed, the Church, hears it. But hearing is an active reception of what is heard. When the Church hears the word of God, revelation overflows Scripture itself and passes into the Church's liturgy, practice, and dogma.[1] When the word is heard the first response is praise (liturgy). The second response is enacting the mission of charity that those who hear the word obediently embrace: first, there is sharing the truth, evangelizing those who have not heard; second, there is enacting the truth in the bodily works of love for the hungry and the naked. A third response consolidates the new articulations of revealed truth that necessarily arise in the faithful mind, and that praise and proclamation and practice themselves contribute to, in the form of dogma. Dogma itself then plays its own role in a repetition of the cycle of hearing and subsequent overflowing. For a fundamental theology, we need to say a

---

1. On the overflowing of Scripture into dogma, see Joseph Ratzinger, "What Is Theology?" in *Pilgrim Fellowship of Faith: The Church as Communion*, trans. Henry Taylor (San Francisco: Ignatius Press, 2002), 29–36.

word first about the Church and then her teaching authority and third about dogma.

Church

The Church was called into existence by the word of God, by saving revelation. We might in fact have considered the Church as the first consequence of revelation since, as we have just said, there is no teaching unless someone is taught and there is no word spoken unless it has been heard. We could then have turned first to the hearers of the Word.

They who hear the word of God and keep it are the mother of Christ (see Lk 11:27–28); the Church is originally the Marian Church, who treasures up what she hears in her heart (Lk 2:51). The Church who is Mother and Bride is also the Body of Christ, and the Body of Christ is the People of God. Notwithstanding the fact that each individually must hear, therefore, each hears as a member of a whole assembly: revelation is public, and we are saved just in our relations to one another or not at all. Revelation addresses a multitude, and makes of it one People.

In her own nature, therefore, the Church is the assembly of people who share the same mind, the mind of Christ, and who live by the same charity poured into their hearts by the Holy Spirit who is given us. The things already spoken of in chapters 2 and 3, the act of Tradition and the things handed on, including Scripture, and a Rule of Faith, a rule of life, and the Eucharist and the sacraments—all these things are doubtless *within* the Church. For this reason too it seems that it would make better sense to have treated the Church first, even before Tradition and Scripture.[2] However, our interest in the Church is fundamental theological. And from this perspective, the Church concerns us as the custodian of revelation, and so as posterior in idea to revelation. She concerns us as the guardian of the *tradita* and the Scriptures, all of which are again logically prior to the idea of the Church.

If we are here interested in the Church in her authoritative role as

---

2. In different respects, Church and Scripture are mutual wholes; see Sokolowski, "God's Word and Human Speech," *Nova et Vetera* (English) 11 (2013): 192, 194.

the guardian of the deposit of faith, then this role, as the Pastoral Letters (1 Tm; 2 Tm; Ti) indicate, is especially the charge of bishops. It is true that revelation is consigned to all the faithful, and the *sensus fidei fidelium* is itself a norm of faith. Even so, authoritative articulations of this norm belong to the magisterium or teaching authority of the Church. The inspiration of the Spirit in virtue of which Scripture is composed passes over, as it were, both into the *sensus fidei* of all the faithful who can recognize the truth of revelation, and likewise into the "sure charism of truth," that is, the truth of revelation itself, possessed by the episcopal successors of the apostles who in their own day can enunciate it in new circumstances.[3]

According to the Church's account of herself in *Lumen Gentium* from Vatican II, bishops are the successors of the apostles by dominical institution (no. 18).[4] The New Testament witness to this is abundant. According to Matthew, the twelve disciples or apostles (Mt 10:1–2) are given authority in the Church to bind and loose (18:18). The mention of the Church here indicates the evangelist's discernment of a dominical intention for an abiding authority within an abiding community. According to Acts, Pauline churches have elders (Acts 20:17), which is to say officers in an institution. The Letter to the Philippians is addressed to "all the saints ... with the bishops and deacons" (Phil 1:1). Timothy is appointed to teach, like Paul himself (1 Tm 2:7, 4:13, 4:16, 6:2–3; 2 Tm 1:11, 1:13, 2: 15), *and to appoint others who can teach* (1 Tm 3:2; 2 Tm 2:1–2). Titus is charged to appoint bishops in Crete (Ti 1:7). And these bishops must be able to teach (1:9), like Titus himself (2:1). Like Timothy, he and his appointed bishops are to follow the "pattern of the sound words" (2 Tm 1:12) and guard the deposit of faith (1 Tm 6:20). And for their teaching, the Holy Spirit is promised them (2 Tm 1:14). In 1 Peter, Peter likens himself to a fellow presbyter (1 Pt 5:1), and exhorts the presbyters to tend their flock like the chief Shepherd, Christ (2:2–4). In the fourth gospel, the risen Lord enunciates a comprehensive principle of succession to apostolic office. He tells the disciples on Easter day: "As the Father has

---

3. St. Irenaeus, *Against Heresies*, in *The Ante-Nicene Fathers*, vol. 1, ed. Alexander Roberts, James Donaldson, and Arthur Cleveland Coxe (New York: Cosimo Classics, 2007), bk. 4, chap. 26, no. 2.

4. Vatican II, *Lumen Gentium, Dogmatic Constitution on the Church*, can be found in Norman Tanner, *Decrees of the Ecumenical Councils*, vol. 2.

sent me, even so I send you" (Jn 20:21). As he was sent with the authority to send others, he sends the disciples with the authority to send others after them, others sharing their own authority. The subsequent history of the Church attests the existence of bishops as far back as there are written witnesses to Church order.

What is the intelligibility of this arrangement? First, there is the social nature of the Church, which rests on the social nature of man himself, and considered precisely in his bodily limitations. Just as the Lord needed other men to propagate his message to more men than he in person could preach to (e.g., Lk 10:1–12), so the apostles also needed those who could be sent to extend the gospel beyond their own personal and bodily limits. Second, also from the social nature of man, no society is one society if it does not have a principle of unity. This principle can be final: all are directed to the same end. It can be formal: all are united by the same mind and will in pursuing the common good of all. But it can also be efficient: all are united by their subordination to one who has care of the common good. Such an analysis of society is, of course, largely Aristotle's, and it was taken up in thinking about the Church by St. Thomas in the thirteenth century. The bishops are the visible governors and rulers of their churches, so that all may pursue the same end of holiness in this life and beatitude in the next, and so that all may share the mind and charity of Christ.

There is also an intelligibility to hierarchical structure discerned by neo-Platonism and adopted for thinking about the Church by Denis the Areopagite. The principle is that the first cause in any order does not influence the last things in that order except through intermediaries. This is a sort of abstract description of the elaborate and many-leveled hierarchies of being, life, and knowledge in the neo-Platonic universe. The Christianization of this principle consists in discerning in the hierarchies of both nature and grace a manifestation of the goodness of God: he so overflows with power and goodness that he makes others to share in the dispensation of his gifts. This principle is harder to appreciate in a culture marked by Enlightenment egalitarianism, but it should recommend itself to whoever prizes charity, in which one rejoices that God has given others even more than he has given oneself.

This intelligibility of the Church such as the Lord has arranged it and left it is a function, not just of beholding God's goodness and the variegated dispensation of his gifts in charity (the previous argument) but also of seeing in the arrangement an opportunity for the *exercise* of charity. Where some have things to give and others have to receive, there is increased opportunity for love and generosity, for greater humility and meekness. In other words, the very shape or structure of the Church conduces to her end, which is charity and growth in charity for all.

Magisterium

The Problem for Which the Magisterium Is the Answer

The abiding presence of hierarchical, apostolic office in the Church is the solution to an important difficulty that maintaining any tradition faces, a difficulty notably formulated by Plato. In the *Phaedrus*, Socrates tells the story of the invention of writing by one of "the old gods," Theuth, and its less-than-enthusiastic reception by king Thamus, who declares that it will destroy the memory of all who use it.[5] For his part, Socrates observes that written words, though they seem to speak intelligently, cannot defend themselves from anyone who questions their sense or truth, since they can say nothing but the same thing they have already said.[6] Moreover, the written word can fall into the wrong hands, the hands of those who cannot understand and will thereupon abuse it, and yet its parent, its author, cannot come to its help.[7] A wise man, therefore, will never consign his serious thought to paper, for the only discourse that can defend itself is that written on the soul.[8]

St. Paul might say that the goal of his mission is to inscribe the teaching of Christ on the soul, "not on tablets of stone but on the tablets of human hearts" (2 Cor 3:3). And he thinks that he *writes* not simply by force of the words of the good news he speaks (Rom 10:14–15), but also with the ink of the Holy Spirit on Christian hearts (2 Cor 3:3). But he is

5. Plato, *Phaedrus*, trans. R. Hackforth, in *Plato: The Collected Dialogues*, ed. Edith Hamilton and Huntington Cairns (Princeton, N.J.: Princeton University Press, 1961), 274D–275B.

6. Ibid., 275D.

7. Ibid., 275E.

8. Ibid., 276A.

there to guarantee his own extrinsic and written word by further and subsequent explanation (1 Cor 5:9–13).

Now, there is apostolic testimony that is consigned to writing, the New Testament, which remains long after its parents, the apostles and hagiographers, are dead. Still, there must be some living voice, some voice that shares the authority of the parent that can defend it, which is to say, interpret it. This is the voice of the bishops.[9] The same Spirit that writes the gospel on the hearts is also promised them so that the New Testament can always be read aright, even in circumstances and for questions unforeseen by its human authors.[10] The idea that the correct interpretation of Scripture is dependent on the Spirit who inspires it is itself to be found in the Old Testament; interpretation is therefore like prophecy itself.[11]

Matthew 16 and the Papacy

For Catholics, the living voice that most readily comes to mind for the declaration of what has been revealed and how to understand it is the pope's. We read Matthew 16 and the promise to Peter back to back with the First Vatican Council's declaration in *Pastor Aeternus* that defines the pope's ability with the help of the Holy Spirit to guard and expound the deposit of faith and infallibly define its meaning in matters that concern both faith and morals.[12]

This express and precisely formulated realization of the pope's role in maintaining the Church in the truth, however, was the fruit of a long history. Just because of the peculiarly modern challenges of doctrinal relativ-

9. An introductory treatment of the magisterium can be found in Avery Dulles, SJ, *Magisterium: Teacher and Guardian of the Faith* (Ave Maria, Fla.: Sapientia Press, 2007).

10. See Jn 14:26, 16:12–15; cf. Acts 20:28; and the prayer of consecration for bishops in the *Testamentum Domini* (5th c., Syrian), which can be found in Paul F. Bradshaw, *Ordination Rites of the Ancient Churches of East and West* (New York: Pueblo, 1990). There is a sense also in which the New Testament cannot fall into the wrong hands. It ceases to be what it is; it self-destructs when read by gnostics or rationalists. The idea that the correct interpretation of Scripture is dependent on the Spirit who inspires it is itself to be found in the Old Testament; interpretation is therefore like prophecy itself.

11. James Kugel, "Early Interpretation: The Common Background of Late Forms of Biblical Exegesis," in James Kugel and Rowan Greer, *Early Biblical Interpretation*, ed. Wayne A. Meeks (Philadelphia: Westminster Press, 1986), 58–62.

12. First Vatican Council, *Pastor Aeternus*, in *Decrees of the Ecumenical Councils*, vol. 2, *Trent to Vatican II*, ed. Norman P. Tanner, SJ (London: Sheed and Ward, 1990), chap. 4.

ism, of historicism, of doubt relative to the metaphysical reach of human language, and skepticism relative to the historical reliability and continuity of Christian sources, it became expedient in the post-Enlightenment world to re-articulate the ancient teaching that the Holy See is the touchstone of communion in the apostolic faith by defining the pope's proper capacity so to teach as to require, but only by force of the ancient revelation he newly articulates, that his definitions be embraced with divine and Catholic faith.

The papal service to the word of God and to the Church formed by that word is, for us today, perhaps only the most salient instrument by which the Lord fulfils his promise to be with us always in his truth to the end of the age. But it makes no sense all by itself, even in what is unique to it, unless we see this service embedded in the wider episcopal task of maintaining the Church in the truth of Christ. The Petrine office is in the first place ordained, with unfailing faith, so that the pope may strengthen his brothers (Lk 22:32). In other words, the Petrine office is first of all the exercise of a primacy within a college, within the communion of the other bishops.

A First Passage of Arms: The Bishops and Gnosticism

Just so, the Second Vatican Council treats of the pope within the context of the college of bishops of which he is the primate in *Lumen Gentium*, numbers 20–25. The wider episcopal task in which the papacy is included is already apparent in the very early days of the Church in the episcopal defense of the New Testament when its integrity was abused and its meaning twisted by the Gnostics of the second century. St. Irenaeus unlocks the Scriptures, Old and New, with the key of the Rule of Faith. The Gnostics do not have that key, and their reading of Scripture, their arrangement of the tesserae of biblical verses, produces rather the face of a dog than that of the King. An important part of his response, however, is his ability to appeal to the Tradition of faith maintained by the bishops in sees first founded by the apostles.[13]

The ecclesial rejection of the Gnosticism of such men as Valentinus

13. St. Irenaeus, *Against Heresies*, bk. I, chap. 9, for the image and the appeal.

and Basilides was the common work of bishops working as it were in their own places, but without the coordination provided by a common consultation. It is an example of what we would today call "the universal ordinary magisterium," the idea of which is that the bishops throughout the world, teaching the same thing on a matter of faith and morals contained in revelation, cannot be mistaken.[14]

Why cannot such teaching of the Church's bishops be mistaken? This is a function of three things: the nature of revelation, the historicity of its reception, and dominical promise.

The nature of Christian revelation, as Cardinal Newman pointed out, is that it comes to us *as* revelation. Revelation there may be, he granted, in every man's conscience, and scattered throughout history, vouchsafed to those who seek God with a pure heart, and who by their circumstances and the interior light of grace are secretly apprised of this or that great truth of the moral life or of the providence of God. By contrast, Christianity comes to us publicly, with public credentials.[15] If it be true, it must be certainly true, and for two reasons. First, it must be true because proceeding from the mouth of the God who cannot lie and who creates men to come to the truth. Second, it must be true, and known certainly to be true as proceeding from God, because otherwise it were unreasonable to risk one's life for its truth, either by living concordantly with its laws and precepts or by shedding a martyr's blood.

Second, revelation cannot always easily be recognized as true because of the historicity of its reception. For it is received in circumstances—cultural, philosophical, economic, social, political—that vary and that change over time. This is the problem outlined in the *Phaedrus*. God's Word became audible to us in the human words of Christ and in the words of Scripture. Just so, they entered into a history that the Incarnation determines for ever more but which does not stop until the Second Coming. The Incarnation is a kind of in-historicization of the Word. Like any other word introduced into history, those who hear it at second and

14. Vatican II, *Lumen Gentium*, no. 25.

15. John Henry Newman, *An Essay on the Development of Christian Doctrine*, 6th ed. (Notre Dame, Ind.: University of Notre Dame Press, 1989), pt. I, chap. 2, sec. 2, "An Infallible Developing Authority to Be Expected."

third remove will have questions that could not be proposed either to the Lord, or to his apostles, or to the hagiographers of the New Testament. There must, therefore, be readings of Scripture that newly actuate the word of God once spoken in another moment of history. The Spirit is promised to subsequent readers of Scripture within the Church, the Spirit in whose power the hagiographers did their work. Even so, because of human finitude and fallibility, not all readings will be equal—equally adequate, equally insightful, or even equally free from error. There must be a recognizably authoritative voice that can distinguish the true from the false.

There is such a voice, and that, in the third place, is the promise of Christ. If revelation is to remain as revelation from age to age, with the note of certainty and infallibility it must bear if it *is* God's revelation, then there must be some living voice accompanying the differing readings that the word of God evokes, a voice able to separate the wheat from the chaff. This voice is the voice of the magisterium. This is the solution to the problem posed by the *Phaedrus*.

In the second century, the rejection of Gnosticism was an exercise of the ordinary universal magisterium of the Church. At the same moment, there were three other like exercises. First, there was the ever more clearly articulated reception of the canon of the Scriptures contested by the Gnostics (and Marcionites). Second, there was the approbation of the Rule of Faith within whose bounds the Scriptures were to be read. And third, at that same moment, the recognition of the very authority of the episcopal successors of the apostles was a sort of self-reflexive but nonetheless discernible exercise of the teaching office of the bishops. The Church came then to a sort of heightened awareness of all three of these intertwined threads that make up the threefold cord of right teaching—Scripture, the Rule, the Magisterium. Coming to such a heightened awareness of a truth already possessed is what would later be called "a development of doctrine." Antecedents for all three threads there had been from the apostolic era on. But there is a clearing of the ecclesial mind in the second century on these fundamental issues, a clearing *within* the rejection of Gnosticism, that determines the structure of authoritative ecclesial preaching and catechesis and theologizing from that time on. And in that way, there is sort of theological incomparability about this first age of the Fathers never matched—never in the nature of things *able* to be matched—by subsequent ecclesial and theological history. With the exception of just one thing, which shows up at Nicaea, the panoply of the Church in the propagation and defense of the gospel is complete, and that thing is the expression of teaching in dogmatic form.

An Ecumenical Council at Nicaea

If the rejection of Gnosticism was an exercise of the universal ordinary magisterium of the Church in the second century, matched by a similar exercise in the rejection of Sabellianism or modalism in the third, there was a new form of magisterial expression in the fourth century. Granted the freedom of the empire already given by Constantine, but threatened by the Trinitarian teaching of Arius in Alexandria, bishops, probably around three hundred of them and mostly from the eastern empire but with a handful of westerners, met at Nicaea in 325 to consider his teaching.

Arianism is nicely distinguished against Sabellianism. Sabellius and other "modalists" (Adolf Harnack's name) taught that the distinction of Father and Son was really only a distinction of how the one God acted. When God created he was Father. When the same God, the very same agent, acted to save us in Christ, he was the Son. In this way, the unity of God and the divinity of the Son were maintained at the expense of the real distinction of Father and Son. This makes it impossible to read such passages as Christ's prayer to his Father in Gethsemane straightforwardly, for now it turns out that he is praying to himself, as Tertullian pointed out in his refutation of Sabellianism.

Arius maintained a real distinction between Father and Son; they were distinct agents. But they were distinct as agents in such a way as not to be equally divine in an unqualified sense. Rather, the Son, the Word of whom St. John speaks at the opening of his Gospel, was created by the Father. Arius did not distinguish between creating and begetting. He made of the Logos or Word of God the first begotten and created instrument by which God fashioned the rest of the universe. Arius maintained the unity of God, like the Sabellians, but now at the price of the real divinity of Christ. The created status of the Word meant that, incarnate in Jesus, it was no longer true to say of Jesus of Nazareth that he was truly divine and truly human. Salvation was carried out by a divine proxy, and could not mean sharing in the life of the uncreated God.

The Council of Nicaea was called at the behest of the emperor. It was not an exercise of imperial power, however, but rather an ecclesial discharge of the duty to guard the deposit of faith. Legates from the Roman See attended, and the ecumenicity of the council was therefore in principle sealed, since communion with Rome was the commonly recognized standard of communion with the Church, as Irenaeus had already recognized in the second century.[16] Such a common and impressive exercise of magisterial authority expressed in a special way the properties of the Church. Because the meeting was ecumenical, including bishops even from beyond the empire, the catholicity of the Church was evident. And because they agreed with moral unanimity as to the teaching they endorsed, the unity of the Church, too, was manifest. Additionally, the bishops were acting in the service of the apostolicity of the Church, defending the teaching of the apostles already to be found in summary form in the baptismal creed they adopted and amended for the purpose of publishing their teaching. The Arian challenge, moreover, enabled the bishops to achieve a more express appreciation of their mission in the Church: it was not fitting for bishops to be instructed by priests (Arius was a presbyter); rather, the bishops individually and corporately were the proper and true judges of the faith.

The fathers at Nicaea—according to legend 318, whose Greek alphabetic numeration, "TIH," stood for Christ and his Cross—condemned Arius's teaching. Perhaps more significant than the fact that they met in concert at one place to do so in a council rightly called "ecumenical," since unlike previous local councils it could claim to speak for the entire Christian world, was the way they reproved Arianism. They did so by asserting the true divinity and the uncreated nature of the Word, and they did this in a novel way, asserting that Jesus, the Word made flesh, was "consubstantial with the Father." When asked why the council had adopted a non-biblical way to respond to Arius, St. Athanasius answered

16. See Ludwig Hertling, SJ, *Communio: Church and Papacy in Early Christianity*, trans. Jared Wicks, SJ (German, 1943, 1962; Chicago: Loyola University Press, 1972).

that Arius's position could not be surely excluded by appeal to Scripture, since he could find a way of interpreting the crucial biblical passages in accord with the idea that the Word is created. So the council adopted a word not found in the Scriptures to speak of the relation of Son to Father, of the Word to the God of Abraham. The consubstantiality of the Son to the Father was something that could not be squared with holding that the Son is created. In this way, the Nicene teaching broke new ground in the way to assert Christian truth. The council invented "dogma."[17]

Dogma

What It Is

A dogma is an authoritative formulation of revealed truth. Dogmas state the redemptive meaning of the pattern of revelation, of the gospel.[18] They declare the truth about the God so revealed by that pattern and about man so called to share in the goods it promises. Dogmatic truths are saving truths and so are to be embraced by divine and Catholic faith. The authority in question is the teaching authority of pope or council or all the bishops precisely as declaring what is contained in the revelation of God in Christ. Examples of dogmatic truths are such teachings as that Christ is true God and true man, or that there is a truly human will in Christ, or that the beginning of faith in God is the work of grace, or that justification works a real change in the justified man.

Above, it was argued that since the text of Scripture can repeat only what it first says, then in order to answer new and unavoidable questions for Christian belief and action that are brought to it, there must be a living interpretive voice to accompany it. Only so will it remain a reliable guide for Christian faith and charity. An interpretation is more than a repetition of Scripture, and yet, if it is a good interpretation, it neither adds something to what is said nor omits anything that has been said. On the other

17. Bernard Lonergan, SJ, *The Triune God: Doctrines*, trans. Michael Shields (Toronto: University of Toronto Press, 2009), 241–55.

18. For Joseph Ratzinger, the canon, as heard by the whole Church and which hearing completes revelation, overflows into liturgy and dogma; see Aaron Pidel, "Joseph Ratzinger on Biblical Inerrancy," *Nova et Vetera* (English) 12 (2014): 319.

hand, interpretations sometimes unfold the implications of a text, bringing out what is latent in the text, or link it up with other equally authoritative texts, explaining how both are to be understood together. Nicaea is a summary of the linking up of many texts, drawing out their common implication, and translating from Scriptural to an extra-scriptural word in order to express the implication.

The reasoning behind Nicaea, for instance, can be summarized so. First, texts that impute creation to Christ, such as Proverbs 8:22f., Hebrews 1, John 1, and 1 Corinthians 6:8, impute a properly divine activity to the Word who became man, an activity also ascribed to the Father; but second, things that have the same properties belong to the same kind of thing, are "consubstantial"; therefore, Father and Son are consubstantial. Of course, "properly" and "properties" and "consubstantial" are not used in Scripture to speak about Father and Son. They are logical markers that give logical shape to assertions first made about Father and Son in the more religiously immediate and direct language of Scripture. Scriptural assertions are intent on a direct expression of the reality in question, but not concerned with the precisions that second order considerations of logic can bring to discourse. In this way, the "interpretation" of Nicaea both says the same thing as Scripture does about Father and Son, and nevertheless says it in a different way. If we want, we can say it is "development," an unfolding of Scripture that is expressed in an enunciation never before used to speak of what Scripture has, in fact, spoken about.

In this way, we come to see the point of dogma. Revelation proceeds from the mouth of God in the language of David the king and of Jeremiah the prophet, in the terms of Second Temple Judaism and of first century Greek-speaking Jews and gentiles, and in the deeds enacted in the history of these peoples. It is expressed in a culturally idiomatic form, for it is addressed first of all to these peoples, at determinate times and places. The Church is universal, however, and so must speak to many cultures. And the Church is one, and must be able to take reflexive possession of the fact that all the members of the Church share in the one mind of Christ (Phil 2: 2, 5; Acts 4:32). She needs, therefore, catholic categories in which to address men of all cultures, trans-cultural and therefore trans-temporal categories that detail the truth of the mysteries of the Trinity, of the Incarnation, of the Church, of the Sacraments. These categories express, as much as can be done by men who hear the word of the transcendent God, the intelligible structure of the mysteries themselves. These categories are those of substance and being, of person and property, of nature and power.[19]

The Authority of Dogma

The authority of dogma is not a human authority. The authority of dogma is not a merely jurisdictional ecclesial authority. The authority of dogma is a divine authority. And this follows immediately from the fact that the Church enjoins us (juridically) to embrace it with divine and Catholic faith. Divine and Catholic faith answers to divine authority and to nothing else. This is not always as immediately evident to us today as it was to the ancient Church. Here is how Yves Congar puts it:

The Fathers and the medieval writers saw all that happened in the Church and could be described as the history or realization of salvation, as what we can call the ever active presence (*actualisme*) of God. An initiative of God is implied in all activity which has some bearing on salvation.[20]

This initiative of God extended to the teaching of the Church, especially her solemn teaching; and the promises of John 14:26 and 16:12–13 on the continual teaching activity of the Spirit in the Church were understood to be fulfilled in the teaching of pope and council. Again:

It follows that the work of manifestation or revelation of himself and his plan, which God initiated through the prophets, and then accomplished in Jesus Christ, to whom we have access through the witness of the apostles—this manifestation continues in the Church, through the action of the Holy Spirit.[21]

---

19. For the notion of "catholic categories," see Bernard Lonergan, *The Triune God: Systematics*, trans. Michael Shields (Toronto: University of Toronto Press, 2007), 35, 63; and for a description of the transcultural problem that dogma addresses, 77–87. For an expression of the magisterial reflexive possession and endorsement of such categories, see Pius XII, *Humani Generis* (1950), no. 16 (J. Neuner, SJ, and Jacques Dupuis, SJ, *The Christian Faith in the Doctrinal Documents of the Catholic Church*, 7th ed. [New York: Alba House, 2001], nos. 147–48); Pope Paul VI, *Mysterium Fidei* (1965), nos. 24–25 (available at the Vatican website under Paul VI's page, http://vatican.va); John Paul II, *Fides et Ratio* (1998), nos. 94–95 (Neuner and Dupuis, *The Christian Faith*, no. 109d).

20. Yves Congar, *Tradition and Traditions: An Historical Essay and a Theological Essay*, trans. Michael Naseby and Thomas Rainborough (New York: Macmillan, 1966), 130.

21. Ibid., 131.

And again:

God acts in the Church, and thus what is there legitimately done is from him. This is the conviction of the whole of Catholic tradition.... For the Fathers and the early Middle Ages, the sacred actions are performed *in* the Church, according to the forms of the Church, and are rigorously sacred as such. But their *subject* is *God*, in an actual and direct way. Ecclesiastical structures are much more the manifestation and form of *God's* action than a subject whose internal quality or power could constitute an adequate basis for the certain production of the expected effect.[22]

Congar distinguishes two ways in which this has been conceived. First, it has been conceived as a function of the living presence of God in the Church, and this up to the twelfth century roughly; second, it has been conceived as a function of juridical powers given to the Church by God and exercised by the hierarchy. If the second way is a function of a heightened appreciation of institution and law, the first is a function of the participationist metaphysics that reigned in the Church till the ascendency of nominalism, but which no effort should be spared to recover as fully as possible.[23]

We can say when we assent to dogma that we are believing the Church. But we are believing the Church because we think God is speaking in her. It is like believing the prophet or the apostle for the same reason.[24]

Development of Dogma

It is not the case that dogma develops only from Scripture, for the gospel has been received in the Church in extra-scriptural forms. The Tradition that transmits revelation contains more than the Scriptures. It contains the Rule of Faith. It contains also the sacraments and the worship of the Church. The Church's worship of Christ implies the Nicene settlement just as much as any reading of Proverbs 8 does. And the Arian distinction

22. Ibid., 134–35.

23. This is the constant object of Matthew Levering's prodigious output, for which one might start with his *Scripture and Metaphysics: Aquinas and the Renewal of Trinitarian Theology* (Oxford: Blackwell Publishing, 2004).

24. See John R. T. Lamont, *Divine Faith* (Aldershot, UK: Ashgate, 2004), 165–69, on the magisterial or exclusively ecclesiastical way of thinking about the authority of dogma; and 169ff. for what he calls the "ecclesial" view, the view up to the twelfth century.

of the Persons according to essence or nature is blocked by the baptismal practice of the Church, since baptism is in the name (one, singular name) of Father, Son, and Spirit, unto one salvation worked by all three Persons. It is not surprising that the fathers of Nicaea should take a baptismal creed within which to assert the consubstantiality of the Son with the Father. On the other hand, the Rule of Faith, as we now have it, is not in its content a-Scriptural (we spoke of the relation of the Rule and Scripture in discussing the Tradition of the Church). The worship of the Church is informed by Scripture, and not just in the Liturgy of the Word. Baptismal practice is undergirded by Matthew 28:19.

For its part, *Dei Verbum* speaks about "growth in understanding [*perceptio*] of what is handed on," the apostolic Tradition of the revelation of God, *before* it takes up Scripture's written witness to revelation.[25] Dogmatic formulation is never independent of Scripture or abstracts from it, but dogmatic development depends not merely on parsing the words but penetrating the reality. So, the constitution says, "what is handed on" is "both the words and the realities they signify."[26] Of course, we do not have cognitive possession of the intelligible real except through the signifying words. Growth in understanding what is handed on, the constitution explains, comes in three ways: first, "through contemplation and study by believers," who like Mary "ponder these things in their hearts" (Lk 2:19, 51); second, "through the intimate understanding of spiritual things which they experience"; and third, "through the preaching of those who, on succeeding to the office of bishop, receive the sure charism of truth." The first two ways are, in principle, common to all the baptized faithful.[27] The last way is proper to bishops. The ways are distinct.

First, there is contemplation and study. Christian contemplation is ordered to beholding the intelligibility and goodness and beauty of revealed truths and realities. This is a matter, often, of the comparison of the things in question to naturally known counterparts.[28] For instance,

25. Vatican II, *Dogmatic Constitution on Divine Revelation (Dei Verbum)*, in *Decrees of the Ecumenical Councils*, vol. 2, *Trent to Vatican II*, ed. Norman P. Tanner, SJ (London: Sheed and Ward, 1990), no. 8.

26. Ibid.

27. See discussion in Yves Congar, OP, *La Foi et la Théologie* (Tournai: Desclée, 1962), 108–10.

28. See First Vatican Council, *Dei Filius*, chap. 4.

St. Thomas likens the charity that is poured into our hearts by the Holy Spirit (Rom 5:5) to friendship. Thus, thinking that Aristotle tells him true about friendship, the crown of the moral virtues, in books eight and nine of the *Nicomachean Ethics*, and knowing the Lord's distinction between servants and friends in John 15, St. Thomas can compare and contrast the friendship that completes our created nature with the more perfect friendship Christ establishes with us.[29] "Study" connotes a more discursive pattern of thought, by which connections are made and inferences drawn. So, for instance, properties are deduced from natures, natures intuited from properties. The human freedom of our Lord, displayed in the gospel, demands that we recognize a human nature perfect both in its capabilities and its exercise. Contrariwise, the recognition of him as a man like us in all things but sin (cf. Heb 4:15) conduces to the confession of two wills in Christ, human and divine, as taught by the Third Council of Constantinople (680/681). Lots of the discussion of dogmatic development in the seventeenth century confined itself to the forms of inference available to produce a conclusion that could be embraced by divine and Catholic faith or a conclusion merely theologically certain.[30] The path to understanding dogmatic development at this level is rather to attend to the acts of contemplative understanding that articulate the fundamental and intrinsic intelligibility of some mystery, or that relate it to the end of man, or that compare it to some naturally known reality.[31] Sometimes, these acts of understanding can be cashed out in demonstrative syllogisms, as with the deduction of the Lord's human will from his human nature. But more often they cannot, and we remain with arguments *ex convenientia*. Many such arguments bearing on the same conclusion, however, can lead to certain knowledge of some doctrine, as do the arguments for the Immaculate Conception. As the first Eve was made without sin, so the second. As the first Eve was drawn wholly from Adam's side, so the second from the sinless side of Christ. It is unbecoming that the author of grace be welcomed into the world by a freedom tainted by sin. And so

29. St. Thomas Aquinas, *Summa theologiae* II-II, q. 23, aa. 1, 3, and 6.
30. Owen Chadwick, *From Bossuet to Newman*, 2nd ed. (Cambridge: Cambridge University Press, 1987), chap. 2.
31. See Lonergan, *The Triune God: Systematics*, 53–57.

on. Such intuitions, especially allied with the experiential knowledge next listed by *Dei Verbum*, and the *pietas* that issues from the Christian's love of Mary, lead the Christian faithful ahead of the magisterium. The faithful Bride who is the Church recognizes the faithful bride who is Mary, just as Elizabeth without the help of the priest Zacharias.

So, in addition to what purely "logical" theories of development can offer to understanding development, where, for instance, properties are deduced from natures, there is also what Cardinal Newman contributes in speaking of the "illative sense"—the sense by which we see how individually non-probative signs of the truth of some particular fact can, when multiplied, produce reasonable ground for asserting the fact. The broken pane of glass does not prove all by itself that there was an intruder. The displaced lamp just of itself does not do so either, nor, individually, the nervous dog or the bread crumbs on the table. But altogether, they do. Also in matters dogmatic, where some strong antecedent theological probability is corroborated by many signs that this probability either has been met or has by previous ages of faith been thought to have been met, then there follows a prudential judgment that intellectual assent can and even ought to be given to some development, that is, to the recognition that the probability is an actuality.[32]

Second, there is indeed a sort of experiential knowledge of spiritual things available to the Christian. St. Thomas recognizes just such a way of knowing things, a "connatural knowledge" of what, because we love it, we thereby experience intimately. So—his example—a chaste man knows without reasoning, but immediately and by the delight of what he loves, what things are opposed to chastity or what sort of behaviors threaten it.[33] He does not have to reason it out; his acquaintance with the beloved virtue and how it unites him to Christ and Mary speaks faster than any discursive exercise of prudence whose point of departure is the express knowledge of the nature of chastity. This kind of knowledge of the reali-

32. For the preeminent presentation of a logical theory, see Francisco Marin-Solà, OP, *L'évolution homogène de dogme catholique*, 2 vols., 2nd ed. (Fribourg: Librarie de l'Oeuvre de Saint-Paul, 1924). For Newman's contribution, see Andrew Meszaros, *The Prophetic Church: History and Doctrinal Development in John Henry Newman and Yves Congar* (Oxford: Oxford University Press, 2016), chap. 2.

33. St. Thomas Aquinas, *Summa theologiae* II-II, q. 45, a. 2, c.

ties of Christian revelation operated in the definition of Mary's Immaculate Conception. Long before theologians worked out the possibility of redemption in virtue of the future merits of Christ, Christians knew that Mary did not come into the world tainted by original sin. This kind of knowledge works also to give certainty in the rejection of some proposed development of doctrine or pastoral practice. Before the historical reconstructions of Church order had been canvassed and before the theological arguments about the structure of orders had been reviewed, those who savored the communication of divine things within the register of sexual symbolism, those who adored the person of Christ represented by the priest at mass, those who cherished the maternal and Marian character of the Church against the foil of a male priesthood knew that the Church could not ordain women to the priesthood, and did not have to wait until Pope John Paul II's apostolic letter *Ordinatio Sacerdotalis* (1994) to learn this. The experiential knowledge of spiritual things, it may be worthwhile to remark, although it renders a verdict without reasoning, is not established without words. We do not learn to love Mary, for instance, independently of the first chapters of Luke.

The experiential or connatural knowledge of revealed mysteries is sometimes thought of as an extra-propositional, extra-linguistic possession of the mysteries of salvation, and this makes it easy to explain the emergence of dogmatic formulas that are not deduced or otherwise easily lead out from the words of Scripture. Such an extra-linguistic possession has been thought to be necessary since otherwise development could not be distinguished from the assertion of something so novel that a denial of the closure of revelation would be implied. However, this is a mistake. There is no human cognitive possession of reality that bypasses language. It is an important mistake, moreover, because it is tantamount to removing the limits on what we can know and say about the mysteries, the limits of Scripture itself. From hearers of the word we soon move to become architects of our own spirituality. The doctrines of the Church become symbols in the modern sense, imaginatively pleasing images on which we hang our hopes and desires—except when they are not pleasant, like the doctrine of original sin, and then we discard such a "symbol" as no longer serviceable for Christian thought and action. In other words, an appeal to a non-linguistically mediated experience of God easily passes into a barely concealed report of what we ourselves think is good for us to think and good for us to do, and forfeits any pretension really to communicate what has been heard from God. The experiential or connatural knowledge of the mysteries, however, means especially our conformation in love to what is revealed—to who is revealed—and it is not established without words, the words of Scripture and tradition and the liturgy.

Third, there is the preaching of bishops. This may seem to be something hard to distinguish from episcopal contemplation of the mysteries and study of theology, but if we understand the form of liturgical preaching, we will see how distinct, and basic, this way of growth in the understanding of revelation is. The lectionary of the Church, ancient and modern, serves up readings from both Testaments for the Eucharistic celebration for Sundays and solemnities (the Sundays of Easter excepted, where readings from the new history of the renewed People of God, readings from Acts, replace the Old Testament reading). Preaching that is full and comprehensive states the realization of the Paschal Mystery or some part or aspect of it realized here and now, this Sunday, this solemnity. And it does so by unpacking the Scriptures Old and New, and precisely by finding the New latent in the Old and the Old realized in the New.[34] That is, preaching is a live repetition, a live realization, of the very pattern of words and deeds that revelation first and everlastingly consists of. It is the slow but sure penetration of the complex, never completely mastered, always surprising pattern and the patterns within the pattern of the economy of salvation.[35] We said above, in arguing for the necessity of a living authoritative voice of doctrinal discernment, that Scripture says always the same thing, over and again. But in another sense, because of the endless complexity of the relation of the Testaments to one another, the Scriptures constantly say new things to those who ponder them in their hearts.[36]

34. Vatican II, *Dei Verbum*, nos. 15–16.

35. For an example, see Matthew Levering, *Mary's Bodily Assumption* (Notre Dame, Ind.: University of Notre Dame Press, 2015), chaps. 3 and 4.

36. See St. Gregory the Great, *Homilies on the Book of the Prophet Ezekiel*, trans. Theodosia Tomkinson (Etna, Calif.: Center for Traditionalist Orthodox Studies, 2008), bk. 1, homily 6, nos. 12–15. In no. 13, the Scriptures are a vast ocean of intelligibility, with innumerable meanings, an

The fruit of that kind of episcopal reading of the two Testaments can be found, for instance, in St. Irenaeus's *Demonstration of the Apostolic Preaching*, whose very point is to manifest against Gnosticism the unity and integrity of the economy of salvation from the Old to the New Testaments, showing that the Father of Christ is the God of Abraham and Moses, and that the prophets foretold what the apostles preached.[37] Or again, St. Cyril of Alexandria's *Commentary on John*, completed probably before 428, arms him as it were beforehand to deal with Nestorius. His commentary on John 6:42, for instance, already contradicts any denial that Mary is the Mother of God; his commentary on the Eucharistic discourse of John 6:52ff. prepares him to see the immediate and disastrous soteriological consequence of that same denial.[38]

The twentieth-century discussion of development often went forward in an atmosphere that did not take due account of the unity of Scripture, the typological and figural reading of the Old Testament on which so much of patristic development of doctrine rested. That is, the sort of appreciation of the virtualities of Scripture that Gregory the Great evinces was lost.[39] That appreciation has been restored especially by Henri de Lubac and Yves Congar.[40]

Development of Doctrine and Assent to Dogma

We have seen that *Dei Verbum* distinguishes three ways in which what is contained in the words and deeds of the original pattern of revelation is unfolded, three ways in which the Church achieves "growth in understanding" of what is revealed, namely studious contemplation of what has been handed on from the apostles, connatural knowledge of divine realities, and episcopal preaching. These ways are the engines of doctrinal

---

ocean we navigate borne up by the cross, the key to all the meanings. He says this apropos of explaining the presence of the New Testament in the Old.

37. Irenaeus of Lyons, *On the Apostolic Preaching*, trans. John Behr (Crestwood, N.Y.: St. Vladimir's Press, 1997).

38. St. Cyril of Alexandria, *Commentary on John*, vol. 1, trans. David R. Maxwell (Downers Grove, Ill.: IVP Academic, 2013).

39. See note 36.

40. For Henri de Lubac, see his *Medieval Exegesis*, 3 vols., trans. Marc Sebanc and E. M. Macierowski (French, 1961; Grand Rapids, Mich.: Eerdmans, 1998–2000); and for Congar, see his remarks on the economy of salvation in *La Foi et la Théologie*, 8–18.

development. None of these ways, however, is the reason why we assent to some teaching of the Church when the Church proposes it to us as dogma contained in revelation, and it is important to be clear on this.[41]

We do not assent in faith to the dogma of the human will and freedom of Christ because this conclusion follows apodictically as naming a necessary property contained in human nature, nor do we assent to the dogma of the Immaculate Conception because such a conception evidently fits the dignity of the Mother of God. Nor do we assent to it because it cannot be discordant with a soul whose love of Mary conforms it to her very image. Nor do we assent to any episcopal teaching because it arises out of the brilliance of the exegesis that links the Testaments one to another. We assent to dogma solely on the ground that the Church proposes it to us as contained in the word of God, and so, as spoken by God. For the divine authority, the authority of God-speaking, is superior to the created mind's perception of necessary entailments. It is above the created beauty of any *convenientia* in the economy of revelation as understood by man. It is beyond the perceived but still created harmony between a holy soul and the Object to which it has been conformed in love. The authority of God-revealing is God, and so is something altogether uncreated, and the assent of faith responds to that and that alone, a point we shall revisit in chapter 7.

The Historicity of Dogma

The idea that there is some wordless apprehension of what revelation reveals is often allied with a second mistake, a wrong understanding of what we adverted to above referring to the historicity of the reception of revelation. Recognition of dogma's development is just one and the same thing with recognizing its historical character, the fact that dogmatic enunciations are assembled not all at once but in time and subject to timely, that is, "historical," influences on those who formulate them just in their formulating them. Dogmatic truths, though warranted by God's speech, are spoken in human terms; and all humanly asserted truths, divinely warranted or not, are historically constituted truths.

41. See Congar, *La Foi et la Théologie*, 115–20.

So, for instance, Aristotle's truth is historically constituted. His meta-physics is conditioned by his physical findings, and the *Physics*, in part, is conditioned by the then-current cosmology and astronomy. But if we no longer think that fifty-five (or fifty-eight) unmoved movers are required in order to account for the motion of the heavenly bodies, if the relation between these movers and the First Unmoved Mover therefore disap-pears for us as anything except an historical problem, it is not the case that the definition of motion is no longer the actualization of what is in potency so long as it is still in potency, or that act is not prior to potency, or that the nature of a natural substance is not more beholden to form than to matter. Basic terms and relations, their fundamentality one of the chief results of Aristotle's analysis, remain the same. And insofar as we ask Aristotle's questions about motion, we will still conclude necessarily to a First Mover. Or again, insofar as we mean by soul what he meant by soul, we shall continue to say that it is the first act of an organic body in potency to it.

Mutatis mutandis, the same is to be said of dogma. One constraint on today's understanding of past dogma is the "catholic" character of fundamental dogmatic categories, and the insight that there are no more basic instruments with which to think the real than such terms as sub-stance and nature, person and property, even where, used of divine things, they must be used analogically. The relevant history of the constitution of some dogma is always necessary for the most exact understanding of what was meant and how that meaning was achieved. But the categories of many dogmatic truths, fundamental as they are to thinking the real, assure a trans-temporal communicability of dogma.[42] We return to this issue in chapter 5.

The Church has not left the issue of the permanence of the meaning and truth of dogma in any doubt. The First Vatican Council teaches that dogma is "irreformable." What the council meant is that, understood the way the dogma was understood by those who, with the assistance of the Holy Spirit, asserted it as a true statement to be received with divine and Catholic faith, the statement remains true. This means that the dogmas of

42. See note 19, above.

the Church remain in play as the true assertions they are for helping us to understand not only all exegetical and theological discourse posterior to them, but even all exegetical and theological discourse *previous* to them, and that they remain unchanging touchstones for judging the truth of any human discourse whatsoever. The "history of dogma" therefore means an excavation of what questions were asked, what the terms of the questions and of their answers meant, why the questions were asked the way they were, and why they were given the form they had. Part of the reason for the assertion of the Immaculate Conception, for instance, was the implication that no one else was so conceived, and that therefore the universal condition of original sin continues to have social and political consequences in the world. This is important for understanding the intent of the dogma, and for discounting those interpretations that try to find in Mary's conception the exemplar of our own. That is not really a possible way in which to take the meaning of the definition.

It can be asked, however, whether this very teaching on the irreformability of dogma really is not itself an illegitimate constraint on how to understand its historicity. Perhaps the historicity of dogma means that even the dogmatic assertion that dogma is irreformable—a kind of meta-dogma—is itself quite reformable, according as we have a proper understanding of the historical circumstances in which *this* teaching was formulated. Only where truth is understood as the conformity of proposition and reality does the teaching of Vatican I have the meta-historical character implied by the teaching that it is irreformable. That is, we have to understand truth the way St. Anselm does in his *De veritate*, as "correctness" or "rectitude," which is how St. Augustine understood it in his *Soliloquies*, which is how Aristotle understood it in book 9 of the *Metaphysics*. It is alleged to the contrary, however, that truth, so understood, is a quite secondary notion of truth, even though presupposed for the long era in which the Church's theology in the West was dominated by scholasticism. It may be urged that the primary and truly fundamental notions of truth are quite otherwise.

For Martin Heidegger, the original sense of truth or *aletheia* was that of the unveiling of being to an historically situated, "thrown" *Dasein* (man taken just as attuned to truth and the being it unveils). But this builds into truth itself a sort of historical character, according to which what human beings take as the real, as being, varies, and must vary, from age to historical age, as Heidegger then proposes to demonstrate in his history of the unfolding of Being in the West. For biblical theologians influenced by Heidegger, furthermore, the truth with which the Bible is concerned is the truth that is *done*: truth is not neutrally beheld by the distant eye of the detached observer, but something performed by the existentially engaged and concretely determined covenant partner of God. For both reasons, anthropological and theological, philosophical and revealed, we ought never to think that truth, even the truth of defined dogma, escapes judgment and so revision in its material articulation, by a gospel that continues to unfold the revelation of God contained in Scripture as it continues to accompany us historically, generation by generation. Revelation is addressed to us, men who change, and it too must change if it is still to be heard by us. Dogma is therefore relative not only to the revelation to which we have access in Scripture and Tradition, as is obvious, but also to the historical circumstances in which that revelation is heard and so repeatedly formulated and reformulated—just as were the formulations first recorded in Scripture itself.[43]

The irreformability of dogma, therefore, is something regional—it holds only so long as some determinate conditions of Dasein's articulation of Being and beings last, and only so long as the situation of man's hearing of the gospel itself lasts.[44] Once they change, dogma is reformable, and just so that the overriding demands of the gospel of salvation and mercy may confront us and be met by our free response.[45] In this way, for instance, the Church's teaching on the indissolubility of sacramental marriage must accommodate, in the contemporary age, the gospel demand to show mercy to sinners and precisely where mercy originates

43. For such an argument, see Walter Kasper, *Dogma unter dem Wort Gottes* (Mainz: Matthias-Grünewald Verlag, 1965), chap. 3.

44. Kasper, *Dogma*, 80: "Die Wahrheit bleibt innergeschichtlich immer Verheissung, sie läst sich nie adäquat in Sätze einfangen, sondern ist offen für die je grössere Zukunft Gottes. Zur Wahrheit im Sinn der Schrift gehört das Moment des Überraschenden, des Neuen und des Überbietenden."

45. Kasper says there is an absolute character to the truth of revelation, *Dogma*, 129; however: "Solche Absolutheit schliesst es aber aus, dass sie gleichsam in einem Satz erfasst werden kann; die Absolutheit des Evangeliums bringt es vielmehr mit sich, dass die Kirche immer unterwegs sein wird, dieses Evangelium auszuschöpfen und zu ergründen." See the discussion in Ignace de la Potterie, SJ, *La vérité dans saint Jean*, vol. 2 (Rome: Biblical Institute Press, 1977), 1021–23.

and is made available to us, by participating in the sacrament of the Lord's Supper.

What shall we think of such a proposed end-run around the Church's once-formulated, and, as it used to be supposed, once-and-forever reliably formulated teaching? The first trouble with such meta-theories of truth is that they want us to accept them on the ground that they are true in the old-fashioned "correctness" or "conforming to reality" way of understanding truth. Is it true that truth is the historically conditioned unveiling of Being? Is it true that revealed truth is the always never completed and therefore never trans-temporally formulable promise of God? But if these sentences are true, then the definition of truth they propose self-destructs. We may have to wait some years, but then conditions will change, and the definitions will be no good—no longer true.

The second trouble is that though there is some sense in saying that the Bible is concerned with our doing the truth, even so, in the same Gospel of John where this is prominent, there is also a concern for truth in the ordinary sense. "Truth" in John's Gospel is the revelation of Christ and to do the truth is no longer to do the works of the law but to believe in Christ.[46] To believe in Christ, to accept his revelation, is to accept the truth that he is the Son.

The third trouble is that this proposal to relativize all Church teaching has been condemned many times in the last one hundred years or so, from Pius X to John Paul II; and the permanence of dogma and the permanence of its formulae maintained.[47]

The ultimate trouble with this proposal is that it means, in the end, that no word has been spoken, no revelation given. We are thrown back on an assurance of God's love, and the rest is up to us to invent. Contrary to what I thought when I embraced the faith, that I had now found guid-

46. See the conclusion to de la Potterie, *La vérité dans saint Jean*, 2:1008–9, 2:1010–11.

47. Pius X, *Pascendi Dominici gregis* (1907), nos. 12–13 (available at the Vatican website on Pius X's page, http://vatican.va); Pius XII, *Humani generis* (1950), no. 16 (Neuner and Dupuis, *The Christian Faith*, nos. 147–48); Paul VI, *Mysterium fidei* (1965), nos. 24–25 (available at the Vatican website on Paul VI's page, http://vatican.va); John Paul II, *Fides et Ratio* (1998), nos. 94–95 (Neuner and Dupuis, *The Christian Faith*, no. 109d). There is also the Congregation for the Doctrine of the Faith's declaration *Mysterium ecclesiae* (1973), no. 5 (Neuner and Dupuis, *The Christian Faith*, nos. 160–63).

ance and help for thinking about how things are and how to live, I found no such thing. No, I am back on my own. And perhaps, even worse, I will be under the thumb, not of some historically transcending truth, not of God, not of the Church, not of Tradition, not of some pope or bishop bound by revelation, by Scripture and past dogmatic articulation thereof, but of whoever gets his hands on the levers of power in the Church and told to think whatever they tell me I must think according to their measure of what they take "our" experience to be.

How should we better think of the historicity of dogma? For there to be a history, something must stay the same, and something must change. For there to be a history of X, X must stay the same; and if the history is recognizable, X must be recognizably the same. What is the X that stays identifiably the same in the history of dogma?

Karl Rahner was fond of boiling the gospel down to the truth that God has come close to us, and that the categorial (historically available) manifestation of this grace is Christ and his Church. The categorial manifestation is *necessary* for the reality of the presence of grace, and the necessary *shape* of this categorial manifestation is Christ, the Word made flesh. Is this enough? Arguably, it is, as long as one is careful about maintaining our ability to identify Christ. That seems right: what revelation reveals in the economy of words and deeds is the form of Christ.

That there be a categorial manifestation of God's grace and truth means, for the Rahner of *Hearer of the Word*, that the dogmatic propositions of the Church be true. That is to say, there is no categoriality without categories. And for *Hearer of the Word*, the revealed categoriality of the God who comes close to us and that remains identifiably the same is located precisely in the dogmatic propositions that the Church proposes to be embraced by divine and Catholic faith.[48]

Past this point, the questions are simple. Is the Arian Christ the same Christ as the Christ of the New Testament? That is, is non-divinity the same as divinity? Is the Christ of Nestorius the same as the Christ of Nicaea? That is, does an eternal agent or does a created agent save us by dy-

48. Karl Rahner, SJ, *Hearer of the Word*, trans. Joseph Donceel, SJ (German, 1941; New York: Continuum, 1994), 40–41, and chaps. 14 and 15. The post-conciliar, "later" Rahner is another matter, of course.

ing on the cross? Is the Christ of Sergius of Constantinople the same as the Christ of Chalcedon and Leo the Great? That is, does a divine person save us by a human obedience and a created charity, or is there no human work worked by Christ for us to imitate? Further along the course of the Church: Does Christ invite all who follow him to share in the very same sacrifice by which he reconciled the world to his Father, or can he only distribute the fruits of that sacrifice to those he cannot include in the very act by which he goes to the Father? Does Christ make all who are saved by his grace members of his one body, or is he a sort of reverse chimera, the unnatural head of many distinct ecclesial bodies?

The X that stays identifiably the same throughout the historical course of dogma is therefore the form of Christ. This is why, in the end, our confidence that the constitution of dogma over time, its "historicity," is not a deformation of the figure of Christ is rooted in the very faith by which we recognize him in revelation. This in turn means that the individual's recognition of the integrity and continuity of Catholic truth is parasitic on the Church's recognition of this same thing.

For Vincent of Lérins (d. c. 450), who first thought carefully about the constitution of the Church's teaching across time, the Church's recognition of the integrity of teaching is most expressly actualized in the ecumenical council. It is the council that serves as the memory of the Church, where, in an assembly that attests both the catholicity (*ubique*) and unity (*ab omnibus*) of the Church, the discernment of the apostolicity of the Church is also possible, and therefore what always (*semper*) has been taught can be manifested, so that we believe what has been taught *ubique, semper et ab omnibus.*[49]

Definitive Teaching

When the Church defines something as contained within the deposit of revelation, it is to be embraced with divine and Catholic faith, in faith's very assent to the God who reveals himself. But there is other definitive

---

49. Vincent of Lérins, *The Commonitory*, trans. C. A. Heurtley, in *The Nicene and Post-Nicene Fathers*, 2nd ser., vol. 11, ed. Philip Schaff and Henry Wace (Grand Rapids, Mich.: Eerdmans, 1982); see Thomas G. Guarino, *Vincent of Lérins and the Development of Christian Doctrine* (Grand Rapids, Mich.: Baker Academic, 2013), 5, 14, 29–33.

teaching that, like dogma, is infallible, but not embraced by faith. This is because there are things logically connected with the truths of faith, ordinary things really connected to revealed realities. And sometimes, it is necessary to speak definitively about these truths and realities, too, in order to guard what has been revealed from being misunderstood or implicitly denied. Such truths belong to the so-called second object of magisterial teaching authority, which will be touched on again when we treat the *praeambula fidei* in part two of this book.

PART II

MAN HEARS

CHAPTER 5

PRAEAMBULA FIDEI

We come now to the second part of this book. The first part considered God speaking a word to us. Now we turn to our hearing of that word in faith. Before faith, however, there are the *praeambula*—the things that walk before it.

For instance, the last topic discussed in chapter 4 was dogma. Dogmas speak of a reality, divine reality, transcendent to the world. This supposes that human language can meaningfully speak of things we do not sense and that cannot be sensed. Furthermore, dogmas purport to speak of this reality in a trans-cultural, trans-temporal way. As we have seen, this supposes there are concepts or categories that transcend the particularities of cultures and times. Neither of these suppositions is uncontested. But both of them can be vindicated philosophically. They count as *praeambula fidei*.

That there are *praeambula* to faith naturally knowable is itself a dogma of faith. The First Vatican Council asserted in *Dei Filius* that "right reason demonstrates the foundations of faith" (chap. 4), having already repeated St. Paul's teaching in Romans that the invisible things of God can be perceived in the things that have been made (chap. 2, Rom 1:20).[1] The constitution also anathematized those who deny that revelation can be made credible by external signs or that the divine origin of Christianity can be proved by miracles certainly known as such (chap. 3, canons 3 and 4). The natural knowledge of God and the vindication of the possibility of miracles are presented here as *praeambula fidei*.

John Paul II recalls this teaching of *Dei Filius* when, in *Fides et Ratio*, he lists the topics that fundamental theology addresses.

With its specific character as a discipline charged with giving an account of faith (cf. 1 Pt 3:15), the concern of *fundamental theology* will be to justify and expound the relationship between faith and philosophical thought. Recalling the teaching of Saint Paul (cf. Rom 1:19–20), the First Vatican Council pointed to the existence of truths which are naturally, and thus philosophically, knowable; and an acceptance of God's Revelation *necessarily* presupposes knowledge of these truths.... Consider, for example, the natural knowledge of God, the possibility of distinguishing divine Revelation from other phenomena or the recognition of its credibility, the capacity of human language to speak in a true and meaningful way even of things which transcend all human experience. From all these truths, the mind is led to acknowledge the existence of a truly propaedeutic path to faith.[2]

We will consider credibility as a property of revelation in the next chapter. But the Holy Father lists also the natural knowledge of the existence of God, repeating the First Vatican Council, and the capacity of human language to speak of divine things among the *praeambula*, something we just noted as presupposed to the knowledge of faith expressed in dogma. As it turns out, in demonstrating a naturally available knowledge of God, philosophical reason, deployed under the direction of faith, at one and the same time vindicates the capacity of language to speak of God. And although we touched upon the capacity of language to speak of God briefly in chapter 1, this chapter will take up the usual exploration of that

1. First Vatican Council, *Dei Filius*, in *Decrees of the Ecumenical Councils*, vol. 2, *Trent to Vatican II*, ed. Norman P. Tanner, SJ (London: Sheed and Ward, 1990).
2. John Paul II, *Fides et Ratio* (1998), no. 67, italics added. I give the translation available at the Vatican website, http://vatican.va. There is another translation in *Restoring Faith in Reason, A New Translation of the Encyclical Letter Faith and Reason of Pope John Paul II together with a commentary and discussion*, ed. Laurence Paul Hemming and Susan Frank Parsons (Notre Dame, Ind.: University of Notre Dame Press, 2003), 1–173, with facing Latin pages.

capacity in the doctrine of the analogical names of God. In the first place, however, we need to show just why it is that, as John Paul II insists, faith *necessarily* presupposes a natural knowledge of God. Second, we need to say a word about the contemporary circumstances prejudicial to the natural knowledge of God. Then we can say something about the natural knowledge of God and about analogical language in speaking of God.

That Revelation Requires the Possibility of Natural Theology

Catholic and Protestant Differences

The demonstration that faith necessarily supposes a natural knowledge of God not only shows the relation of natural theology to revelation and so to theology, but also demarcates important philosophical agreements and disagreements between Catholics and Protestants. Both Martin Luther and John Calvin granted a natural knowledge of God, following Paul in Romans 1:19–20, and like Paul pointed out its insufficiency: we may come on our own to know God as creator, but this is not to know him as saving.[3] That is, on our own, we do not know God as he wants us to know him through the revelation of his Son. And again like Paul, both were aware of sinful man's proclivity to distort the natural knowledge of God, to forget it, to prefer a knowledge of a man-made and man-imaged god. There is nothing remarkable here in early Protestant thought—that is, there is nothing novel here over against Catholic teaching, which likewise follows the plain sense of Romans (and the Book of Wisdom, and Psalm 103, and so on).

But there are two further Protestant thinkers that argue for things unacceptable to Catholic thought. First, Immanuel Kant (1724–1804) sought systematically to show that human reason cannot make any valid claim to a knowledge of God.[4] Knowledge is a function of applying what he called

---

3. For Luther, see his *Lectures on Romans*, trans. Walter G. Tillmanns and Jacob A. O. Preus, ed. Hilton Oswald (St. Louis: Concordia, 1972), 153–70. For Calvin, see *Calvin: The Institutes of the Christian Religion*, trans. Ford Lewis Battles (Philadelphia: Westminster Press, 1956), vol. 1, bk. 1, chaps. 1–6.

4. Immanuel Kant, *Critique of Pure Reason*, trans. Norman Kemp Smith (New York: St. Martin's

the categories of understanding, such as substance and cause, unity and existence, to sensory intuitions of objects. Since there are no such intuitions of divinity, there is no knowledge of God. Moreover, if there were knowledge of God strictly speaking, God would be introduced into the deterministically governed causal relations of the things of this world where freedom cannot be recognized. However, just as there can be a practical postulate of our own freedom, there is also a practical postulate of God as the supreme guarantor of the moral order, without which we would be in despair. Such postulation is not knowledge. But then, oddly, we do not really want knowledge of God, for otherwise the world would not be safe for moral faith; such faith would be proscribed by a reason that sees only determinisms and that cannot recognize human freedom and a free God. The faith for which the world is now safe, of course, no longer expresses itself in teachings or dogmas that tell us any true thing about God in addition to his hoped-for rule as guarantor of the universal moral law known in our experience of obligation. As distinct from morality, an ethical religion, one that does not foster superstition and clericalism, becomes largely a matter of imaginatively shoring up what would otherwise be a wavering and ineffective commitment to obey the moral law.[5] Kantianism is a sort of Averroism for the eighteenth century, where religion satisfies the imagination but only philosophy meets the requirements of mind, and minus Averroes's tenet that metaphysical knowledge of God really is knowledge.

Kant's strictures on the knowledge of God were the seedbed of Freidrich Schleiermacher's attempt to find a feeling or intuition of God that could support something more in continuity with historical Lutheranism, as well as of subsequent liberal Protestant denials of the objectivity and truth of the Church's dogma as in Adolf von Harnack, Ernst Troeltsch, Auguste Sabatier. We return to this strand of modern theology in the last chapter.

To the Kantian critique one can respond theologically by appeal to Romans 1:19–20 and Wisdom 13, or philosophically by deploying the argu-

---

Press, 1965), 485–531, esp. 528–530; and for the necessity of speaking of the world *as if* it is created, see 550.

5. Immanuel Kant, *Religion within the Limits of Reason Alone*, trans. Theodore M. Greene and Hyt H. Hudson (New York: Harper and Row, 1960).

ments of natural theology while noting the difficulty in Kant's critique of natural theology, which has to do not so much with what he says about "existence" not being a predicate, or with his view on the relation of the cosmological to the ontological argument for God's existence, but rather with the inherent difficulty of setting a limit to human inquiry. It is hard to delimit a boundary for thinking short of the principle of non-contradiction. Kantians are deceived by the metaphor of a limitation within or horizon of a visual field: I may not be able to see beyond a wall or even fruitfully imagine what is on the other side. But thinking does not have limits like that; it is not bound by anything in the world except "being," which is to say it is not bound at all.

The second Protestant thinker of note here is Karl Barth (1886–1968), who takes things in a similarly radical direction. Contrary to Kant, he maintains that the word of God really does teach us, and it teaches us true; and "dogmatics" in his *Church Dogmatics* is meant to reassert the objectivity and truth of the knowledge of God that God imparts to us in Christ. In Christ, God "commandeers" both our capacity to know and our language so as to give us real knowledge of him.[6] But this is no return to a pre-critical, that is, pre-Kantian, position. With Kant, Barth also wanted to deny the natural knowledge of God, and not only on philosophical but on theological grounds, too. The very attempt at such knowledge is misguided and sinful, forsaking the only ground upon which God can be known, which is God himself and his word.[7] And this rejection of natural theology, together with its companion doctrine that such knowledge is analogical, Barth erects into the great and, for him, saving barrier between genuine Christianity and Catholic adulteration of the word of God with human words, a barrier likewise between genuine theology and the Catholic adulteration of it with philosophy.[8]

Arguably, Barth's view of God's word, where the conditions of hearing it are supplied wholly from the Creator, implies a God who is epistemi-

6. Mats Wahlberg, *Revelation as Testimony: A Philosophical-Theological Study* (Grand Rapids, Mich.: Eerdmans, 2014), 84–85, citing Bruce McCormack.

7. Karl Barth, *Church Dogmatics* (Edinburgh: T and T Clark, 1956–75), vol. 2, pt. 1, 179, 196, 204ff.

8. For the rejection of natural theology, see Barth, *Church Dogmatics*, vol. 2, pt. 1, 86–128, 134–78.

cally inassimilable by us. The issue of the natural knowledge of God has therefore been fraught since at least the eighteenth century, and marks a sort of parting of the ways for many contemporary Protestants between Christianity and its Roman Catholic corruption. Evidently, we misconceive things if we think of it merely as a question about which philosophy a theologian thinks more theologically employable—Kant or (say) Aristotle. The real question is whose description of the scope of human reason is true. Even so, there are many valuable things that Kant and Barth call to our attention by their strictures on natural theology.

In the first place, the knowledge of God naturally available to us cannot be quite the same in all respects as our ordinary knowledge of the ordinary world. Can the doctrine of the analogy of being be deployed in such a way as to take satisfactory account of this? Catholics have always thought it could be. Second, there is something bracing about the intransigence of Barthian mono-theo-epistemicism, according to which there is no knowledge of God except exclusively on the personal terms that God himself settles on and discloses to us in making himself known in Christ. Can that personalism be taken into account in a description of the "natural knowledge of God"?

The Necessity of the Natural Knowledge of God

So there are things Kant and Barth usefully alert us to. On the other hand, the flat denial that there is any natural knowledge of God cannot be entertained, first because it contradicts the word of God and Catholic Tradition and dogma, and second because it is incoherent and makes a hash of the reasonability of the act of faith. While it is easy and salutary to consult Romans 1:19–20, Wisdom 13, St. Athanasius, St. Augustine, St. Thomas, the First Vatican Council, and *Fides et Ratio* on this issue, it is in the end more urgent to explain why the possibility of a successful natural theology is, to use the word John Paul II employs, *necessary*.

Thomas Joseph White has tried to make this plain in dialogue with contemporary Barthians by arguing from the content of faith, the presuppositions of Christological faith.[9] White deploys his argument in three

9. Thomas Joseph White, OP, "'Through Him All Things Were Made' (John 1:3): The Analogy of the Word Incarnate according to St. Thomas Aquinas and Its Ontological Presuppositions,"

steps, and begins by first observing, what is only self-evident, that there exists a properly human knowledge that is distinct from and not derived from revelation. It cannot be that all we know is revealed in the way the Trinity and the Incarnation are revealed. This may seem obvious, since it is evident not only from our experience as we straightforwardly take it, but also from the real distinction of human nature from divine nature. We are not God. We are knowers. But even as knowers we are not God, and have a distinctive, properly human knowledge of the world. Obvious as this may seem to some of us, moreover, it is well worth saying to Barthians, since for them not only do we know God only on the basis of revelation, but we know the world as truly existing only on that same basis.[10] Even so, White's position amounts to insisting that the gratuity of God's bestowal of a revealed knowledge requires a natural knowledge from which it is distinct.

According to White, "If the revelation is given gratuitously, it is also something that is not possessed according to our ordinary form of human conceptuality."[11] In the second step, however, White argues that if the revelation of such things as the Trinity and the Incarnation is to be really and truly heard by us in faith and integrated into our up-and-running consciousness of what we already know about ourselves and our neighbors and the world, then that requires that we recognize it *as* the revelation it is. It is to be given a home in the way we knowingly take reality; even, it is to take the highest and architectonic place in how we knowingly take reality. But it remains in itself a gift of God and must be appreciated *as such* and integrated into our knowing selves just as such. This is to say that in relating revelation to what we already know we have to be able to contrast it to the non-revealed, natural knowledge we already possess.

So, as White illustrates, if we assent to the truth that the Word that was with God in the beginning is God and became flesh, then, if we are

---

in *The Analogy of Being: Invention of the Antichrist or the Wisdom of God?* ed. Thomas Joseph White, OP (Grand Rapids, Mich.: Eerdmans, 2011), 246–79, esp. 267–72; reprinted with some modifications in White, *The Incarnate Lord: A Thomistic Study in Christology* (Washington, D.C.: The Catholic University of America Press, 2015), chap. 4, "Why Christology Presupposes Natural Theology."

10. For the necessity of revelation to guarantee our knowledge of the world and ourselves and others as truly existing, see Barth, *Church Dogmatics*, vol. 3, pt. 1, 345–49.

11. White, "Analogy of the Word Incarnate," 269.

to think this through as much as we can and it deserves, we must be able to marvel at the sameness and greater difference there is between the divine Word and a human word. Or again, we have to think about what it means and what it could not mean to say that a divine person "becomes" something. This means, centrally, we have to think it through in such a way that we do not make the ascription of the work of creation to the Word (Jn 1:3) impossible. We would do that, for instance, by supposing that "becoming" here means change, either by way of diminishment or augmentation. For if that is how the Word "becomes" flesh (Jn 1:14), then the Word is being thought of as just one more thing within the world, and that is not coherent with thinking the Word as creating the world, which is to say being unconditionally responsible for the totality of its being.[12]

To think rightly of the divinity of the Word, therefore, "we must have an intrinsic natural capacity to recognize such revelation as something exceeding the scope of our ordinary natural powers of reflection and knowledge."[13] But then a third step takes us home. As we have just seen in illustrating how the knowledge of revelation is to be related to our natural human knowledge, such that we can say we have really received the revealed word, then we are ineluctably engaged in the task of thinking about divinity just on its own, and thinking about it just on our own—that is, by force of our own native, natural powers. That is, we are engaged in a "natural theology," which turns out to be a sort of sub-routine required by faith itself within the all-inclusive theological program. We could put it like this: since God reveals *himself*, after all, we can appreciate this self-revelation as the revelation it really is only against a logically prior knowledge of him from the "outside," as it were. Only with such a knowledge will the revealed knowledge of God be intelligible to, and so assimilable by us as what it is. And this logically prior knowledge is "natural theology." Without such knowledge, the terms of revelation will either be indistinguishable from the terms in which we know the world, or some alien body whose equivocal claims cannot be related to what we are and

---

12. Nor, on the other hand, can one creature become another without ceasing to be itself, as Robert Sokolowski points out in *The God of Faith and Reason: Foundations of Christian Theology* (Notre Dame, Ind.: University of Notre Dame Press, 1982), 36.

13. White, "Analogy of the Word Incarnate," 270.

what we desire.[14] For White, the vindication of natural theology is just the flip side of the defense of the analogy of being.

It is to be noted that this natural knowledge of God is not necessarily to be exercised prior to revelation. What is asserted is a possibility, a natural capacity, not the actual exercise of the capacity—though some such exercise Aquinas certainly recognized in Plato and Aristotle.[15]

Faith Requires the Possibility of the Natural Knowledge of God

White argues from the content, the Christological content, of faith. There is also an argument from the act of faith itself. Its point of departure is the observation that the credibility of revelation depends on its reasonability. That faith be reasonable is necessary if faith be not something that destroys but rather perfects the intellect, as grace in all its modalities perfects human nature as a whole. If our nature is rational, it must be possible rationally to believe. And this means that revelation must be able to be recognized prior to faith, just as *Dei Filius* teaches.

Garrigou-Lagrange sets forth in careful detail how the divine origin of Christianity, the fact of revelation, can be certainly known.[16] Moral certitude is sufficient for the individual believer,[17] but there is a need for scientific demonstration for the collective faith of the Church as a whole.[18] Now, nothing is rationally credible for divine faith except it be evidently and not merely probably credible.[19] And nothing is evidently rationally credible for divine faith unless it appears to reason from certain signs to be supernaturally revealed by God.[20] For this minor premise, three things

14. For White, the vindication of natural theology in a Thomist frame is the flip side of a defense of the analogy of being. See also his *Wisdom in the Face of Modernity: A Study in Thomistic Natural Theology* (Ave Maria, Fla.: Ave Maria Press, 2009), 252–54, according to which the natural knowledge of God, apophatic and analogical as it may be, is necessary lest the knowledge of God in revelation be something extrinsic to our nature and our natural desire.

15. See for instance St. Thomas Aquinas, *Questiones disputata de potentia Dei*, in St. Thomas Aquinas, *Quaestiones Disputatae*, vol. 2, ed. P. Bazzi, M. Calcaterra, et al. (Rome: Marietti, 1949), q. 3, a. 5.

16. Reginald Garrigou-Lagrange, OP, *De Revelatione per Ecclesiam Catholicam Proposita*, 5th ed. (Rome: Desclée et Socii, 1950), 1:491ff.

17. Ibid., 1:494–97.
18. Ibid., 1:515.
19. Ibid., 1:491.
20. Ibid., 1:491.

are required: first, that something be known as in fact revealed by God; second, that God be known to be truthful; and third that God be known to be infallible.[21] That something be known as revealed, moreover, follows as the First Vatican Council taught from the knowledge of miracles and other signs. Therefore, prior to faith, there must be possible in principle the knowledge of God's existence, of his nature as veracious and all-knowing, and of the possibility of miracles. As to the last: "God is the free and omnipotent cause from which depends the application of all the hypothetically necessary laws, nor is he bound to them."[22] So we are heavily involved in a natural theology that will know God's existence, his knowledge and truthfulness, his power and freedom.

Messages in Bottles

In 1959, Walker Percy wrote an essay titled "The Message in the Bottle," which has us imagine a castaway who receives messages in bottles washed up on the shore.[23] Some of the messages count as knowledge, knowledge that is in principle verifiable by the canons of the modern empirical sciences. Some of the messages count as news: matters of fact, but all of them contingent truths, not scientifically necessary truths, but some of them crucial for the prospect of getting off the island and finding one's way back home. However important the message may be for homecoming, Percy expects us to see that the bare presentation of the message by itself as found in the bottle is not sufficient for us to assent to it; rather, a piece of news "requires that there be a newsbearer."[24] However detachable the bearer of *knowledge* from the knowledge he brings—since the empirical test of the knowledge has nothing to do, in the end, with who first enunciates or repeats the knowledge in question—the piece of *news* is not in that way detachable from its bearer. At least we must have the apostle, the one sent, personally present to us. An apostle is not a genius, scientific or otherwise, and we do not believe him because his mind has dominated

21. Ibid., 1:492.
22. Ibid., 2:49; for three orders of miracles, see 2:65ff.
23. Walker Percy, "The Message in the Bottle" in Percy, *The Message in the Bottle: How Queer Man Is; How Queer Language Is; and What One Has to Do with the Other* (New York: Farrar, Straus and Giroux, 1982), 119–58. The essay first appeared in *Thought* 34 (1959–60): 405–33.
24. Ibid., 136.

and delivered up to us the intelligibility of some region of being; rather, "we believe him because he has the authority to deliver the message."[25]

There is a difference between science and authority, therefore. However, Percy recognizes that the traditional apologetic discourses on the historical evidences for the authenticity and authority of Christ and the Church must be accompanied by philosophical approaches to God and his nature.[26] Showing this shows the necessity of natural theology, a natural *knowledge* of God.

Let us alter Percy's story just a little, and say that, rather than a message in a bottle, we have a message in a book—or let us say the book, the whole book, arrives in a bottle—a rather large bottle, to be sure, since the book is the Bible. But the supposition is the same. We are supposing that all we have is the message itself: a word that presents itself to us as God's word. Will an evangelist—not an original apostle but a contemporary evangelist—have any success presenting it to us so? Think of the epistemic situation we would find ourselves in.

"Here's a message for you from God about your eternal destiny."

"God? Eternal destiny?"

"Yes; pay attention—it's in this Book."

"Destiny?"

"Yes; it's a matter of whether or not you will find everlasting happiness."

"That sounds good. But who is 'God'?"

"The maker of heaven and earth, who can give you eternal life, just as the Book explains."

"Oh. Great. How do you know the message is from him?"

"Because he spoke it through prophets and apostles, as recorded in the Book, and there were great signs and wonders to prove it was him speaking."

"Like what?"

"Well ... There was the Exodus of Israel from Egypt, and there was Jesus of Nazareth and his mighty works and his resurrection from the dead."

"Wow. And how do we know about these warrants for the message?"

"They're written down, in the Book, in the same Book as tells us the message."

"But how do I know the message is likely to have come from a creator of heaven and earth?"

25. Ibid., 146–47.
26. Ibid., 140.

"It's congruent with what he says about himself in the Book as merciful and good."

"And I know he can work miracles because …"

"Because like the message, such works are congruent with the way he speaks about himself in the Book as creator and redeemer of men."

"Is there any access to the words and deeds of God apart from the Book?"

"No, not really."

"So we are stuck with the message in the Book, and the signs that validate the message as coming from 'God' are reported only in the Book?"

"Right."

"And there is really no other way of access to him except the Book?"

"No; but that's explained in the Book, too. To think we had independent access to God would be to mistake our own capacity to know him, and to forget that, if God is known, he can be known only from himself, given his own decision to speak. God is such that the only way to know him is on his own terms, which is to say, just as he presents himself in the Book."

"Maybe some other day …"

The just imagined dialogue goes on with the evangelist presenting no credentials except the message itself. This, Percy says, will not work. Will things change if the evangelist presents himself as an agent of the Church founded by Christ, himself the keystone of the arch of the historical pattern of salvation? This is to add Tradition to what must otherwise be a very lonely Scripture.

"Perhaps I should emphasize that the Book has never been, as it were, unaccompanied. It has always and uninterruptedly been in the custody of a community of faith, the People of Israel and the New Israel, the Church."

"So you are confident of the continuity of Israel and the Church and the messages they bear from the time they were first fully enunciated?"

"Yes, I am."

"How does this strengthen your epistemic position?"

"Like this: it's not only that we have a record of the over-all message and its miraculous warrants, we have as well a record of the reception of the message and its warrants in an historically continuous community of faith."

"That's very impressive in its own way, of course. But you yourself are in the same position relative to the historically continuous, custodial community of faith as you are to the Book, right?"

"What do you mean?"

"I mean that, in the same way that you trust the Book, so also you trust the keepers of the Book who themselves trust the Book."

"Well, yes; but doesn't the very existence of this continuously existing custodial community provide a sort of perpetual and extraordinary, not to say miraculous, witness to the truth of the message of the Book and the warrants contained therein?"

"But you can't say that unless you are outside the Book and its keepers, looking on both as just one fact. Before, every access to God was supposed to be inside the Book. But now you want me to recognize something here and now, something present, something beyond the record of the Book as miraculous."

Thus, even the ecclesially accredited custodian of the Book will not be enough to make a reasonable case for assent to the message. He has to appeal to something beyond the message and beyond the custodians in their purely custodial capacity. That is, he has to appeal to some access to God beyond the Book and the Church.

The priority of speaker to what he speaks has to be able to be dealt with on its own terms—we cannot just have this Speaker in his speech, where that is the only thing we have of and from him. Thus, "that God has spoken" cannot be recognized unless God can be known to exist and unless it can be known that he might have something to say.

We could put the point as follows. God cannot simply announce himself to us in his self-revelation if it is impossible for us to have any other cognitive access to him. How would we relate such an epistemic meteorite to what we know of reality? If it fits happily into the periodic table we have already constructed, then of course nothing new has been introduced into consciousness. On the other hand, if it is so completely unlike what we know of the real that we cannot relate it to what we already know, then once again, nothing new has been introduced into consciousness, nothing has been said in such a way we can *hear* it. It must rather be that, if the atomic weight and number are hitherto unexperienced by us, we can at least relate them to the periodic table we know. Something new will have been said, and something newly heard will be registered. But this requires being able to imagine something beyond the periodic table we know.

Because God has spoken to us, we must be able to know him independently of his address to us. This is a necessity of manifestation. Even as with a purely human speaker, it is not the speech alone that shows that the other speaker exists. Otherwise, we would not be able to distinguish him from ourselves, or from some voice in our heads that, for all we know, is just another form of (a schizophrenic) us. To say that we have a written word that, in the absence of a living voice, shows us his existence is no good. If all human beings had from him was a scrap of paper with words said to be God's, that would not tell us that God exists. Positive revelation demands a natural revelation, natural theology. And this is precisely why the Scriptures come to us with affirmations of its possibility. While He identifies himself in the words and deeds recorded in the book, He shows us in the book how we can also identify him *outside* the Book. He shows us this, just so that we may recognize his identification of himself in the words and deeds recorded in the Book.

Positivism

The Abiding Positivism of Contemporary Culture

The foregoing was an argument to the effect that faith requires the possibility of a robust natural theology that can demonstrate the existence of God, his providential governing of his Creation, and his capacity to show himself by miracles. In the contemporary world, however, it is hard to locate a space where such natural theology can be credited or even entertained. Today, materialism is the default metaphysical position of popular and very much of university culture, at least if we may judge according as popular culture finds expression in mass market magazines and according as learned culture finds expression in the writings of Christopher Hitchens (*God Is Not Great: How Religion Poisons Everything* [2009]), Richard Dawkins (*The God Delusion* [2006]), and Daniel Dennet (*Consciousness Explained* [1991]; *Breaking the Spell: Religion as a Natural Phenomenon* [2006]). Consciousness and religion are treated as things epiphenomenal to the entities postulated by physics, and reductive explanations of their existence and nature, not quite complete as yet, are soon to be perfected by some constellation of empirical sciences.[27]

Contemporary materialism is mostly an effect of a sort of uncritical positivism. Critical or self-conscious positivism supposes that, if there is something real but not knowable by the empirical sciences, then we human beings shall never know it, since our only access to the real is the empirical scientific method. Uncritical positivism more robustly asserts the existence only of what is accessible to empirical scientific methods. Positivism, materialism, naturalism—and precisely in the half-formed, half-realized way they are popularly entertained—have all the same deadening effect on natural theology; they seem to make all arguments for the existence of God stillborn. It does no good to point out that logical positivism itself as a philosophical movement in Anglo-American philosophy was declared dead in the 1970s. It may indeed have had its day in philosophy departments, but it continues to supply the architecture of contemporary thought in its resistance to Christianity. When people say that "modern science" has made belief in an immortal immaterial soul and a transcendent God impossible, they are really expressing the old, undead, positivist philosophical approach, materialism in an epistemological form.

John Paul II speaks of the current dangers to authentic philosophy in chapter 7 of *Fides et Ratio*, and lines them up as follows: eclecticism, historicism, scientism, pragmatism, and nihilism (nos. 86–90). Earlier, tracing the history of the separation of philosophy and faith, the list is: rationalism, idealism, positivism, nihilism, and the limitation of reason to a purely instrumental function, that is, one necessarily subsequent to will and choice and decision (nos. 45–47). Reason limited in such a way is a consequence of scientism or positivism, since the empirical sciences cannot deploy any idea of nature whose finality proposes ends to human choice. Scientism "rejects as invalid all those forms of knowledge which are alien to the positive sciences and therefore relegates to the area of pure imagination both religious and theological knowledge, as well as ethical and aesthetic knowledge" (no. 88).

27. Among many rejoinders, there are David Bentley Hart, *Atheist Delusions: The Christian Revolution and Its Fashionable Enemies* (New Haven, Conn.: Yale University Press, 2010); and Edward Feser, *The Last Superstition: A Refutation of the New Atheism* (South Bend, Ind.: St. Augustine's Press, 2008).

Scientism is just a more relaxed but no less confident positivism. The Holy Father rightly adverts to its epistemological incoherence. If the only propositions that are meaningful must be verifiable either as logical deductions or empirical observations, then positivism in this its most restrictive form is itself meaningless, since it is verifiable in neither way. Notwithstanding the demise of positivism in philosophy departments, however, its looser, more labile form, "scientism," occupies the public ground today; and the Holy Father is right to end his list of "dangers" by returning to it. "It remains true that a certain positivistic cast of mind continues to nurture the illusion that, thanks to scientific and technical progress, man may live as a demiurge, single-handedly and completely taking charge of his destiny" (no. 91).[28] Earlier, he had characterized this "demiurgic power" as demonic (no. 46), and one may think that is a more satisfactory characterization: together with the omnipresent solicitation of sexual gratification, it is how the ruler of the age prevents the gospel from being heard.[29]

Making Positivism Public Not as Science but as Philosophy

Therefore, the first order of business in discussing the *praeambula* today is to bring positivism out of the shadows into the light. Without this, philosophical demonstrations and theological observations cannot have the force which is natively theirs. The hearer may be interested, but will remain skeptical, simply because the demonstrations and observations are so far removed from what can be said in public without apology.

The self-defeating character of logical positivism, as touched on above, is a good place to begin. But the newer, less articulate forms of positivism, must be pointed out, as the Holy Father indicates, such as they are to be found in contemporary reductive accounts of consciousness and mind and moral norms.

One must first of all point out what is only obvious, that there are no reductive accounts of consciousness or of such things as sensory knowledge.[30]

28. This is the translation at the Vatican website, http://vatican.va.
29. For a characterization of technocracy, see Pope Francis, *Laudato Si': On Care of Our Common Home* (Frederick, Md.: The Word Among Us Press, 2015), nos. 106ff.
30. See Conor Cunningham, *Darwin's Pius Idea: Why the Ultra-Darwinists and Creationists Both Get It Wrong* (Grand Rapids, Mich.: Eerdmans, 2010), 320–23.

There are alleged accounts. But the always ever postponed *completion* of these accounts is to be insisted on. The postulation that such completion is possible is a philosophical, not a scientific, postulate. Clarity can then begin to be attained when one points out the fact that it is not eyes that see, or the optic nerve, or the area of the brain where the optic nerve ends, but rather only the animal, the cat or dog or chimpanzee, that sees. No one has any evidence whatsoever to impute "seeing" to rods and cones, the retina, the optic nerve, the brain. The one thing in our experience that sees is the whole dog, the whole cat, the whole animal. It is tiresome, if nonetheless still necessary, to observe that mere correlations of brain events with conscious experience are not accounts of conscious experience. Correlations of material modifications of the human being with conscious experience have been known, in a rough and ready way, since grapes were fermented and beer brewed. They did not move Plato and Aristotle to misapprehend the quite astounding phenomenon of human awareness and knowing.

Life

It follows also that it is inadequate to characterize life or consciousness as an "emergent property of complex multi-celled organisms."[31] In the first place, "organism" itself is doing more duty than scientism allows it in such a statement, if it is true to its own drive toward reductive accounts of consciousness and knowledge. For an organism is already a whole entity, where the organs are instruments of the whole of which they are parts. An organism is not an accidentally occurring machine assembled of sub-machines, as is an automobile. The parts of such a machine, the sub-machines such as the transmission, the oil pump, the fuel pump, the brakes, and so forth, are not instruments of the whole. The whole thing, and all the parts therein, are instruments of the human being who uses it.

Once the dis-analogy between a living animal and a machine is recognized, the very point of thinking of living animals as naturally occurring accidental, chance, machines is lost, which was to make a reductive account of animals thinkable in the first place.

31. On emergence, see Timothy O'Connor and Hong Yu Wong, "Emergent Properties," in *The Stanford Encyclopedia of Philosophy*, summer 2015 ed., ed. Edward N. Zalta, http://plato.stanford .edu/archives/sum2015/entries/properties-emergent/.

Life, or livingness, can, however, be characterized as an emergent *form*, where form makes the whole what it is, and where the parts (organs) are instruments of the whole of which they are parts.[32] This is important for Catholic doctrine and Christian philosophy, which cannot make sense of man and his origin and his destiny except that the soul or form of the whole can be supposed to be ontologically prior to the material it dominates and gives unity to, not as one material part to another (say, the heart in respect to the stomach), but the way the intelligibility and unity of the operative powers of the whole are prior to the operative powers. Only on this basis can we further an intelligible account of the unity of man as a material substance in which two things will be true.

First, the immateriality of a mind that subsists in and is a power of the soul alone will make credible Catholic teaching on the survival of persons after death. A human soul so conceived will not evidently be subject to annihilation when the whole man suffers corruption at death. Conceiving the human form in this way is the natural correlate of biblical and Catholic doctrine on the immortality of the soul. Second, the natural and intrinsic unity of soul and body, united as is an act intelligibly prior to the body to a body which is capable of being so organized, means that an integral hope for a human happiness encompasses the whole man, both body and soul. The matter-form composition of man is the natural correlate of the doctrine of the resurrection of the body.

On the other hand, Catholic doctrine cannot make sense of soul or form in a world in which biological evolution is true unless such a form or souls be thought of in some way as indeed *emergent*, which is to say in some way something temporally subsequent to some previously produced material structure they then animate and inform and therefore order as living bodies. Just so, Pius XII taught that Catholics are entirely free to embrace "the doctrine of evolution, in as far as it enquires into the origin of the human body."[33] The difference between Catholic thought and

32. On form, see Robert Sokolowski, "Formal and Material Causality in Science," *American Catholic Philosophical Quarterly* 69 (1995): 57–67.

33. Pope Pius XII, *Humani Generis* (1950), no. 36 (J. Neuner, SJ, and Jacques Dupuis, SJ, *The Christian Faith in the Doctrinal Documents of the Catholic Church*, 7th ed. [New York: Alba House, 2001], no. 419).

evolutionary biology has more to do with the correct description of the *product* or term of evolution—the animal, the human being—than with evolution itself.[34]

Sensory Knowledge

Insofar as some evolutionary account is proposed for the assembling of the relationally complex collection of material entities that are the ancestors of the animals of our immediate experience and to which we impute such activities as seeing and hearing, then the question is to be raised about how the one who proposes such an account thinks he knows it within the strict confines of positivism. Evolutionary accounts of the constitution of the senses rely on the utilitarian or pragmatic value of sensory knowledge. Such knowledge and the sensory organs that gave it conduced to the survival of those animals that possessed such senses. The pragmatic value of such senses is evidence for their objectivity. Only those structures that delivered the right stuff, which was the true stuff, survived. Such accounts seem the stronger when we think of touch and taste. A sensory apprehension of the hot and the dry gives the animal warning to seek shade. A sensory apprehension of the wet, the smell of the water, directs the animal to the creek.[35]

When we add the property of consciousness to such activities as touching and hearing and seeing, however, evolutionary accounts of sensory knowledge are less promising. The watery animal seeks the water that sustains it, very well; it is easier to imagine chemical-mechanistic accounts of the senses so functioning. But sensory knowing is conscious. What does consciousness seek? It seeks what is good for the thing that is conscious. Which is to say that consciousness first seeks the self, and that it is of the self, of the whole to which it belongs. And it is much harder to propose a reductionist account of consciousness. The watery nature of the animal and the water in the creek help us to think about the sensory perception of

---

34. See Robert Sokolowski, "Soul and the Transcendence of the Human Person," in *What Is Man, O Lord? The Human Person in a Biotech Age*, ed. Edward J. Furton (Boston: National Catholic Bioethics Center, 2002), 49–63.

35. This does indeed seem to make soul a temperament, for the difficulties of which view see St. Thomas Aquinas, *Summa Contra Gentiles, Book Two: Creation*, trans. James F. Anderson (Notre Dame, Ind.: University of Notre Dame, 1975), chap. 63.

things once we come to understand both the watery animal and the water in the creek as being in some sense the same thing. But unless panpsychism is true, the conscious act of sensing is not seeking conscious elements or compounds in its environment.

The trouble is in the very statement of the bridge that the reductionist account has to build: it has to go from atoms and compounds whose description by the physicist or chemist in terms of atomic weight and number and ionic and covalent bonds *never* includes the note of "consciousness" to the activity of an organically complex animal which is conscious in its hearing and seeing. The bridge has not been built. Nor should anyone alive to the nature of consciousness suppose that it can be built—it just is not the kind of thing of which we could expect to have a chemical explanation or a multi-cellular explanation, although it evidently has chemical and multi-cellular presuppositions.

There was no reductive explanation of conscious, sensory operations when the defining qualities of the elements were the hot and the dry, the wet and the cold. There is no reductive account of conscious seeing and hearing when the distinguishing qualities of the elements are atomic radius, electron affinity, and ionization energy. It is not the sort of thing that anybody alive to differences would expect.

Reason

When we come to what properly distinguishes human beings, however, the odds for fulfilling the hope for a naturalist, materialist account of reason approach zero. The general argument against naturalistic accounts of human beings and their works and words was worked out by C. S. Lewis. Naturalism (positivism, scientism) holds that everything that happens is caused by non-rational causes—material things impact one another and react with one another, and all according to law, such that every event must be as it is. And this includes our thoughts and our scientific theories and our philosophical views of things—like naturalism or positivism. We may think that we assert naturalism because of evidence, because we have reasons to think it true. But the push-pull of elementary particles— whatever they may be—is indifferent to reasons and evidence. Thus, no thought is *known* to be valid, although it may *in fact* be valid, if all we know of it is that it is fully explained by nonrational causes. It may be valid, in other words, by chance. Thus Lewis's argument.[36]

(1) A thought that is fully explained by nonrational causes is valid only by chance.

(2) But naturalism holds that all thoughts are fully explicable as a result of *non*rational causes.

(3) Therefore, naturalism is committed to hold that any thought is valid, if it is, only by chance.

(4) But naturalism is a thought.

(5) Therefore, naturalism, if valid, is so only by chance.

(6) But it is unreasonable to hold theories that, if true, are so only by chance.[37]

Suppose that, because of naturalistic, materialistic, mechanistic, reductivist views, I doubt whether human inquiry and reason really give us the truth about the natural world. There is really nothing to be done. Human reason is the only way to know or to measure reality that we have. It is as if I doubted whether my twelve-inch ruler were really accurate, although it is the only ruler left in the world. In fact, there is a standard of the ruler—say, the platinum-iridium bar stored in some Swiss vault, or some way to count the wavelengths of some decaying isotope. But what is like the platinum-iridium bar next to human reason as a measurer? St. Augustine knew—it is the necessary truths we glimpse when we inquire as to the certainty and necessity of our knowledge. Even so, we should never be in such a position as to be thrown off our mental balance by such tales as told by evolutionary epistemology and EEM—evolution of epistemological mechanisms. Are the "mechanisms" metaphorical machines, or really and truly mechanical? The latter, for positivism. Then we are so distracted as to forget the natural light (a metaphor) by which Aristotle and Plato knew the nature of mind, and that it was not material.

Thomas Nagel notes the self-evidencing character of rational argu-

36. For which, see C. S. Lewis, *Miracles: A Preliminary Study*, rev. ed. (New York: HarperCollins, 2001), chap. 3, "The Cardinal Difficulty of Naturalism." This edition contains his modification of the original 1947 argument in light of the criticism of G. E. M. Anscombe.

37. For a more recent version, see Conor Cunningham's discussion of Thomas Nagel et al., *Darwin's Pius Idea*, 212–17, and 335–45 for discussion of Alvin Plantinga and John Searle.

ment and inference, a character that lifts it into another order than the phenomena explained by contemporary evolutionary accounts of organisms. He grants the consistency of maintaining an evolutionary account of the senses and having confidence in their objectivity. He continues:

By contrast, in a case of reasoning, if it is basic enough, the only thing to think is that I have grasped the truth directly. I cannot pull back from a logical inference and reconfirm it with the reflection that the reliability of my logical thought processes is consistent with the hypothesis that evolution has selected them for accuracy. That would drastically weaken the logical claim.... It is not possible to think, "Reliance on my reason, including my reliance on *this very judgment* [of its reliability], is reasonable because it is consistent with its having an evolutionary explanation." Therefore any evolutionary account of the place of reason presupposes reason's validity and cannot confirm it without circularity.[38]

And again:

In ordinary perception, we are like mechanisms governed by a (roughly) truth-preserving algorithm. But when we reason, we are like a mechanism that can see that the algorithm it follows is truth-preserving. Something has happened that has gotten our minds into immediate contact with the rational order of the world.[39]

Moral Norms

Last, there is the question of moral norms. The scientistic utilitarianism of evolutionarily pragmatic accounts of moral norms does not measure up to the phenomenology of moral value and supposes an account of "good" as merely useful. But there are three problems here.

First, the phenomenology of moral values gives us absolute norms, not useful norms. Just as there is no smooth path from the useful to the true, so there is no smooth way from the useful to the morally good. Second, if the meaning of the good cannot rise above the useful, useful as encouraging the multiplication of forms of life governed by these norms, then the evolutionary account itself cannot be but useful, or at least cannot be known to be more than useful. For the point of proposing such an

---

38. Thomas Nagel, *Mind and Cosmos: Why the Materialist Neo-Darwinian Conception of Nature Is Almost Certainly False* (Oxford: Oxford University Press, 2012), 80–81.
    39. Ibid., 83.

account is to propose it as true. And measuring up in thought and speech to the true is a moral norm. Therefore, if the account cannot be known to be more than useful, then it cannot reasonably be presented as true in the ordinary sense, where the true is distinguished from the advantageous and is indifferent to utility. Third, the useful is useful for something. What is the something for which the pragmatically accounted-for moral norms are useful? If it can only be the multiplication of the forms of life abiding by such norms, then the reductive account of the good as the quantitative is already built into the argument from the beginning. It is not a result of the argument.

But in this way, the original point of departure—that only the positive sciences give knowledge of the real—is itself abandoned. It cannot be sustained by the application of the positive sciences to an evolutionary understanding of man himself.

The positivist influence on the course and interpretation of the empirical sciences has the unintended effect of making science as a whole, all the sciences, including the sciences that consider man himself in any way, a production of merely useful views, views of reality that are conducive to some outcome (whose privileged position as an "outcome" cannot on positivist terms be made good except as "something that is temporally posterior"). Science is itself good only as useful, and there is no real knowledge of anything except of the immediate point of self-consciousness that cannot be denied on pain of declaring the Cartesian *cogito* deceptive. The self of which we are conscious therefore has no knowable connection with what science knows. The self is radically alienated from the unknowable *other* that is beyond immediate self-consciousness. And since there is nothing normative for our own actions in the empirical construction of the world thus created, there is no limit on what and how we will. We become ourselves the demiurgic, demonic will John Paul II spoke of in connection with positivism and scientism. We will have made ourselves after the image of quite another god than the God of Abraham.

The regnant and omnipresent positivism of contemporary intellectual life in the West is an important impediment to faith today. But clearing it away opens a path to inquire of a truth beyond worldly truths, as important as such truths may be both scientifically and politically. Is there some

Truth that would satisfy every desire for truth and make us happy with another-worldly happiness?

Natural Theology Deployed: The Existence of God

The rational path to affirming the existence of God does really prepare for faith. If done fully and rightly under the (extrinsic) direction of faith, it should lead us to anticipate a word of revelation from God.

The Existence of God

First, the existence of a transcendent and uncaused Cause who is responsible for the otherwise inexplicable existence of the beings of our experience is affirmed. The things of our experience exist, but they do not have to exist. If the question as to their existence is a possible question, a meaningful question, then one has as good as granted the existence of God. For as Herbert McCabe says, he just is the answer to the question, "Why is there anything at all?"[40]

Kant objects to the legitimacy of the question since it anticipates an exercise of reason that takes us beyond the realm of sensory data. Such an exercise would be illegitimate if we had no way to conceptualize and speak of this "beyond" in a way that does not surreptitiously reduce God to one of the things of the world. It is the point of the doctrine of analogy to explicate this way. Hume objects to the question, since it can be answered neither by "any abstract reasoning concerning quantity or number" nor "does it contain any experimental reasoning concerning matter of fact and existence."[41] But this is nothing but a classical statement of the positivism already discussed and suffers from the same self-referential inconsistency. Hume's fork is neither a demonstration of abstract nor a product of experiential reasoning. George Steiner avers: "Nothing in science or logical discourse can either resolve or ostracize Leibniz's question

40. Herbert McCabe, "Creation," in McCabe, *God Matters* (Springfield, Ill.: Templegate Publishers, 1987), 5–6. On which question see Denys Turner, *Faith, Reason and the Existence of God* (Cambridge: Cambridge University Press, 2004), chap. 11, "Why Anything?" For comparison of McCabe to St. Thomas, see White, *Wisdom in the Face of Modernity*, 260–68.

41. David Hume, *An Inquiry Concerning Human Understanding*, ed. Charles W. Hendel (Indianapolis: Bobbs-Merrill, 1980), 173.

of all questions: 'Why is there not nothing?' The positivist edict whereby an adult consciousness will only ask of the world and of existence 'How' and not 'Why?' is censorship of the most obscurantist kind."[42] For McCabe, simply acknowledging the legitimacy of this fundamental question contains everything a rigorous theism desires. How can this be? Its point of departure is the puzzling fact of the existence of things that do not explain their own existence.[43] The features and sometimes even the nature of things can, in principle, be explained by factors discoverable within the world. That is the aim of the empirical sciences, to show how things are. But nothing within the world explains existence itself.

If there is no antecedent reason to suspect the question and declare it a bad question, then we shirk our intellectual responsibilities in not asking it. Maybe we will learn that, in considering its answer, we are led into contradiction, and then, on the basis of that capital sin against the light, know that the question is bad. But in fact, the postulation of an answer to the question brings immediately in its train a sort of guarantee that the answer cannot be self-contradictory. For if God is understood carefully just as such, as the answer to the question why there is anything at all, then it immediately follows that he cannot be any of those things, or like any of those things; and that is to say that he escapes the limitations of any of the things that are included in "anything." At the same time that we assert his existence as the answer to the question of why anything, we have at one and the same time a perplexing confession that we do not know what he is. For we know what things are only according as we play their features and their limitation off against one another. But if God is distinct from the world not as things within the world are distinct from one another, then we do not and cannot know what he is. The account of the existence of the things in the world, cannot itself be one of the things in the world. God is therefore outside the world.

42. George Steiner, *Errata: An Examined Life* (New Haven, Conn.: Yale University Press, 1998), 186. Steiner is no theist, but he does not settle comfortably into the cheerful atheism of the day.

43. This is arguably a better point of departure today than, say, the fact of motion or of efficient causality—the departure points of the first and second ways to prove the existence of God of St. Thomas. Many commentators tell us how much St. Thomas liked the first way, as the most evident. But motion for moderns has been rendered problematic; see Edward Feser, "Motion in Aristotle, Newton, and Einstein," in *Aristotle on Method and Metaphysics*, ed. Edward Feser (New York: Palgrave Macmillan, 2013), 236–58.

God is distinct from the world and things of the world; he is "outside the world." What does this mean? It means a lot of denials. If he is not of the world, it means first of all that the species-individual structure of the sensible things of our experience—according to which things come in kinds, and there can be many individuals of a kind of thing—does not characterize him. He would not be a *kind*, and that is hard for us to think, since everything we meet in the world falls into a kind. He is beyond the limits of things that make kinds distinct from one another, that make them determinate, limited, realities. Neither could he then be an instance of a kind. He is beyond the logic of kinds and instances.

In the second place, he would not be material, since it is materiality that enables there to be many instances of a formally identical kind—many individual persons but all of them united in being men. Third, if God is not material he would not be temporal. Being temporally measured depends on the actualization of potency which is still in potency, and this is a function of materiality. God is therefore outside time. That means, he is not measured by time, and his duration has no beginning or end. In the third place and more basically, since he is responsible for what is in any way, where the *way* something is does not tell us *that* it is (for only so was the question of why there is anything at all really a question), neither will this distinction apply to him, else he would not be able to account for it as the answer to why things exist rather than nothing. So, there will be no distinction of way and reality in him, of essence and existence; there will be no distinction between what is able to be and its being. And that exclusion precludes any distinction of substance and accident, which are similarly related as potency to act, as what is determinable to its determining realizations.

In sum, God is not a kind of thing or instance of a kind (therefore is God unique); he is not material and so has no material parts; he is eternal; and he is utterly simple as something wholly in act. And since his being is beyond all the limitations of the things of the world, it is in principle beyond any such limitation whatsoever. And his being or existence will be infinite.[44]

44. For this paragraph, see St. Thomas Aquinas, *Summa theologiae* I, q. 3, on the simplicity of God; and q. 10, on the eternity of God.

In the fifth place, the Cause of the beings of our experience must be intelligent. For the beings of our experience are intelligible. In whatever region of material reality we look, things turn out to be patient to the probings of the mind, hospitable to intellect, just as the successful pros-ecution of the empirical sciences (not *scientism*) demonstrates. Is this in-telligibility imposed on material reality by the enquiring human mind? Scientists do not suppose so; they think they are discovering empirical laws and correlations, not inventing them. But there is no intelligibility of caused things without the practical intelligence of an artificer. Therefore, the first Cause of things must also be intelligent.[45]

But since he is prior to the things of the world as accounts are prior to what is accounted for, he therefore understands the things of the world first in understanding himself—there being nothing else except himself to understand prior to the existence of the things that are not him, the things of the world. It cannot be that he comes to the perfection of understanding things only once he has produced them, for then he would be dependent on what depends on him, and what is caused and therefore owes all that it has to its cause—a worldly thing—would then impossibly add something to its cause. His understanding, like his being, will be infinite.

He must also, in the sixth place, be free. For the things of the world need not exist—that was our point of departure. Therefore they proceed from God not necessarily, but contingently. But contingent productions of an intelligent agent are free productions. God could create, but then again, he did not have to. None of the realities and intelligibilities of the things of the world add to the reality and intelligibility of the one who understands them in understanding himself. All the contingently exist-ing intelligibilities of the world are included in his active understanding of what he understands, whether the world exists or not. Whether the things of the world exist or not makes all the difference to them, but none to him. He is the unlimited understanding of unlimited intelligibility, as well as the unlimited reality of unbounded existence.

In the seventh place, the world of our experience is temporal, which

45. See Hugo Meynell, "The Intelligibility of the Universe," in *Reason and Religion*, ed. Stuart C. Brown (Ithaca, N.Y.: Cornell University Press, 1977), 23–43; and Ed Miller, *God and Reason: A Historical Approach to Philosophical Theology* (New York: Macmillan, 1972), chap. 5, on the fifth way.

is to say that the things that inhabit it realize themselves in time, which is to say that they reach and realize their perfection by the gradual actualization or realization of their potential unto those perfections. The end of a tadpole, the perfection of a tadpole, is a frog. One of the ends of sodium is, with chlorine, to make salt. But the end or perfection of anything is what is good for it. This sort of relation is intelligible, and falls within the compass of the first Intelligent Cause. He therefore orders things to their good. And since all the things of the world are in an intelligible relation to one another, he orders the universe to its good. But whatever intelligently orders things unto their good ends is itself good. And if we say he is unlimitedly good, as unlimitedly intelligible, then all the goods of the created order will be pre-contained in him, finite copies of what already exists infinitely in him, participations of him.

Summing up, it turns out that none of the intelligibilities of our experience and none of the goods of our experience add anything to God. He would be in undiminished intelligibility and goodness and being whether the world existed or not. We neither add anything to his goodness and happy intelligent enjoyment of it, nor, if we did not exist, would his happiness be diminished. This is very important for distinguishing Christian philosophical theology from the views of Hegel and other post-Christian metaphysicians who in one way or another offer us a picture according to which God needs to make the world in order to come to his own fullness, or according to which the world adds something to God and therefore we ourselves add something of value and goodness to God which otherwise he would not have possessed.

In the eighth place, the good of human beings is the knowledge of truth, since all men desire to know, and to know truly. Therefore, the first intelligent and good Cause of things must also compass that particular good of conscious and intelligent creatures and himself be Truth in the way that he is Intelligibility and Good and Being, which is to say, in an unlimited way, since he is beyond all the limited forms of being and goodness and truth in our experience. The "true" adds to "intelligibility" the note of "intelligibility as known." Since God is an intellect, then his own good will be this very conscious possession of himself as intelligible; and so his good will be truth. And the end of the world will likewise be truth, since it proceeds from one whose good is truth.[46] This means that, according as our own end is truth, the reflex possession of the intelligible as such, then we are made in the image of God.

Ninth, it cannot be the case that the world created by God has no created persons within it. We may say that the motive of infinite Goodness in creating finite, good things is to share his goodness. Well and good. But it is not shared in a real sense unless it is known to be shared. This is easier to express in the language of manifestation. The world of created intelligible, good, and beautiful things declares the glory of God, just as the Psalm says (Ps 19:2). To whom does it declare it? God does not need this declaration; it adds nothing to his perfect possession of his intelligibility in the truth which he is. Therefore, there is no point to Creation unless there are created persons who can behold the glory of God, and in so doing, come to their own perfection, which is to say, their own glory. There must be angels and men, both in the image of God according as they are intellectual, so that there be some receiver of the manifestation of God's goodness and glory. The full share of God's goodness is therefore the community of angels and men just insofar as they know his truth and goodness. This state of affairs is inscribed in the very idea of "glory," which implies a relation of what is being shown to one to whom it is shown.

Tenth, let us return to the question of the "personalism" of our knowledge of God, an issue raised by Barth. Evidently, God's revelation of himself to Israel and to the Church in Christ is very personal indeed, since it depends on his freedom so to do, and bears with it the astounding realities both of our invitation to adoptive divine filiation and of the Trinity of persons. What of the natural knowledge of God? Is it right to characterize it as "impersonal"? The natural knowledge of God is not personal in the sense just delimited. "The things that have been made" and from which we know God are not words spoken to us the way the words of Scripture are. Still, in coming to the natural knowledge of God, we know that creation is a free act, and that there must be rational or intellectual creatures within the created order for it to make sense and have a point.

---

46. See St. Thomas Aquinas, *Summa Contra Gentiles: Book One: God*, trans. Anton C. Pegis (Notre Dame, Ind.: University of Notre Dame, 1975), chap. 1.

Therefore, God freely and so "personally" makes himself known to us in the book of nature.

The Anticipation of a Word from God

In the eleventh place, it follows from the fifth, sixth, and seventh things (unlimited intelligence and intelligibility, freedom, goodness of God) that God can speak to us should he choose. Since he is infinite, there is much he does not and cannot "say" simply in creating the world. Whatever world he creates will be finite and must be, if distinct from him; whatever world he creates can therefore manifest only some of his intelligibility and goodness. And no created rational or intellectual nature, just as such and in its own intelligible finality, can be ordained to enjoy the divine goodness as God himself enjoys it. But he is free, and so he can speak more than what he manifests of himself in Creation, and he can give more than is inscribed in the natural order, since he transcends it. And he is good, with a goodness beyond our capacity to measure. The eighth and ninth things, moreover, make it fitting that God speak to one who is by his nature made to his image.

In the twelfth place, given our misery, we his creatures might all the more expect him to speak, since he is both our creator and is good. We may expect him to speak to us about our misery and to help us find a way out of it. By our misery I mean: (1) the universal human propensity to violate the natural moral law and to commit unjust, intemperate, cowardly acts; and (2) our being consigned to a death beyond which it is difficult to see any satisfactory existence fitting for human persons; and (3) the relative blindness that sin and despair induce whereby it is difficult to come to the natural knowledge of God.

This expectation that God may speak to us follows from what we may know naturally of God. It follows not with necessity, but with fittingness. But the fittingness is very strong.[47] Of course, it does not anticipate in any way what the word of revelation actually contains, which is in fact an invitation to friendship with God, for which nature must be elevated by grace,

47. Pius XII, *Humani Generis*, no. 3 (Neuner and Dupuis, *The Christian Faith*, no. 145), speaks of a "moral necessity" whereby God would reveal to us naturally knowable moral and religious truths.

nor can it anticipate the revelation of the intimate and tri-personal reality of God, for the apprehension of which supernatural faith is required.

In the thirteenth place, if God speaks to us, we can make a guess as to how he might speak to us. He will speak to us in a way that acknowledges the very nature of man he himself has made. So, first, he shall speak to us in our own words since it is by words alone that we have cognitive possession of the real. Second, he will speak to us as social beings, creatures who do things for one another even and especially in the orders of truth and the communication of truth. We may expect then that he not speak immediately to every man, but to all men through some men. Third, it will likely mean he will speak to us as political beings, that is, men whose natural good is realized in a city whose citizens contribute to and benefit from the common good and whose rulers enact and enforce the laws that guarantee this good. And fourth, that is to say that he will speak to us "historically," inasmuch as cities are historical things, things that take time to make and common effort to maintain through many generations. Fifth, he will speak in a large way open to and inviting the inspection of everyone, and this is included in saying that he will speak to us as historical beings. And yet, he will not speak in such a way as to yell or to coerce the notice of anyone. Sixth, speaking in words and historical deeds and realities, he will install a sort of large "word," a pattern or economy within human history taken as a whole. We cannot anticipate the contours of this pattern. This pattern may not from the beginning obviously include the whole of mankind in its various nations and tribes. But it will stand out among all, later if not sooner, as a *signum levatum in nationes* (Is 11:12). The unmistakable character of the manifestation of the word of God to all will, we may suppose, itself have a history. But that there will be such a pattern seems relatively likely. The very inscription of such a pattern in man's history will bespeak much about God: about his eternity as a presupposition for making a pattern that transcends the agencies of any and all human beings; about his wisdom in fashioning the intelligibility of such a pattern; about his goodness.

The Nature and Conditions of Natural Theology

The previous arguments about God and what he is not and what he may do are put in no technical form but in a form proximate to ordinary language. And insofar as fundamental theology overlaps with apologetics, that is the right way to put things. The apologist or fundamental theologian, moreover, should be unapologetic about the force of such illations. It is bad to approach arguments for the existence of God with too much handwringing and too many lamentations over their difficulty. It is a strategic error and gives way too much away to Hume and Kant and the modern ethos. What is true is that arguments for the existence of the truly transcendent God who freely creates all that is not him *were* speculatively difficult before revelation. But now, they are not. The difficulty we face now is that the force of the arguments for God is blunted by a post-Christian culture, which is to say, a culture that systematically wishes to bracket Christianity and the Christian God, to *not look*. In one way, this is nothing new: the mind darkened by sin has always closed its eyes to the light, and this is the teaching of both the Book of Wisdom and the Letter to the Romans. But now we are speaking of a culture, Western culture, that has decided to be blind. It is for this reason that, as John Paul II taught, it is the province of faith to give shelter to metaphysical reason,[48] repeating the teaching of Balthasar who said: "the Christian is called to be the guardian of metaphysics in our time."[49]

Once we know what we are talking about when we say "God," and mean the creator of heaven and earth, he who could be alone and by himself without any diminution of his infinite being or truth or goodness, then his existence is not in itself difficult of demonstration.[50] What is hard is introducing the distinction between God and the world in the first place and so conceiving God as that than which nothing greater can be conceived.[51] In fact, the distinction between God and the world, and so the perfect knowledge of the transcendence of the creator, both depend on revelation itself for their completion and clarity. This is true both as a truth of history and as a necessity of the manifestation of such a God who does not need the world in any way whatsoever.[52] Nevertheless, it is

48. John Paul II, *Fides et Ratio*, nos. 55–56.
49. Hans Urs von Balthasar, *The Glory of the Lord: A Theological Aesthetics*, vol. 5, *The Realm of Metaphysics in the Modern Age*, trans. Oliver Davies et al. (German, 1965; San Francisco: Ignatius Press, 1991), 656.
50. Sokolowski, *The God of Faith and Reason*, chap. 9.
51. Ibid., chaps. 2 and 3.
52. For the historical argument, consult Gerhard May, *Creatio Ex Nihilo: The Doctrine of*

a distinction of such scope and fundamentality that it provides the frame not only for the understanding of the reveled mysteries of the Trinity, the Incarnation, grace, and the sacrament—as Robert Sokolowski rightly insists[53]—but also, and quite paradoxically, for the very fact of revelation itself. Revelation cannot be made epistemically coherent until, given the Christian distinction, we can establish the existence of God independently of revelation, just so that revelation may be recognizable as what it is: the word of the God who could be, in unexampled majesty and infinite glory, all that he is whether the world existed or not. If reason alone were sufficient to raise our minds to the things of God in our fallen condition, there would have been no need for the Incarnation, and for the Word to lead us by temporal and changing things to eternal and unchanging reality.[54]

Analogical Predication of God

If God speaks to us, it must be the case that our words are capable of meaningfully referring to God and the things of God, transcendent though he be to our experience and world. If any theory of language seems to make this impossible or implies that it is, then that theory is wrong. For by faith, we know that God has spoken to us, and our faith is more certain than any theory of how language works.

The right way to think about the analogy of names suited to God is simply to follow the arguments for his existence carefully and notice how the words used to indicate him are themselves products of the argument and not presupposed to it. That is, it is a mistake to begin with an analysis of certain transcendental terms—terms that range over and are not confined to one or another Aristotelian category such as substance or quality, terms such as being or good or true—and then ask whether they

---

"Creation out of Nothing" in Early Christian Thought, trans. A. S. Worrall (London: T and T Clark International, 1994); for the phenomenological argument, see Robert Sokolowski, *Presence and Absence: A Philosophical Investigation of Language and Being* (Bloomington, Ind.: Indiana University Press, 1978), chap. 15.

53. Sokolowski, *The God of Faith and Reason*, chap. 5.

54. St. Augustine, *Of True Religion* (*De vera religione*), in *Augustine: Earlier Writings*, ed. and trans. J. H. S. Burleigh (Philadelphia: Westminster Press, 1953), nos. 13–14, 19, 30, and 47. Augustine recapitulates the teaching of St. Paul in the first part of Romans that the moral quality and direction of a person's life very much qualifies his ability to hear an argument for God.

will serve us for speaking about God. This is a bad strategy, for we end up subsuming God and other things under a term understood prior to asking whether he exists. But if we fit God into what we suppose is an already sufficiently tested concept, we risk reducing him to the level of the other things included under that term. Such is the great accusation against Christian discourse about God leveled by Martin Heidegger and others with the term "onto-theology." The charge is that Christians think of God as already encompassed within being when being is already known metaphysically. Such a god is not beyond the being of our experience, and so it will be contradictory to end up affirming in the Creed that such a god, one being among others, creates beings of the same rank as himself.[55] That some Christian thinkers have fallen into this incoherence is certainly true. But that revelation or the natural knowledge of God commits us to this way of proceeding is false.

St. Thomas's own presentation of how we rightly speak about God avoids this debacle. Speaking about the names of God in the first part of the *Summa theologiae*, he says that we cannot speak of God and creatures with words meant in the exact same sense, for then we will very obviously not be speaking of God, nor can we use words taken in absolutely disparate ways when said of God and of creatures, for then nothing will be communicated. And then article 5 of question 13 continues:

Now names are thus used in two ways: [1] either according as many things are proportionate to one, thus for example "healthy" predicated of medicine and urine in relation and in proportion to health of a body, of which the former is the sign and the latter the cause: or [2] according as one thing is proportionate to another, thus "healthy" is said of medicine and animal, since medicine is the cause of health in the animal body. And in this way some things are said of God and creatures analogically, and not in a purely equivocal nor in a purely univocal sense. For we can name God only from creatures [as was argued in article 1]. Thus whatever is said of God and creatures, is said according to the relation of a creature to God as its principle and cause, wherein all perfections of things preexist excellently. Now this mode of community of idea is a mean between pure equivocation and simple univocation. For in analogies the idea is not, as it is in

55. For the onto-theological innocence of both Aristotle and Aquinas, see White, *Wisdom in the Face of Modernity*, chaps. 2 and 3.

univocals, one and the same, yet it is not totally diverse as in equivocals; but a term which is thus used in a multiple sense signifies various proportions to some one thing; thus "healthy" applied to urine signifies the sign of animal health, and applied to medicine signifies the cause of the same health.[56]

This is a subtle text. He distinguishes two ways of analogizing, a first way in which many things are related to one thing, and a second way in which one thing is related not to many but to just one other thing. It is only the second way that serves to name God. But then he returns to speaking of many things relative to one thing at the end of the exposition, and he illustrates both ways with the same field of things that can be called healthy.

Why is it the second way, the relation of one thing to one other thing, that serves to explain how we name God? God is known only as the cause of the things of our experience. The health caused in an animal body by some medicine tells us something about the medicine; if, say, it heals by cooling, then it has the power of cooling. If God causes the beings of our experience, is he therefore being? He is, but evidently, not in the same sense as the beings he causes, just as the power of cooling may not itself be cool. This sense of being is by no means evident to us; it is known positively as something real and powerful, but more exactly only by the successive denial of such limitations and conditionalities we are acquainted with in the beings of our experience. The term positively asserted of God, "being," is supposed from the outset to connote something of a higher order than the thing caused, and this connotation is given precision by denying that God's being is composed of matter, or with any potency whatever, even a distinct principle of essence.

If we go back to St. Thomas's own demonstrations of the existence of God, then the first names said of God are a First Mover that is not moved, a First Efficient Cause, a Necessary Being, Maximal Being and Goodness and Truth, and an Intelligence that directs natural things to their end. In each case, we grasp something true and informative of God, but not something we have insight into. We understand "first" and "mover," and see that "unmoved" does not contradict "mover" (though it implies he is not material). But we do not see how the First Mover moves, and so are

56. Thomas Aquinas, *Summa theologiae* I, q. 13, a. 5.

left with no quidditative knowledge of God. From all the arguments we arrive at something that is the first principle of the motions and causings and grades of goodness and so on in the things of our experience, but we do not have insight into how God effects any of these things. His causing is not distinct from himself, and is similarly unable to be included in some super category of causing that encompasses both his causing and the causings of our experience. The sense of "being," "mover," "cause," and so on we end up with is produced in the very movement of the argument: we have an assertion of the existence of God as mover and cause and intelligent director, but no satisfactory definition of divine moving, causing, necessary existence, or directing.

As deployed by St. Thomas, the doctrine of analogy is not a standalone teaching. It makes sense and has its full force only as allied with an account not only of how we know things, by abstracting form—something that functions as act—from the potency of matter, but also as allied with a metaphysics of participation. It is only in a world where what is caused shares some likeness with its causes, and with its ultimate Cause, that language will stretch also to speaking meaningfully about God.

Trans-Cultural and Trans-Temporal Language

It is objected to the Catholic idea of dogma that a proper grasp of the historicity of man and the particularities of human culture make impossible teachings that can be understood everywhere and in all times. It is true that the ability to speak trans-culturally and trans-temporally is an achievement that not all cultures foster. But it is an ability that all men are able to cultivate.

We addressed the issue of the historicity of dogma in chapter 4, defending the First Vatican Council's teaching that dogma is "irreformable" against radical historicism. There is also something to say about the genesis of trans-cultural, and in that sense "catholic" concepts.

The ability to speak trans-culturally and trans-temporally is the ability to speak Greek; that is, it is the ability to speak in the way that Plato and Aristotle and other ancient cultivated Greeks did. This is sometimes obscured by the characterization of ancient Greek culture as one culture among many—the ancient Assyrians, Chaldeans, Persians, Phrygians, Egyptians, and also Greeks. "Culture," moreover, means particularity, and means it in two ways: there is first the cultivation of the land, and the particularities of land and geography distinctively stamp a people; second there is *cultus*, the cultivation of the divine, and indeed, from place to place, the worship of distinct deities. In this light, Greek culture is one among many. On the other hand, it is the culture that formulated the problem of the one and the many; it is the culture that learned to distinguish nature and culture, that is to say, nature and convention, *physis* and *nomos*. That discovery just is the discovery of a reality prior to, and for Plato and Aristotle, normative with respect to, culture—normative with respect to all cultures. It is not a discovery within philosophy, really; it is the discovery of philosophy.

The discovery is provoked by Greek encounter with alien cultures and religions. Leo Strauss explains how this encounter encourages an application of two pre-philosophic distinctions: first, the distinction between the actual inspection of something, personal acquaintance or "eyewitness" knowledge, on the one hand, and hearsay, on the other; and second, the distinction between what we make (artifacts), and what we find lying at hand prior to our arranging it into artifacts (stuff).[57]

Suppose I discover that the account of the gods and the world that I hold and the pattern of right conduct that I hold to on the authority of the tradition of my city do not match the account and the pattern of some other city. How shall I explain this difference? The difference can, after all, be contradictory. I can think that the other city is wrong, that its tradition is faulty and has no real authority; I can think that my city and I are right. On the other hand, I might place both traditions in question, and try to work out an account of things independently of tradition, and think about the pattern of right conduct independently of what I have been taught. I start to consider tradition as hearsay; I prefer to find out things on my own, on the basis of my own experience of the world and of human action. Second, I wonder whether different traditions and different laws and human ways of arranging society and worshipping the gods

57. For what follows see Leo Strauss, *Natural Right and History* (Chicago: University of Chicago Press, 1953), 86–90.

and judging human conduct are just as artificial as clothing and buildings. Just as the houses are different over yonder, so is the religion and law. The stone and the wood are the same, but the houses are different. And just as houses are artifacts, so perhaps also are religion and religious stories and human laws. These things have not, perhaps, been discovered, the way we discover wood or wool, but are made, the way we make chairs and tables or the way we cut cloth. And again, perhaps the "hearsay" of the tradition is not the speaking of a god, but nothing more than the fancyings of men. Carpenters make tables and tailors tunics; just so, poets make the gods and priests make the laws. What do they make them out of? What is the stuff that precedes the artifact of culture?

At this point, then, we can begin to call what we find out on our own, what we can discover, independently of human mores and laws, "nature"; and we can call the social and political and moral and religious artifacts that men construct "convention."

Before the distinction, the ways of men—the men of my city—and the ways of the animals and plants were all equally given simply and un-problematically as the ways in which things operate and display them-selves, and show themselves to be the kind of thing they are. But now, while the ways of the animals and the plants may still be taken to disclose what they are, their true origin from their ancestral stock, their "nature," man turns into something highly problematic. His nature turns out to be covered over by and radically other than the manner of his action. At least, it *may* be. And the wisdom in the ancestral accounts of the gods and their relation to the world and their institutions of cities and laws turns out to be a just-so story.

Of course, we know from the workshop that some artifacts are in ac-cord with nature in that they respect the materials they are made of and bring out latent perfections in them, and some artifacts are not. If nature and convention are distinct, still, is there a social order, a moral and po-litical order, a religious arrangement, that is in accord with nature? It is with respect to this last question that the sophists and Socrates differ. The sophists answer the question with a No; Socrates and Plato answer with a Yes.

More than any set of technical terms such as substance and accident, form and matter, act and potency, essence and property, and important as these may be in constructing a philosophical account of the world and man, it is the distinction between nature and convention that is fundamental. This is so because, otherwise expressed, it is the distinction between what is prior in itself and what is prior to us, between the reality that is causal, and the caused phenomena that first meet the eye and solicit our touch. The nature of a cow requires her to eat grass. So also, the nature of man and natural need is causal with respect to economic cooperation and political regime. They are casual, but not determinative. So, while the differences between cities can be noted, they cannot be understood without the knowledge of the nature of man, a nature that the many opposed and even contradictory cultures serve as much to hide as to express.[58]

How does this story prepare for the trans-cultural and trans-temporal character of Catholic dogma? Catholic dogma, encompassing the teaching of Nicaea and Constantinople I on the Trinity, the teaching of the Christological councils from Ephesus to Nicaea II, the teachings of Lateran IV and Vatican I on God, the teaching of Vienne and Lateran V on man, the teaching of Trent on the Mass and the sacraments—Catholic dogma formulates the *priora in se* of the Christian mysteries.[59]

For example, what meets us first in our knowledge of Jesus the Christ are the gospels and letters of the New Testament. How shall we put into a coherent picture the entire gamut of things said of Jesus of Nazareth in the canonical Scriptures? The fathers discovered that it was wise to distinguish things said of Jesus Christ insofar as he is man, and things said of him insofar as he is God. Without this, smushing all the predicates together as if they manifested one kind of thing, we end up with an Arian Christ, neither truly divine nor properly human. But by distinguishing between things said of Christ as man and things said of Christ as God, we have a sure guide for assembling the course of Christ's life in which we behold a man like us in all things but sin progressively manifesting, first, who he is as the divine Son of God, and second, what we all are called

---

58. See ibid., 123–34.

59. Bernard Lonergan, *The Triune God: Systematics*, trans. Michael Shields (Toronto: University of Toronto Press, 2007), 83–85, 89–99.

to be and how to get there as we see the trajectory of his life from the humiliation of the cross to the glory of the Resurrection. The key, then, is to read the Scriptures distinguishing the natures, divine and human, and asserting the unity of agent or person. And this is all nicely summed up at Chalcedon and Constantinople II where we confess one hypostasis or person subsisting in two natures, divine and human. That is the *prius in se* to which the *priora quoad nos* of Scripture lead us.

It does not take too much reflection on the gospel to see the inevitability of the Church's use of Greek philosophical thought for its own purposes. The gospel proposes a common and supernatural end for man, one for which we prepare by faith, hope, and charity in this life, and which ends in the vision of God through Christ in the Holy Spirit in the next. But how human flourishing is to be conceived, how the virtues lead to and share in it, and how a community conduces to it are the topics of classical Greek ethics and political philosophy. The relations of body and soul, and of the role of form in human intellectual knowledge, were topics of Greek philosophical anthropology. Most obvious, Aristotle's metaphysics is the science of being *qua* being. How could it not help Christians think out the themes both of Creation and of Creation through Christ? Here is James McEvoy speaking of the Fathers of the Church.

They appreciated philosophy's purifying critique of polytheism. They saw that the philosophical standpoint had made possible for its adepts a critical distance regarding their own Greek or Latin culture. They realized that this standpoint resulted from the philosophical search for the transcendent, unique divinity, or Logos, or One. The Christian mind met Greek and Hellenistic culture, not in the purely particular features of the latter but at the point where it was moving beyond itself in the direction of universality.[60]

The Church thus borrowed certain Greek and Latin terms in which to express her mind as to the innermost core of the revealed mysteries, terms that, because of their fundamentality relative to human experience, were transportable from culture to culture and across the ages. It is a mistake, however, to think that the Church adopted these categories

---

60. James McEvoy, "Commentary," on *Fides et Ratio*, in Hemming and Parsons, *Restoring Faith in Reason*, 191.

ready-made, so to speak, *prêt-à-porter* and ready to clothe the Christian mysteries. Think of the last mentioned topic, Creation. The science of being introduces clarity into thinking about Creation, not because it is a science whose subject includes God, but on the contrary, just because God is beyond the being that is the subject of metaphysics. Correlatively, the magnificent vision of metaphysical continuity and necessity between the One and all the things that emanate from it quite sharpens our view of Creation, which smashes the continuity, denies the necessity, and apprehends the freedom with which God, who could abide in splendor and undiminished glory did he alone exist, creates the world and so shares his glory unto our but not unto his further good.

Then also, the Greek appreciation of the person was not ready for immediate expression of the doctrines of the Trinity and the Incarnation and Christian subjectivity made to the image of God. "Person," too, like "being," had to be adjusted to Christian revelation. What this means is that it is not Hellenism or philosophy that frames the gospel; rather does revelation project a horizon beyond which no further horizon can be thought: the God who is before Greek being, so transcendent to it that he can enter into the world in the Incarnation, so generous that he can raise up created persons to share in his own tri-personal reality.

We would not be mistaken to see in St. Paul, the apostle to the gentiles, the one who already in the New Testament so engineers the shape of Christian preaching as to make it trans-cultural, truly universal. It is not merely that, according to Acts 15, he provokes the express judgment of the apostles that Christians are free from the particularities of the Mosaic Law in its legal and ritual enactments. When he turns to the Athenians in Acts 17, he engages them not as speaking about the God of Abraham, Isaac, and Jacob, which would be meaningless to them; he turns from the particular history of Israel to the cosmos, and speaks rather of the God who made the world and is Lord of heaven and earth and who will judge all men. The universal appeal of the gospel is therefore already set afoot in the earliest preaching of the apostles. It is set afoot by appealing to the very culture-transcending possibilities discovered by the Greeks, who sought philosophical answers to the question of the cause of the world.

CHAPTER 6

CREDIBILITY

The credibility or believability of divine revelation is a property that follows from its nature. God does not speak unless he can be heard, and he does not command unless he can be obeyed. The actuality of hearing what God says is the topic of the chapter on faith. Between the speaking and the hearing, however, there is this third thing, the credibility of what is said: the ability of revelation to be heard as what it really is, its capacity to be taken as true by the hearer.

There can be distinguished a created and an uncreated credibility. Uncreated credibility is the very authority of the divine revelation itself, which, just because it is divine, is "self-credible." That is, the fact of God's speaking, since it is God himself, is rendered credible by nothing else than God, and the attempt to make it credible in some other way is either confused or tantamount to blasphemy. There is no one more to be relied on, more to be trusted, more to be taken at his word, than God. There is no measure to which his word can be subjected. The authority of God's speaking is therefore absolute for whoever hears. Just as the vision of God saturates the mind's capacity for intelligibility and truth, its capacity to "see," so the word of God to us now saturates the mind's capacity to hear and believe. Just as all things will be seen in the Word in the beatific vision, and seen for what they are more truly than if directly looked upon, so now, in this life, although we do not hear all things in hearing the word of God in faith, we hear that word such that it judges and orders all other words, and if this does not occur, then we have not heard it. The uncreated credibility of God is known in this life in knowing the fact of revelation itself, and that knowledge is the knowledge of faith. That is to say, the act of faith believes not only what God says, but the very fact that God is saying it. The self-credibility of the revelation of God, however, is a topic not for this chapter but for the next.

Created credibility, on the other hand, is the credibility of revelation beheld prior to the act of faith, the credibility that is accessible to reason. It is something that accrues to the created manifestation of the revelation of God in the economy of salvation, to its manifestation in Tradition and Scripture, in the Church and in dogma. The rational credibility of revelation is a difficult notion; rational credibility shares in the self-credibility of the divine speaking, but has to be accessible to reason. The idea is that supernatural, uncreated credibility, available only to faith, manifests itself *prior* to faith in a rationally apprehensible, created credibility. Just as, relative to content, God's word is spoken in human words, so, more formally, his own credibility shows itself in a created credibility available to natural reason. In a similar way, the Son manifests himself, his person, in a human nature. The same structure belongs to the mysteries of revelation, of the Incarnation (the apex of revelation), and of the faith that receives it.

Why must we expect this credibility to be provided for in the providence of God? There are two reasons. The first is in the nature of an act of communicating something to men. The second has to do with the moral responsibility with which a man is required to approach the possibility of faith.

First, the credibility of Christian revelation is something public and so serves as a sort of advertisement that revelation has been made. It is a sort of invitation to those who pay attention to what may reasonably be hoped for as the end of human destiny, promising a word that addresses the questions of the permanent value of the person (immortality of the soul), the catastrophe of death (resurrection of the body), and human moral evil (satisfaction for past sin and restored moral uprightness), and all three of these in relation to the divine mind and will.

Second, the credibility of Christian revelation is required so that proceeding to the act of faith may be a morally praiseworthy act. Failing this credibility, a credibility open to reason's questions, faith becomes unreasonable, and therefore morally irresponsible, an exercise of credulity repugnant to the God who makes reason, and offensive to the common good of civil society. This implies that revelation, the gospel message, is rationally credible. The judgment that revelation is credible is therefore always at least implied in the act of faith, even if it is not an explicit object of consciousness. Moreover, what is explicitly conscious to the believing mind of the credibility of revelation can be something that touches only one part or aspect of its credibility and may yet suffice for a reasonable assent to the gospel. This is a function of the manifold and exceedingly powerful credibility of revelation.

The First Vatican Council teaches the necessity of the rational credibility of revelation most expressly and formally in chapter 3 of its *Dogmatic Constitution on the Catholic Faith (Dei Filius)*.

in order that our submission of faith be nevertheless in harmony with reason [cf. Rom 12:1], God willed that exterior proofs [*argumenta*] of his revelation, viz., divine facts, especially miracles and prophecies, should be joined to the interior helps of the Holy Spirit; as they manifestly display the omnipotence and infinite knowledge of God, they are the most certain signs of divine revelation, adapted to the intelligence of all people.[1]

The explication of the rational credibility of Christian revelation will proceed as follows. First, this credibility accrues to the economy of salvation as a whole in its internal elegance and coherence. It accrues to this

---

1. J. Neuner, SJ, and Jacques Dupuis, SJ, *The Christian Faith in the Doctrinal Documents of the Catholic Church*, 7th ed. (New York: Alba House, 2001), no. 119; see canon 3: "If anyone says that divine revelation cannot be made credible by outward signs, and that, therefore, people ought to be moved to faith solely by each one's inner experience or by personal inspiration, A.S." (Neuner and Dupuis, *The Christian Faith*, no. 128). This teaching is recalled by Pius XII in *Humani Generis*, no. 29 (available at the Vatican website, http://vatican.va): "it falls to reason ... to prove beyond doubt from divine signs the very foundation of the Christian faith." The "demonstration" required by faith need not be apodictic; its nature will be taken up in the chapter on faith.

economy, however, also and necessarily according as the words and the deeds that constitute the pattern are convincing and real. This is a matter, finally, of the culminating words, the words of Jesus, and the culminating deeds, the cross and resurrection. Therefore, second, the credibility of the words of Jesus, his teaching, must be examined, as also, third, the credibility of his resurrection from the dead.

Since both the second and third forms of credibility depend on the witness of Scripture and the manner of its tradition to us, as retailing reliable eyewitness accounts of the resurrection, and "ear-witness" reports of his teaching, then fourth, for Jesus to be known to be credible to us in his word and his resurrection, the reports of these things such as we have them in *Scripture* must be credibly eyewitness reports. This credibility is intimately bound up with the temporal conjunction of these reports with the original apostolic witness and its accessibility in the tradition of the apostolic and immediately post-apostolic age. Some of this we have already touched on in chapter 3, but now we need to make it more explicit.

Fifth, of the Church, especially the apostolic Church, that mediates the witness of the Tradition and Scripture, it must be credible that she was founded by Christ with the authority to guard the deposit of faith in her dogmatic teaching, and, sixth, there must be a credibility intrinsic to the content of dogma.

The credibility of the pattern of revelation as a whole depends on its internal coherence and elegance, which itself as factually established in history depends crucially on the credibility of the word of Jesus, which itself depends on the credibility of the resurrection, which like the credibility of the fact of his having said what he did depends also on the credibility of the Gospels as eyewitness accounts. The credibility of the Christ's foundation of the Church is a matter of the continuing credibility of the gospel message from the Ascension to the Parousia, since no revelation is in fact given to those dependent on its reception across time without the possibility of its definitive and institutional interpretation. And these interpretations in whole and in part, the sum of the dogmas of the Church, must return to the economy and in themselves reflect the coherence and beauty of the original pattern.

The Credibility of the Pattern or Economy of Salvation

St. Irenaeus expressly offered his *Demonstration of the Apostolic Preaching* as a manifestation of the credibility of Christianity. "We have not hesitated to speak a little with you [Marcianus], as far as possible, by writing, and to demonstrate, by means of a summary, the preaching of the truth, so as to strengthen your faith."[2] He first sets forth the main line of the history of salvation, from creation to the Fall, and thence from Noah to the patriarchs and Moses and the prophets, ending with the Incarnation and Cross. These elements of Christian creed and Christian story are then corroborated by their having been foretold by the prophets. That is the burden of part two of the *Demonstration*, for the Old Testament manifestations of the Son and the prophetic anticipation of Christ's earthly career give us rational assurance of the truth of the gospel. As he says: "That all those things [about Christ] would thus come to pass was foretold by the Spirit of God through the prophets, that the faith of those who truly worship God might be *certain* in these things, *for whatever was impossible for our nature ... these things God made known beforehand by the prophets*."[3] Blaise Pascal thought to reproduce this same kind of argument in the seventeenth century. But the apologetic plan of which the *Pensées* are the relic did not presuppose in its intended audience the same confidence in the existence of God and his providence that Irenaeus could count on.[4] Irenaeus had only to activate this common belief in God by recounting the first chapters of Genesis. Augustine, too, had only to preface his exposition of the economy of salvation in the *First Catechetical Instruction* with a brief meditation on the end of man.[5] But Pascal had to invent some engine of destruction to pierce the fortifications of practical atheism and explicit skepticism of seventeenth-century French high society: hence his attention to the distinction of the orders of matter and mind to break the

---

2. St. Irenaeus of Lyons, *On the Apostolic Preaching*, trans. John Behr (Crestwood, N.Y.: St. Vladimir's Press, 1997), no. 1.

3. Ibid., no. 42; italics added.

4. Blaise Pascal, *Pensées*, trans. W. F. Trotter (New York: Modern Library, 1941).

5. Augustine, *The First Catechetical Instruction*, trans. Joseph P. Christopher (New York: Newman Press, 1946).

grip of materialism; hence also his construction of the Wager to concentrate the mind of the *bon vivants*.

We are today in a spot like Pascal's. Secularly educated man is tempted to place the Bible within some scientifically constructed framework: first, the framework constructed in equal measure by the history of religions and cultural anthropology; second, the framework of physical and evolutionary anthropology; third, the framework—beyond which there can be no greater for the contemporary mind—of astrophysics and stories about the Big Bang.

Unless these frameworks are dismantled as providing the most suitable presuppositions for understanding man, unless they are themselves situated within a framework that recognizes the irreducibility of mind to matter, a framework also presided over by the God who in the beginning created the heavens and the earth, then it is difficult for the argument from prophecy and typology to get any traction. If we are thinking apologetically, therefore, the credibility of the gospel thus displayed in this the hallowed argument of tradition is much beholden to an express treatment of the *praeambula fidei* such as was discussed in the previous chapter.

That being said, the fuller apologetic argument demonstrating the credibility of the gospel can be outlined as follows. First, the happiness of human beings is bound to their possession of truth and their exercise of love, unto which they are ordered seemingly without limit. Second, there is therefore no prospect of a humanly satisfactory possession of truth and exercise of love apart from God, who is the Truth and the Good. Third, we should consequently expect the God who makes us also to tell us how we are to know him and how we are to possess him and how this love of him is related to our love of other men, to which our happiness is also bound. Fourth, the knowledge and love of God that God makes available to men must have also somehow to overcome sin and death, which do not intrinsically limit our ordination to truth and the good, but do in fact so qualify it as to tempt us to despair.[6] Fifth, there is therefore an antecedent probability that God, who is good, and who could create us

6. See the partial execution of this program in Charles Morerod, OP, *The Church and the Human Quest for Truth* (Washington, D.C.: The Catholic University of America Press, 2008); and in Luigi Giussani, *At the Origin of the Christian Claim*, trans. Viviane Hewitt (Montreal: McGill-

only for the good, would address us, and that he would address us in such a way that those who seek can find him. Then, sixth, such arguments as that of Irenaeus in the *Demonstration*, or that of Augustine in *The First Catechetical Discourse*, or in a more modern form, that of Balthasar in the sixth volume of *The Glory of the Lord* can be deployed, arguments which, it should be noted, are in their own order very powerful and are neglected to catechetical and evangelistic ruin.[7]

And *that* being said, we should not discount the possibility of beginning from the sixth point and working back. There are many mansions in the Father's house and many ways to them. For after all, if one reads the promises in Isaiah that all the nations shall know God and bring themselves to Jerusalem (e.g., Is 60:3), and then beholds the Church of many nations worshipping the God of Abraham, Isaac, and Jacob, then one might think a dangerous thought, dangerous to the suffocating secularism and positivism of the age.

However, we need not think exclusively apologetically at this point. Irenaeus writes not to induce but to strengthen faith. And the contemplation of the pattern of revelation just as credible does that for all believers.

The Word of the Lord

Whatever the elaborateness and richness with which the economy of revelation is displayed, the keystone of the arch is Christ. As the pattern is a pattern of words and deeds, so he must be the key in both ways. The credibility of the pattern depends signally on the credibility of his claim to be who he is (and the very fact that he made such a claim). Only then can the pattern be what Christians say it is.

The words of Jesus come to us with a self-authenticating power. This is to be contrasted with how the ordinary words of ordinary human beings come to us. Ordinary words come to us with the presumption that

---

Queen's University Press, 1998); and his *The Religious Sense*, trans. John Zucchi (Montreal: McGill-Queen's University Press, 1997).

7. See Sean Innerst, "Divine Pedagogy and Covenantal Memorial: The Catechetical *Narratio* and the New Evangelization," *Letter and Spirit* 8 (2013): 161–88, who pays particular attention to St. Augustine's *First Catechetical Instruction*.

we should give them the benefit of the doubt, which is to say, we should give the speaker the benefit of the doubt, not questioning either his competence to know whereof he speaks or his veracity in telling us what he knows. This is described from the other direction by maintaining that someone who hears another make a claim about the world has a presumptive right to suppose him trustworthy. Hearing him, I should be taken to know what he tells me, without further ado and without argument. That is, I should be taken to know what he tells me, and without reducing the claim his assertion makes on me to follow along with what he says and assent to it back to some general and logically prior consideration of the human propensity to tell the truth and of the signs my interlocutor gives both of his competence and his personal veracity.[8] In other words, if it is true that "I heard that p," "heard" should be taken as a factive verb, just as the verbs in "I know that p" or "I am convinced that p" or "I see that p." Without so understanding things, then the entire world constructed by testimony and belief in that testimony is destroyed, and I am no longer capable of saying things such as "I know that Caesar crossed the Rubicon" or "I know that the atomic number of carbon is 6" or "I know that I was born in America." Doubting the trustworthiness of testimony, taking everything as merely "hearsay," would mean confining ourselves to the remarkably small world of the space we can see with our own eyes, just as doubting the trustworthiness of memory would confine us to just as small a temporal world of the last ten minutes, or hour, or (maybe) day. But the unexperienced world of years and decades would disappear into uncertainty and conjecture.[9] Without trusting the testimony of the millions of people whose reports are contained in conversation and newspapers and books, the world mediated by human language would come to look no larger than the environment of a clever animal.

Our Lord's words, however, come to us with more than the expecta-

8. See the discussion of this point in Mats Wahlberg, *Revelation as Testimony: A Philosophical-Theological Study* (Grand Rapids, Mich.: Eerdmans, 2014), chap. 4, relying especially on the work of John McDowell. For the heard sentence as a signal to follow along with the speaker's syntax, and the conditions under which this following along are suspended, see Robert Sokolowski, *Presence and Absence: A Philosophical Investigation of Language and Being* (Bloomington, Ind.: Indiana University Press, 1978), chap. 10, "The Sentence as a Signal for Propositional Achievement."

9. See Wahlberg, *Revelation as Testimony*, 127–28, on Michael Dummett on memory.

tion that we shall meet them with the presumption that he is trustworthy when he speaks of the things of this world and his experience of them. They come to us with a more powerful claim to our credence. There have been countless individuals, not yet Christians, who have picked up the Gospel according to Matthew, read it, and believed before the last page was turned. Matthew himself notes this self-authenticating power at the end of the Sermon on the Mount: "for he taught them as one having authority and not as their scribes" (Mt 7:29). It is not an exegetical, learned, scribal authority, parasitic on the authority of a prior text. It is not the authority borrowed from a text one is commenting on; rather: "Ye have heard that it was said, Thou shalt love thy neighbor, and hate thine enemy: but I say unto you, Love your enemies, and pray for them that persecute you" (5:43–44). The text is set aside, or bracketed; the authoritative word is his own. Who then is he? Who gives him the authority to speak so? When the priests and elders ask him where his authority comes from (21:23), he asks them rather about John's authority. Of his own authority he says nothing, for there is nothing to say about a self-authenticating authority if it really is self-authenticating.

In this vein, Michel Henry notes an important break in the Beatitudes between two theses they propound. The first thesis is about how to understand men who are pure of heart, meek, and poor in spirit: such men are children of God. As Henry puts it, a divine genealogy is substituted for their natural human descent and lineage. The kingdom of heaven is populated exclusively by the sons of God. As the Fourth Gospel says, we must be born "not of blood nor of the will of the flesh nor of the will of man, but of God" (Jn 1:13). The second thesis is even more provocative and has to do with Jesus' own relation to this divine generation, for he must surely know how it is that God generates sons and daughters in order authoritatively to declare it for the poor and the meek and the peacemakers.[10] But how could he know such a thing? It is surely a knowing parasitic on a prior being since he speaks of the being of men and does so with authority. The difference between Jesus and other men must then consist in the very way they realize divine filiation. Moreover, our filiation

10. Michel Henry, *Words of Christ*, trans. Christina M. Gschwandtner (Grand Rapids Mich.: Eerdmans, 2012), 44.

will depend on his, and our relation to Christ, according to Christ's word, will be one with our relation to God.[11] In sum, his very capacity to declare that the good and the just are children of God therefore depends on his own divine filiation, just as St. Paul concludes that men can be sons of God only because the Spirit of the Son is sent into their hearts (see Gal 4:6).

The question of who Jesus is, the question of his authority, is treated at length in John. Jesus presents himself as one not subject to that law according to which no man can render testimony to himself (see Jn 5:31).[12] He thus presents himself as one who cannot accept, because he cannot be validated by, any human testimony, even that of the Baptist (5:33–36). The testimony he accepts is from the works he has been given to do from his Father (5:36) and from the Father himself (5:37), whose voice has never been heard nor his form seen by man. So, he bears witness to himself and so does his Father (8:14–18). Just in this way, his manner of presenting himself is a claim to self-validation. Moreover, he is credible *only* if he presents himself in this way, for God can be justified by no man. If he offered some other, extrinsic validation, some validation by way of any human authority whatsoever—political or philosophic—or the authority of any prophet (even the Baptist), then he *could not* be who he says he is. His manner of presenting himself would contradict the self that is to be presented.

The foregoing implies also that the apprehension of him as who he is and the acceptance of his testimony about himself as true and worthwhile can only be grasped in one and the same act of faith. As the presentation of things in the Fourth Gospel makes plain, we believe Jesus because of who he is, and we know who he is because we believe him.[13] Only faith can see both him and the rightness and truth of his manner of presenting himself as self-credible, as self-authenticating.

The power of Christ's word, if not measured by any man, is measured only by him, which is to say it is measured by how he lives according to it,

11. Ibid., 46; see Luke 9:24; 12:8.
12. Ibid., 63.
13. See Juan Alfaro, SJ, *Esistenza Cristiana*, 2nd ed. (Rome: Gregorian University Press, 1979), 9–11.

by his faithfulness to it, and in the end, validating his word about himself in his blood, in his faithfulness to it unto death. His life's blood is offered in proof of his life's word—they measure each other.

The claim about himself is such also that we make a response to it whether we want to or not. He himself already somehow includes us, as Matthew 25 shows. He is to be met in every needy person, the hungry, the thirsty, the sick, and the naked. And insofar as we ever are ourselves needy, then we are already in him. The authoritative self-authentication of the Son of man means he is somehow every man. And from the other side, therefore, and even if we would, we cannot escape him: either we feed and clothe him or we do not, but whether for weal or woe, we have to do with him. And this must be true, if he is the God who enters history as one of us. Thus, he cannot be *just* another one of us, but must be the one with whom always we have to do. If we are in the pattern of revelation—as we must be since it is a universal pattern—then we have always to do with the Key to it. But the claim to be such and to be the one with whom we always have to do, as he makes in Matthew 25, is scandalous, which is to say it provokes a response in faith or non-faith, even as the poor and the needy provoke, or do not, a response in charity. We cannot, then, be indifferent to him. That is, it is not possible to be indifferent to him, both because of what he says about himself and because we cannot not meet him in the poor and the needy. The possibility of scandal is a necessary part of the credibility of Jesus' claim about himself.[14]

This scandal is described by Luke. Even when he matches himself to the prior word of God, as he does in the synagogue in Luke 4, reading Isaiah 61—"the Spirit of the Lord is upon me"—and even though the crowd marvels at "the gracious words which proceeded out of his mouth" (Lk 4:22a), St. Luke immediately moves to reporting that the people of Nazareth reject him. He is, after all, merely Joseph's son (4:22b). How can the graciousness both be perceived and yet not win the day for faith? Were we not fallen, the self-authenticating word of Jesus would immediately recommend itself to us in its truthfulness and super-credibility unto faith. But we are fallen, and so cannot take Jesus' word just as it is. The darkness cannot grasp it. His

14. This is a theme important to Søren Kierkegaard. See his *Philosophical Fragments*, ed. and trans. Howard V. Hong and Edna H. Hong (Princeton: Princeton University Press, 1985).

word therefore has also to be validated for us, which is to say he has also to be validated for us; and this he does by his miracles and especially the resurrection.

If we had not fallen, we would have believed. But if we could have believed, he would not have needed to come among us as a man. The rejection of the pure word of Jesus by those who heard him is, however, built into the plan, just as St. Paul says: the rulers of this age did not understand the wisdom of God, "for if they had, they would not have crucified the Lord of glory" (1 Cor 2:8). Nor did those ruled by these rulers understand, and so they consented to his death. But the death is necessary so that there can be resurrection.

Unfallen, we would have accepted the words of Jesus with, as the phrase is, "doxastic responsibility." Fallen, we are more benighted and cannot enter into the self-authenticating word he preaches on its own terms. So that we may be doxastically responsible, however, he gives us a sign.

The Resurrection of Jesus

It is usually supposed that the main problem in apprehending the credibility of Jesus' resurrection is in weighing the credibility of the reports of the appearances of Jesus and the reports of the empty tomb. To be sure, these reports are to be carefully considered. There are multiple and independent reports for both the appearances of the risen Lord and the emptiness of his tomb.

But the credibility of these reports is not, in fact, the main issue. The main issue is finding the categories with which to understand the brute fact of the return to life of the murdered and dead Jesus—the categories which make the fact no longer brute, but intelligible. This is clear from Luke 24: the disciples on the road to Emmaus have firsthand reports of the empty tomb, reports of angelic testimony that Jesus is alive, and their own sensory perception of the One who accompanies them on the road. But they have not attained to faith in the resurrection of Jesus. What are lacking are the proper forms, the proper terms, with which to understand the reports of the women and the message of the angels and the deliverances of their own eyes and ears. Once the Lord gives them these categories, by interpreting the Law and the Prophets and Psalms in reference to himself, then they believe.[15]

This is to say, therefore, that the main burden of the credibility of the Lord's resurrection falls, not on the "sensory data" available either first hand or by report—for us, by report—but on the capacity to understand, with the right notions, what has gone down. This the Lord supplies, together with the interior grace ("did not our hearts burn") that is necessary to understand them and their application to the reports they have already heard. This is to say, in the end, that what is most important is to fit the resurrection into the comprehensive pattern of revelation, of its economy, whose entire form is Christ.

So yes, while we break down the analysis of credibility into discrete topics, including separate consideration of the Lord's words and now his resurrection, it all comes back to a certain whole thing perceived as a whole. And this will be true also, in its own way, when we come to consider the Church's role and the role of her Tradition in the establishment of credibility. For the Church is *part* of the pattern.

For the sake of analysis, we might put it like this. There are two blades that cut the paper. The upper blade of perceiving the credibility of the resurrection does indeed depend on such historical considerations as the following: (1) the multiple attestations of appearances in the synoptic Gospels, and in Paul, who reports an appearance to more than five hundred (1 Cor 15:6); (2) the reports of the empty tomb, which must be reliable, Pannenberg noted some time ago, if the resurrection of Jesus was preached in Jerusalem;[16] and (3) the vigorous missionary activity of the apostles and the rise of the Church, which are otherwise inexplicable except on the supposition that the many people responsible for this activity very firmly believed in the Lord's resurrection.

All these things work together. But they work against the other blade, the lower blade of the theological categories with which to understand why the Christ must suffer and why death could not hold him. That is,

---

15. Jean-Luc Marion, "'They Recognized Him; and He Became Invisible to Them,'" *Modern Theology* 18 (2002): 145–52.

16. Wolfhart Pannenberg, *Jesus—God and Man*, 2nd ed., trans. Lewis L. Wilkins and Duane A. Priebe (Philadelphia: Westminster Press, 1977), 100.

they work against the other blade which in its entirety consists in the pattern of revelation established in the Old Testament. The history and the theology work together in apprehending the credibility of the resurrection.

The evidences and arguments that constitute the "upper blade" have been conveniently summarized in compact form by Dale Allison. He marshals all the arguments for and against the historical reality of the resurrection of Jesus which theologians, historians, scripture scholars, and sceptics have employed since the Enlightenment and assesses their contemporary living force.[17] He notes what Pannenberg notes, the impossibility of preaching the resurrection of Jesus in Jerusalem if the tomb had not been empty, and adds the following: (1) the story of the soldiers guarding the tomb in Matthew 28 supposes that the tomb was in fact empty as Christians claim; (2) there was no Christian veneration of Jesus' tomb; (3) 1 Corinthians 15 supposes an empty tomb, where Jesus' burial supplies a foil to his resurrection; (4) Mark 16 is theologically undeveloped, which is to say untouched by Old Testament allusion; (5) visions of Jesus by themselves could not alone have supported the fact that he was risen; (6) the first witnesses of the empty tomb are women, unlikely candidates for an invented story.[18]

The fifth point, on the relation of the empty tomb reports to reports of the appearances, has been developed in a powerful way by N. T. Wright. He maintains that neither the empty tomb nor the appearances could by themselves generate an announcement that Jesus was raised from the dead. Both are required. A tomb may be empty for many reasons. Appearances may or may not presuppose the visibility of the very body in which Jesus suffered and died. But together, the empty tomb and the appearances are tantamount to a sufficient condition for asserting resurrection, and in fact leave very little choice except to affirm it, unless the gap between the death and burial of Jesus and the missionary activity of the Church is simply con-

---

17. Dale Allison, "Explaining the Resurrection: Conflicting Convictions," *Journal for the Study of the Historical Jesus* 3 (2005): 117–33. He does this from pages 117 to 124, most compactly on page 122, after which he reviews the articles that make up the rest of this fascicle of the journal. A good summary of arguments for the truth of the resurrection can be found in Gary Habermas, "Affirmative Statement," in Gary R. Habermas and Antony G. N. Flew, *Did Jesus Rise from the Dead? The Resurrection Debate*, ed. Terry L. Miethe (San Francisco: Harper and Row, 1987).

18. Allison, "Explaining the Resurrection," 123–24.

signed to a black hole.[19] Moreover, without the fact of the resurrection, then the enquirer will often be in the position of having to assert two intrinsically *unrelated* hypotheses to explain, first, the appearances (hallucination or some such) and second, the reports of the empty tomb (the women got mixed up on the location). Both hypotheses—empty tomb and seeing Jesus—would concur just by *chance* in the Christian announcement that Jesus was in fact raised.[20]

The Credibility of the Gospels as Containing Apostolic Witness

The resurrection comes to us via the testimony of the apostles and first Christians, who report their news to the evangelists and whose own testimony to what they themselves saw and heard we read in the Gospels. The resurrection is a miracle, of course, which is to say, a preeminent sign of the presence and power and communicative intention of the Creator within his creation.[21] Transcendence of the natural order bespeaks the presence of the only one who does transcend it, its Creator. But our knowledge of the resurrection comes via the witness of men—just as does our knowledge of the world of physics or of eighth-century China or of the current politics within the Washington beltway. Thus, the illuminating deed of the transcendent God is clothed in the flesh of the human way of coming to know the world in which we live. Grace, the grace of revelation, does not disdain nature, but presupposes it and adapts it to its purposes.[22] Such a structure we may expect for the manifestation of the crowning event in the career of the Word made flesh.

We have already approached some of the considerations to be made here in speaking of the canonical principle in chapter 2. We need to take

19. N. T. Wright, *The Resurrection of the Son of God* (Minneapolis: Fortress Press, 2003), 686–88.

20. Wahlberg, *Revelation as Testimony*, 210.

21. There is an extended discussion of miracles and the resurrection in ibid., 158–65, 182ff.

22. See Thomas Joseph White's review of Wahlberg's *Revelation as Testimony*, "Trust Witness," *First Things* (November 2015), 61: "The fact that God reaches us through the personal testimony of creative human beings does not make the Bible less credible but shows us that Christian revelation is about the human race having a shared human life with God in real historical time."

up this matter again, however, under the formality of credibility since the credibility of the resurrection is bound to the credibility of the Gospels, as is also the credibility that Jesus really said what he said.

This issue is crucial. It stands at the parting of the ways in the eighteenth century between Christianity and the modern liberal world. It is easy to see why. In criminal cases, any alleged evidence is worthless unless the chain of custody has been maintained: from the first collection of the evidence—blood or bullet, car or clothing—the prosecutor must be able to show that it has been kept safe from any alteration or tampering; there has to be a record of where the evidence was kept and who was responsible for keeping it. Apart from this, the evidence is no longer evidence; it does not show anything with sufficient certitude either to convict or to exculpate.

There has to be a similar chain of custody for the evidence of Jesus' words and deeds up to the time the public availability of the Gospel texts preclude any tampering. This was one reason why the Church could never endorse the principles of the form critical analysis of the Synoptic tradition undertaken in the twentieth century under the leadership of Rudolf Bultmann and Martin Dibelius and others.[23] Form critical analysis seeks to find out how Christian tradition modified this or that story about or saying from Jesus in order to meet the needs of diverse and supposedly relatively isolated early Christian communities. Thus, it has built into it the idea that there has been "evidence tampering" all along the line of oral tradition, and this even before (as it has been supposed) the final and unknown redactor put things together for his and perhaps quite different purposes in composing his Gospel.

The importance of the eyewitness testimony of the apostles is recognized in the Gospels themselves, and there is a claim to eyewitness testimony in 1 John 1:1–3, 1 Peter 5:1, and 2 Peter 1:16–18. The importance of such testimony has consequently—and by the very nature of extraordinary things recorded by the Gospels—always been recognized by the Church. St. Thomas notes that it is the office of an apostle to bear witness,

---

23. See the Pontifical Biblical Commission's instruction "On the Historical Truth of the Gospels," *Sancta Mater Ecclesia* (April 21, 1964), which insists on the trustworthiness of apostolic witness as recorded in the Gospels. This text can be found at the Vatican website, http://vatican.va.

commenting on John 21:24.[24] John accordingly takes care to identify himself as an eyewitness, St. Thomas explains, because he wrote his Gospel after the death of all the other apostles and after the other Gospels had been approved by them, especially the Gospel of Matthew (another eyewitness). John takes this care, therefore, lest his Gospel seem to have less authority than the other three.[25] Further, when he says "*we* know his testimony is true" (Jn 21:25), John speaks in the person of the whole Church who received his Gospel as true.[26]

What then is the authority of the apostles who wrote or otherwise testified to Jesus and endorsed the Gospel accounts? It is both supernatural and natural. It is supernatural, for it is part of the *officium* of the apostle, as commissioned by Christ, so to witness. The apostle speaks with the authority of Christ, and with the help of the Holy Spirit, the Spirit of truth, who helps him remember and guides him into all truth (Jn 14:26, 16:12). But it is also natural, or rather, it speaks to a natural desire, a sort of natural right on the part of the *hearer* of the witness, to be assured that the witness is giving an eyewitness account.

This natural right follows from what has been called the "uniquely unique" character of the events of the gospel.[27] These events are so extraordinary that there is no possibility of reasonably crediting them without eyewitness assurance of their actuality. We should otherwise be doxastically irresponsible were we to believe without such assurance. The revelation of Christ in word and deed, therefore, demands assured eyewitness testimony if it is to be credible, and this demand follows from the very nature of the revelation in question, in both its content as spoken by Christ and in the proofs that manifest it as coming from God, especially the Lord's resurrection from the dead. As to the latter, who would believe this resurrection unless we can be assured of the accounts, as coming from those who saw the risen Lord, saw the empty tomb? As to the

24. St. Thomas Aquinas, *Super Evangelium Sancti Ioannis Lectura*, ed. Raphael Cai, OP (Rome: Marietti, 1952), no. 2654.

25. Ibid., no. 2655.

26. Ibid., no. 2656.

27. Richard Bauckham, *Jesus and the Eyewitnesses: The Gospels as Eyewitness Testimony* (Grand Rapids, Mich.: Eerdmans, 2006), 492–93, relying on Paul Ricoeur. See the symposium on Bauckham's book in *Nova et Vetera* (English) 6, no. 3 (Summer 2008).

former, who would believe that Jesus of Nazareth claimed to be, not just the promised heir of David, not just the prophet like unto Moses, not just the Messiah, but the very Word of God, the very Wisdom of God, and that the engine of salvation would consist of his obedient submission to death? It is not enough that Isaiah provides the vocabulary. The vocabulary has to be applied, to Jesus, and if he is who he is, he is the only one who can credibly apply it to himself. And we must know, on the reliable witness of those who were with him, that he did so apply it. Only then can the self-authenticating words of Jesus be set free to do their work of indicating his identity.

All the Gospels themselves make a claim to eyewitness authority. They do so directly and expressly as does John (Jn 19:34–35; 21:24), or implicitly as does Matthew (Mt 9:9), another one of the twelve, both of whom appear as witnesses to the events described in the Gospels attributed to them.[28] Or they make a claim to eyewitness authority directly but at one remove, as does Luke (Lk 1:1–4), or implicitly and at one remove, as does Mark. Mark does not just speak about the apostolic mission as a continuation of Jesus' mission (Mk 3:14–15; 6:7–13, 30–32; 9:17–18), but also makes his own Gospel a continuation of it, a sort of performative witness to Jesus.[29] Since these Gospels were received by the Church from about 69 to 100 AD, still within the fading glow of the lived memory of the first witnesses, the subsequent Church has always been confident of the reliability of their testimony. The witness of St. Irenaeus, who heard Polycarp who heard John, captures this glow and preserves it for us.

So also does that of Papias of Hieropolis, who searched out those who heard those who heard the apostles. With Papias, who reports in the first decades of the second century the link between Mark and Peter alleged by "the Elder," we are again within a generation of someone much closer to the origins of whatever is passed along about Jesus orally, and who vouches for the Petrine authority of Mark. That the Gospels could be re-

---

28. For a satisfying discussion of the authorship of the fourth Gospel, see Joseph Ratzinger, *Jesus of Nazareth: From the Baptism in the Jordan to the Transfiguration*, trans. Adrian J. Walker (New York: Doubleday, 2007), 218–38.

29. Denis Farkasfalvy, *Inspiration and Interpretation: A Theological Introduction to Sacred Scripture* (Washington, D.C.: The Catholic University of America Press, 2010), 37.

ceived by a Church with apostolic memory is the most important link in the chain of the custody of the evidence. It is how God's credibility uses human credibility.

When we realize that Christian communities were not isolated from each other and that the local traditions they enjoyed could be tested by the larger Church,[30] and when it is further realized that never were the Gospels ascribed to anyone else than to the four "traditional" evangelists (see below), then that tradition can no longer plausibly be construed as legendary.

The confidence of the Church in the testimony of the Gospels is expressed through all the ages. We looked just above to St. Thomas's reception of John's Gospel in the thirteenth century: the question for him is why St. John mentions his eyewitness status, not that status itself. Here is Cyril of Alexandria in the fifth century:

Christ had to be patient with Thomas, as usual, ... as well as with the other disciples with him, who thought he was a ghost or apparition. He had then to show all of them for their satisfaction the print of the nails and his pierced side. He had also and without needing it to take some food, so that no excuse for their unbelief might be left to those who sought to gain the benefits of his death. But it was essential for him to care also for the certainty of our faith ... so that those who come at the last times should not easily be drawn into unbelief.... But if a man accept what he has not seen, and believe that to be true which the words of his teacher brings to his ears, then he honors with praiseworthy faith Christ who is preached. Blessed, therefore, will be the lot of every man who believes through the voice of the holy apostles, "who were eye-witnesses" of Christ's actions, and "ministers of the word," as Luke says. We must listen to them if we want life eternal, and cherish in our hearts the desire to abide in the mansions above.[31]

How does such confidence withstand the sustained critical scrutiny of the nineteenth and twentieth century historical examination of Christian origins? Just as we should expect: with enough evidence to satisfy the mind

30. Richard Bauckham, "For Whom Were the Gospels Written?" in *The Gospels for All Christians: Rethinking the Gospel Audiences*, ed. Richard Bauckham (Grand Rapids, Mich.: Eerdmans, 1998), 9–48, esp. 32–44.
31. St. Cyril of Alexandria, *Commentary on the Gospel according to S. John*, vol. 2, trans. Thomas Rendell (London: Walter Smith, 1885), at John 20:29. I have modified the translation.

of those whom the Holy Spirit moves to believe, but without sufficient evidence to compel belief in those who choose to perish.[32]

As to the resurrection, what of the charge that the very things St. Cyril mentions—touching the wounds of Christ and Christ's eating fish as proofs of his resurrection—are physicalizing and apologetic additions to original accounts that make the resurrection more an event of consciousness in the heated minds of the apostles than an event available to their senses? Such a question already supposes that we are not reading eyewitness accounts; it supposes that the bodily resurrection of Christ is a fabrication. It is a question that presupposes the large scale, intricately worked out suppositions of the form critical analysis of the Synoptic tradition.

The form critical approach to the Synoptic tradition is no longer the exclusive or regnant instrument of analysis that it was fifty years ago.[33] But its influence was mighty, and lingers on outside the field of New Testament studies in ways still calculated to provoke skepticism about the reliability of the Gospels. It is therefore useful to consider it head on. The form critical approach to the Gospels can be summarized as follows:

(a) The Gospels are not biographies

(b) and were written by unknown writers,

(c) who composed them mostly or exclusively from material passed down orally, in whose tradition Jesus' stories and sayings had already been adapted to community needs,

(d) and who further shaped the whole story primarily for their own theological and community concerns

(e) and were chosen from among many candidates by a Church unconnected to apostolic memory.

32. See Pascal, *Pensées*, W. F. Trotter (New York: Modern Library, 1941), no. 430, *ad fin.* (= Lafuma, 149): "It was not then right that He should appear in a manner manifestly divine, and completely capable of convincing all men; but it was also not right that He should come in so hidden a manner that He could not be known by those who should sincerely seek Him. He has willed to make Himself quite recognizable by those; and thus, willing to appear openly to those who seek Him with all their heart, and to be hidden from those who flee from Him with all their heart, He so regulates the knowledge of Himself that He has given signs of Himself, visible to those who seek Him, and not to those who seek Him not. There is enough light for those who only desire to see, and enough obscurity for those who have a contrary disposition."

33. See, for example, John Barton, "Biblical Studies," in *The Blackwell Companion to Modern Theology*, ed. Gareth Jones (Oxford: Blackwell Publishing, 2007), 18–33.

This approach opposes at every point the traditional view of things:

(a') The Gospels are biographies,

(b') and were written by the named people the Church has always attributed them to

(c') and were composed from eyewitness accounts of Jesus' teaching and actions passed down by people interested in what Jesus himself said and did

(d') and were shaped primarily to remember Jesus faithfully and accurately and elicit faith in him,

(e') and were received by a Church still connected to the memory of the apostles.

The third point in the summary of the form critical approach touches on the malleability of oral tradition. This was a foundation of form critical analysis; but the analysis of oral traditions has now become so sophisticated and detailed that there is no simple line to be drawn between Norwegian and German folkloric tradition and tradition of historical intent.[34] Evidently, the assessment of the reliability of orally preserved history varies according as one evaluates the importance that the accurately remembered facts have for those who pass them on. For the Christians, this importance is hard to overestimate, since they believed that their relation to God and their share in eternal life depended on what Jesus had taught and done in the flesh. This concern also governs an assessment of the reliability of the "redactors" of the Gospels, the evangelists themselves. As to the first thing, the nature of the Gospels, they fit well within the genre of Greco-Roman *bioi* of the Hellenistic period.[35] As to the fifth thing, we have already dwelt on the opportunity of the early Church to pass judgment on the historical accuracy of the Gospels.

This leaves us with the second point, the attribution of the Gospels to those to whom the Church has always attributed them. Martin Hengel

34. For an introduction to these issues, see Jan Vansina, *Oral Tradition as History* (Madison, Wis.: University of Wisconsin Press, 1985); also, the discussion in Birger Gerhardsson, a critic of form criticism, in *The Reliability of the Gospel Tradition* (Peabody, Mass.: Hendrickson Publishers, 2001), 9–14, on oral tradition; 29ff. for criticism of Bultmann; and throughout, on the historical reliability of the of the Gospels; and Bauckham, *Jesus and the Eyewitnesses*, chaps. 10, 12, and 13.

35. Richard Burridge, *What Are the Gospels? A Comparison with Graeco-Roman Biography* (Cambridge: Cambridge University Press, 1992).

has observed that there is no evidence that the Gospels at any time *ever* circulated anonymously; that had they done so we should expect many attributions for each Gospel, and certainly attributions to those of more authority than Mark or Luke; that anonymous Gospels would have no authority either generally or for worship; and that the fragments of Papias reliably take us back to the end of the first century for the attributions of the first and second Gospels.[36]

Outside the canon, Papias is concerned with the authenticity of apostolic witness and as contained in the Gospels; within the canon, 2 Peter is also concerned with the same issue of the authenticity of apostolic witness in written form.[37] They are concerned at just the same time, the first quarter of the second century, which is exactly when the credentials must be nailed down and beyond which they cannot be fixed with certitude.

It is hard to separate the apostolic origin and therefore historical authenticity of the Gospels as something known by history from the same things as known by faith. In the first draft of what became Vatican II's *Dei Verbum*, the text says that the Church has constantly believed and held that the Gospels are of apostolic origin and were written by the men whose names they now bear. *Dei Verbum* in the end says formally only that the Church holds to the apostolic origin (no. 18) and historicity (no. 19) of the four Gospels and says that the apostles and apostolic men passed down in writing what the Lord charged them to preach (no. 18). By saying that the Church "holds" to these things, the council maintains that they are accessible to reason when it considers the provenance of the gospels. But from the constant preaching of these same things—apostolic origin, historical reliability, attribution to the usual authors—both explicitly and implicitly, in the liturgy, in councils ecumenical and local, by popes, by bishops, by theologians, by learned and unlearned men, and in fact by all the faithful everywhere and at all times, we have such a massive assertion of tradition—difficult to find one more extensively and explicitly asserted—that the objects in question cannot really be excluded from the contents of Catholic faith.[38]

36. Martin Hengel, "The Titles of the Gospels and the Gospel of Mark," in *Studies in the Gospel of Mark*, trans. John Bowden (Philadelphia: Fortress Press, 1985), 64–84.
37. Farkasfalvy, *Inspiration and Interpretation*, 44.
38. See Anthony Giambrone, OP, " The Quest for the *Vera et Sincera de Jesu*: Dei Verbum no. 19

The Credibility of Christ's Foundation of the Church

The credibility of the Gospels makes credible Christ's foundation of the Church and so the credibility of the Church's teaching authority.

When Jesus announces the presence of God's Kingdom (Mk 1:15) and does those things that prove its presence, such as cleansing lepers and giving sight to the blind (Mt 11:4–5; see Is 35:5–6), driving out demons (e.g., Mk 9:14–29), and forgiving sin (Mk 2:5), then he is restoring Israel to her ancient integrity, as the appointment of the twelve signifies, and preparing her for her eschatological welcome of all the nations into her own covenant relation with God. He is sent only to the lost sheep of the house of Israel (Mt 15:24), but this is to ready Israel for the blessing of all nations through Abraham (Gen 12:1–3; cf. Lk 13:28–29). Equivalently, the restoration of Israel and the preparation of her for eschatological service is the end of her exile, the end of the time of her double payment for all her sins (Is 40:2).[39]

Equivalently, the restoration of Israel and making her the place of God's hospitality to all the nations is the foundation of the Church. This "foundation" is so exclusively the end of every word and action of Jesus that it is difficult to know how there can be a question about Jesus' historical foundation of the Church. What was outside the divine intention, though not of an all-encompassing divine providence, was the refusal of Israel to cooperate in this restoration and preparation. For insofar as the refusal is sinful, it is outside the divine will. But insofar as it is foreknown by God, it can be included both in the way eschatological grace is in fact merited by Christ, and in the way that it will be dispensed in history. It is included in the way that grace is merited, since the Jewish leaders who reject Jesus conspire with the Roman authorities to kill him, and the Messiah's death completes the nation's payment of the debt of punishment for

---

and the Historicity of the Gospels," *Nova et Vetera* (English) 13 (2015): 117–18. Someone may observe at this juncture that the traditional attribution of Matthew to an eye-witness complicates the Synoptic problem. At what point does literary theory, form-critical or source-critical, trump historical testimony? Surely there can be no general answer to such a question.

39. See N. T. Wright, *Jesus and the Victory of God* (Minneapolis: Fortress Press, 1996), summarily, 472–74, 538–39, 645–53; and Brant Pitre, "The 'Ransom for Many,' the New Exodus, and the End of Exile: Redemption as the Restoration of All Israel (Mark 10:35–45)," *Letter and Spirit* 1 (2005): 41–68.

sin. That is, the generation of Jews who reject Jesus arrange for the satisfaction that his suffering and death make before God not only for Israel but for all men of all nations. Further, this rejection of Jesus is included in the way grace is dispensed throughout the rest of history as St. Paul outlines in Romans 10 and 11.

Since the Kingdom is a final thing, the already begun fulfillment of the Kingdom that Jesus brings with him also connotes a kind of finality, and does so both in the order of revelation and in the order of grace. This twofold finality requires a novelty, whereby the last step beyond which there is no further step to take in history is signified, but at the same time a step within a continuity marked out by the previous path of Israel's history. According as this novelty is verified by the words and deeds, or "institution," of Christ, then there is verification of his founding or instituting the Church.

In the order of revelation, and since the words of the Lord are the words of the absolute Word of God, Jesus fittingly says that heaven and earth would pass away before his words pass away (Mt 24:35). He anticipates a time after the Paschal Mystery but before the perfect arrival of the Kingdom. The saying anticipates the time of the Church. Since the words of the Lord are words of eternal life (Jn 6:68), words according to whose reception in faith (Jn 6:40) and in sacrament (Jn 6:56–58) we will be judged eschatologically (Lk 12:8; cf. Jn 6:61), according as our reception accords with that of the twelve premier witnesses of his teaching and life (Mt 19:28), then it is altogether to be expected that the permanence of these words in time is ensured by the authority he grants to the twelve and especially to Peter (Mt 16:18; 18:18). Since he grants this authority to Simon the son of John insofar as he is "Peter," in terms, that is, of his function within and for the Church, it is an authority that passes to his successors. And since the twelve are likewise given authority in that they are judges discharging an office, so here, too, their authority is not personal but official and passes to their successors. Such an authority to bind and loose, to gage the correctness of the reception of faith, is an eschatological one, and therefore something new, although evidently within the path of teaching already marked out in Israel. The granting of such authority counts as a "founding" act.

In the order of grace, the advent of the Kingdom in time means the availability of the grace of forgiveness and the grace of sonship. The graces of forgiveness and sonship are accomplished by the passion and death of Christ. His passion and death are satisfaction for sin, since they proceed from his own created charity, greater in worth than all the good things forfeited by sin: he offers a more than equivalent worth outweighing all sin of all time, which, according as we are included in his charity, forgives our sin and releases us from the debt of hell. At the same time, this redemption is accomplished by way of sacrifice, as he explains at the Last Supper. As the Supper anticipates the sacrifice of Calvary, so the Mass recollects it and applies it to those who offer themselves with Christ and feed on his Body and Blood. The dominical command, "Do this," anticipates a time after Calvary, a time after the resurrection, the time of the Church just as does the Great Commission. It counts as a "founding" act. Those who obey the command to celebrate the Mass are in the first place witnesses to the risen Body of Christ; members of the Body of the Church, they renew themselves in making the Lord's Body and Blood sacramentally present.

The test of whether the Church is founded by Christ and so divinely instituted is enunciated by Gamaliel in Acts: "if this counsel or this work be of men, it will be overthrown; but if it is of God, you will not be able to overthrow them" (Acts 5:38–39). It follows that, if it could not be overthrown, the propagation and flourishing of the Church was a work of God. This invites us to remember St. Thomas's argument for the truth of the gospel and the authenticity of the Church at the beginning of the *Summa Contra Gentiles* implying the historicity of the miracles of the apostles.

This wonderful conversion of the world to the Christian faith is the clearest witness of the signs given in the past; so that it is not necessary that they should be further repeated, since they appear most clearly in their effect. For it would be truly more wonderful than all signs if the world had been led by simple and humble men to believe such lofty truths, to accomplish such difficult actions, and to have such high hopes.[40]

In this context, St. Thomas remarks on the absence of miracles in the propagation of Islam since it was the work of the sword and conquest.

40. St. Thomas Aquinas, *Summa Contra Gentiles, Book One: God*, trans. Anton Pegis (Notre Dame, Ind.: University of Notre Dame Press, 1975), chap. 6.

At the same time, he draws attention to the fact that the teaching of Islam appeals rather to the concupiscence of the body than to the desire of the mind. And this leads us to a last issue in presenting the credibility of Christianity.

The Credibility of Dogma Enunciated by the Church

The Church's dogmatic authority is included in the foundation of the Church: the grant of that authority counts as a founding act; and part of the Church's mission is to teach Christ's word. It is necessary that, if the Word made flesh teaches something that is to remain in time until the his return in glory, he will give the Church whatever it takes to keep that word available, which is to say to keep it as a word that is credibly his word and so certain as a word of divine revelation. Earlier, in chapter 4, we recounted Newman's argument from antecedent probability that a revelation given *as* revelation must be accompanied by an infallible interpretive authority.[41] Such considerations go far in establishing the credibility of the Church's dogmatic teaching.

Of old there used also to be an argument for the credibility of revelation from the "sublimity" of Catholic doctrine. What did this mean? R. Garrigou-Lagrange explains that the sublime "properly signifies something most high and most extraordinary in the order of the beautiful, especially of intellectual and moral beauty." Here is the application to doctrine:

A sign of the divine origin of doctrine proposed in God's name is found in that it wonderfully unites the highest and the lowest things, supernatural and natural things, the riches of divine mercy and the misery of the human race while maintaining the rights of justice, and in that it is at one and the same time proposed to all men of all nations and times, uniting the most ancient and the newest things, and such that the mysteries so proposed, even if obscure, appear marvelously connected with each other and with the last end of man.[42]

41. John Henry Newman, *An Essay on the Development of Christian Doctrine*, 6th ed. (Notre Dame, Ind.: University of Notre Dame Press, 1989), pt. 1, chap. 2, sec. 2, "An Infallible Developing Authority to Be Expected."

42. Reginald Garrigou-Lagrange, OP, *De Revelatione per Ecclesiam Catholicam Propositam*, 5th ed. (Rome: Desclée et Socii, 1950), vol. 2, 14; see in more detail 225–42.

The definition of Chalcedon, for instance, unites supernatural divinity and natural humanity in the one Person of Christ; this doctrine is itself to be read off the saving event of the cross, where the highest and the lowest things, the majesty of God's tribunal and the lowliness of a humanity ravaged by sin are united in one act of divine mercy alleviating the misery of the human race while maintaining the highest justice. While the cross declares the Trinity, something beyond the reach of reason alone, it also manifests at one and the same time both the nobility and the mysterious misery of man: his nobility, since human nature can be joined to the Word; his misery, since the remedy for our fallen estate requires so great a medicine as the death of God; and nobility again, since this death is willed not only by the divine will but the human will of Christ in an act of charity than which no greater is possible. The charity of Christ, extended also to us for whom he died, is a surpassing realization of the supernatural end to which man is called.

Garrigou-Lagrange is not content merely to juxtapose the extremes united in Catholic teaching. Rather, he says that they are *wonderfully* united, and that their connection is *marvelously* apparent. The wonder and marvel have to do with the fact that the juxtaposition is effected in such a way that the lowest things are the most adequate manifestation conceivable of the highest things to which they are connected. For instance, the justice of God is most manifest in his mercy, as St. Anselm says, because his justice is first of all just relative to his own goodness.[43] Or again, the Trinity is most manifest in the distance that the abandonment of the cross (Mk 15:34) shows us between sin-conditioned flesh and the Father of mercy as Balthasar tells us.[44]

This kind of observation develops what St. John says in his first letter, namely, that he saw with his eyes and touched with his hands the Word of Life that was from the beginning, because it was made manifest in the flesh of Christ (1 Jn 1:1–2; cf. Jn 1:1, 4, 14). To recall this gives St. John "joy," and sharing it with those to whom he writes makes his joy "complete" (1 Jn 1:4).

43. St. Anselm, *Proslogion*, in *St. Anselm: Basic Writings*, trans. S. N. Deane, 2nd ed. (LaSalle, Ill.: Open Court, 1962), chap. 10.

44. For instance, Hans Urs von Balthasar, *The Glory of the Lord*, vol. 7, *Theology: The New Covenant*, trans. Brian McNeil, CRV (German, 1969; San Francisco: Ignatius 1989), 202–35.

The joy is elicited from knowing something sublime, wondrous, marvelous, and being conscious of it with others (which is a sort of new motive for it).

St. Augustine on 1 John 1:1 expounds:

Therefore Life itself was manifested in the flesh, for it was put in the way of manifestation, so that what can be seen by the heart alone might be seen also by the eyes in order to heal the heart. For the Word is seen by the heart alone: but the flesh is seen by the bodily eyes. Whence it was that we should see the flesh, but not the Word. But the Word became flesh which we could see so that there might be healed in us whence we should see the Word.[45]

The eyes behold the flesh of the Word, especially the suffering flesh of the Word, so that the heart, by faith, may touch the Word. So to speak, the high and the majestic and the divine are made to shine forth to the eyes of flesh in the low and the miserable and the human. The categories of the low and the miserable and the human are made, in being broken, to pass over and communicate the high and the majestic and the divine.

"The sublime" is an aesthetic category, as Garrigou-Lagrange notes; and he appeals to St. Thomas's explication of the beautiful in terms of integrity, proportion, and clarity. The wonderful union and marvelous connection he observes calls attention especially to proportion. In the modern age, the sublimity of doctrine has been thought to have to do with the breaking of our ordinary categories of understanding and the indication of a disproportion in order that God may speak of himself to us; it has very much to do with presenting to us so intuitively saturated a phenomenon, the phenomenon of the bodily humanity of Christ, that the only category capable of declaring its truth is the non- or super-category of divinity. Neither of these ways of approaching the sublimity of doctrine need exclude the other.

The sublimity of doctrine is also connected to the *praeambula fidei* both as completing them, but as completing them in a way not to be anticipated before the completion. This is true on both the speculative and the moral

---

45. St. Augustine, *Commentaire de la première épître de saint Jean*, ed. Paul Agaësse (Paris: Les Éditions du Cerf, 1994), 1:1: "Ergo manifestata est ipsa vita in carne; quia in manifestatione posita est, ut res quae solo corde videri potest, videretur et oculis, ut corda sanaret. Solo enim corde videtur Verbum: caro autem et oculis corporalibus videtur. Erat enim videremus carnem, sed non erat unde videremus Verbum: factum est Verbum caro, quam videre possemus, ut sanaretur in nobis unde Verbum videremus."

order. Speculatively, it is within the compass of natural reason to demonstrate the existence and unicity of God. Still, revelation delivers these things to us, reconstructing what reason could do before the Fall, and can do again, once guided extrinsically by revelation. Moreover, revelation, that is to say, God, anticipates the best that we might think, with our natural powers, of his nature and existence, and how they are indistinct in him. This is the upshot of Exodus 3:14, where God discloses his name to us as "He who is," *haec sublimis veritas*, as Aquinas styles it in the *Summa Contra Gentiles*. The intersection of this name of God with a culture that asks about being then produces the conception of God as Subsistent Being, the truth that God is beyond the being that is the subject of Aristotle's metaphysics.

Still, even this truth is surpassed by the revealed reality of God in the New Testament. While neo-Platonism could think of plurality and difference only as something subsequent and posterior to the One, not so the New Testament. Difference and distinction are not derogations from divine perfection, but included within it. And the Trinity of Persons, precisely in their distinction from one another, becomes the ground of the distinction of things from God and from one another.

In the moral order, the Ten Words declare to us in the main the dictates of the natural moral law (with the third commandment positively specifying how God is to be worshipped). The revealed word greets what conscience has already surmised about murder, adultery, theft, lying, and dishonoring one's parents. For those who are clear that no metaphysics can be true that does not make possible the objectivity of such moral norms as are written on the second tablet, and that such norms in their truth and majesty are clues to the intelligibility of the being of the universe, their deliverance in revelation is a powerful argument of its credibility. Revelation and reason converge, therefore, and in this way, revelation strengthens reason's grasp of the injustice of the murder of the unborn, of infants, of the aged and diseased self by the Promethean self.

Even so, these truths of the moral order are surpassed in the New Testament, which locates the law of love as the soul of the virtuous discharge of the commands of the second tablet. Virtuously discharged, that is, discharged in such a way that I make the good of the other my own good, the commands lead to the happiness of friendship, the friendship of charity.

FAITH

In the introduction to the previous chapter, it was observed that the word of God received in faith has a certain preeminence over all other words: it judges and orders them. That is, the knowledge of God in faith is a higher knowledge than any other, both as to its content and as to its way of knowing. As to its content: it tells us of the intimate things of God, his triune life which otherwise we could not know, and of his will to invite us to share this life, and of the way to this goal. As to its mode or way of knowing: faith relies on the pure word of God conveyed by the Church; its knowledge is a participation in God's own knowledge, and so it is a higher mode of knowing that any science modern or ancient, including the phenomenology of Husserl or the metaphysics of Aristotle. These two created wisdoms can lead us to ask questions about what God has said and the God who says them. But they do not include God in their natural formal scope. They do not judge what God says or the fact that he says it. They do not project a larger whole in which the knowledge of faith is a regional part. Rather, the contrary is true.

The nobility and superiority of the knowledge of faith are therefore evident. They are evident, however, only to the one who has faith. To the one who has not, faith seems quixotic and risky, even unreasonable, something unbecoming a person in possession of his faculties. Even more, to the one who has not, it can seem a duty of humanity and of common fellow feeling to disabuse of his mistake anyone who has faith. The Christian shares in the mission of Christ and the apostles and so it is incumbent on him to lead all men to the obedience of faith. Even so, the non-Christian who is convinced in his own mind of the irrationality of faith has a mission conferred on him by his humanity to free those who believe from a yoke that diminishes their humanity. Faith either perfects nature and exalts the person, or it corrupts and debases. There is no middle way between these two alternatives.

This simply reports the New Testament's apprehension of things. For gentiles, the foolishness of the cross Paul preaches means a radical failure to live according to reason, to find one's perfection in so living—it is missing the end that human nature sets for us. For Jews, the scandal of the cross constitutes a kind of radical blasphemy and sin against the goodness and wisdom of God (1 Cor 1:23). This is nothing except to replay the scandal that Jesus himself evokes by his claim about himself, his message, his works: "Woe to you, Chorazin; woe to you, Bethsaida, for if the mighty works performed in you had been done in Tyre and Sidon, they would have repented long ago in sackcloth and ashes" (Mt 11:1). Again, that Christ is the Bread come down from heaven and gives us himself as true Bread is a hard saying, and who can bear it (Jn 6:60)?

This chapter begins with collecting some New Testament teachings about faith, and then organizes them with the help of Juan Alfaro. This in turn will lead us to some of the Thomist theses about faith.

The Nature and Properties of Faith according to the New Testament

In the New Testament, faith, *pistis*, has the sense of trust, as when *pisteuein* (to believe) is used with the dative of a person, a construction equivalent to our saying that "I have faith in Jeremy," or "I believe in you." Faith is fiducial: it is trust in a person.

Pistis also has the sense of taking someone's word for something, as when *pisteuein* is used with a following *hoti* (that) clause that states what it is that is being accepted as true. So also, in English, "I believe (that) Jordan is in Chicago." The two senses work together. "I believe Jordan is in Chicago—Mark said so." I trust someone and so take what he tells me as true. "I believe you" means I accept what you say (because I trust you). Faith is cognitive: it is an assent to a proposition.[1] This is the ground of the ability of the Church to propose further dogmatic articulations of revelation.

As depending on what is told us, (1) faith bears on what is not seen, not evident. Just as any act of trust, (2) it is freely done. These are the first two properties of faith. And also, (3) faith is obligatory; it may be that we ought to trust someone, and indeed, we ought to trust God. It is therefore an exercise of obedience, and so also (4) it is meritorious. Further, (5) faith depends on an interior grace, for we are punching above our weight when we believe, and (6) faith brings certainty about what it accepts, a divinely grounded certainty. In addition, (7) faith is reasonable, for it is a matter of our *logos* sharing in the *Logos* of God; and, just as such, sharing his mind (8) faith is also obscure, mysterious. Last, (9) faith is personal. These things are easily verified in the New Testament.

(1) The act of faith bears on what is not seen. "Faith is the assurance of things hoped for, the conviction of things not seen" (Heb 11:1). What is seen is what we know naturally, now in this life, or what we shall know, supernaturally in heaven. What is seen now makes for science in Aristotle's sense, where the science of X is the certain knowledge of the causes of X. But faith is not science in that sense—it does not see the evidence for what is asserted; it does not have causal knowledge of it. Here is how St. Thomas reworks the passage from Hebrews: "faith is a habit of mind by which eternal life is begun in us, making the intellect assent to what is nonapparent."[2]

(2) Faith is free. That is, it is something we freely do; we choose to believe; we choose to trust the person speaking to us; we choose to assent to what he is saying. Faith is evidently dependent on the exercise of our

---

1. For the New Testament senses of faith, see Avery Dulles, SJ, *The Assurance of Things Hoped For: A Theology of Christian Faith* (Oxford: Oxford University Press, 1994), chap. 1.
2. St. Thomas Aquinas, *Summa theologiae* II-II, q. 4, a. 1.

freedom, since we see in the gospels that some believe the Lord, and others do not. Further, the Lord could not exhort us to believe were we not free to do so: "Repent, and believe in the gospel!" (Mk 1:15). The freedom of faith has been defined by the Church.[3]

(3) Faith is free, but it is not something to which we can be indifferent, something we can take or leave. Rather, it is obligatory, and those who do not believe are cursed. "Woe to you Chorazin; Woe to you Bethsaida." The Lord Jesus is someone we *ought* to trust, and he *commands* us to believe in the gospel (above, Mk 1:15). St. Paul speaks of bringing men to "the obedience of faith" (Rom 1:5), indicating that to believe is to obey God. God commands us to believe the gospel. To "obey," of course is to hear (*ob-audire*), and to hear truly, to take in what God reveals, in the way he wants us to, will be just of itself to accept what he says, because he is saying it, and to believe. See John 8:43 where Jesus says to the unbelievers, "Why do you not understand what I say? It is because you cannot *bear to hear* my word." To bear to hear is to agree to hear; to agree to hearing is to assent to what is heard. To hear is to obey is to believe. So also, the good sheep hear the Lord's voice and follow him (Jn 10:27).

Faith is obligatory such that without it we cannot be saved. "He who rejects me and does not receive my sayings has a judge," says the Lord; and he continues, "the word that I have spoken will be his judge on the last day" (Jn 12:48). The Lord says he has a commandment from the Father to speak what he does (Jn 12:49), and we are likewise obliged to receive what he teaches by the same authority, his Father's authority, by which he teaches it. "And I know that his commandment is eternal life" (Jn 12:50). Again, faith is evidently obligatory in the Letter to the Hebrews, where those who fall away from faith are cursed (Heb 6:4–8).[4]

(4) Obedience is pleasing to the one who commands. So, faith is meritorious and those who believe are praised. By faith "the men of old received divine approval" (Heb 11:2). And see the stories of Old Testa-

---

3. See the Council of Trent, *Decree on Justification* (1547), chap. 5 and canon 4 (J. Neuner and Jacques Dupuis, *The Christian Faith in the Doctrinal Documents of the Catholic Church*, 7th ed. (New York: Alba House, 2001), nos. 1929, 1954); and First Vatican Council, *Dei Filius* (1870), chap. 3, canon 5 (Neuner and Dupuis, *The Christian Faith*, nos. 120, 129).

4. See also Rom 1:16, 3:26, etc.

ment faith, which culminate in the example of Christ's perseverance, in Hebrews 11, and see how the discourse ends with the exhortation to have faith, which exhortation includes the promise of salvation at the close of chapter 12.[5]

(5) Faith depends on hearing the word of God; also, it depends on an interior grace. The Fourth Gospel adverts to this interior grace. "No one can come to me [believe me] unless the Father who sent me draws him [by the interior attraction of grace]" (Jn 6:44).[6] The necessity of grace for faith has been defined.[7] We will return to this in more detail, but in general, we can see from the outset that we need help to share the mind of God.

(6) Faith is certain. That is, when we assent to the articles of the Creed by divine faith, we do not therefore end up thinking it is more likely that they are true than not. We are certain that they are true. We do not think it more probable than not that God created the heavens and the earth. We are certain that he did so. This is clear from the New Testament expectation that we are to die for the faith, and should bear any suffering or deprivation, even that of death, rather than forsake faith.[8] It would not be reasonable for us to risk death rather than deny Christ unless faith were certain. Moreover, it is unreasonable, and therefore not meritorious but rather blameworthy, to bet the ranch on a mere likelihood or some poor probability.

That faith is certain in the sense indicated in the New Testament makes it both like and unlike ordinary trust in someone's word. When we take someone's word for something—John tells us that Jordan is in Chicago—our assent is certain. Other things being equal—the absence of any reason to suspect John's motives in telling us this or to suppose he is misled—then we take what John tells us neat, and assent to it. "Yes, I'm certain Jordan is in Chicago; John told me." Certain knowledge is not infallible knowledge, however, as is divine faith.

(7) Faith is reasonable. That is not to say that it is a product of reason,

5. See also Rom 10:10, etc.

6. See also Eph 2:8, etc.

7. See the Second Council of Orange (529), canon 5 (Neuner and Dupuis, *The Christian Faith*, no. 1917); and the Council of Trent in its *Decree on Justification* (1547), chap. 5 and canon 3 (Neuner and Dupuis, *The Christian Faith*, nos. 1929, 1953).

8. See Heb 4:12; and the example of Stephen in Acts.

that it follows deductively from a consideration of reason. How could it? But it is to say that it is not contrary to reason. Rather does it perfect reason, by making us share in the knowledge of God who created our natural reason. The reasonableness of faith is clearly indicated where its obligatory character is noted. See, for example, Matthew 11:21–24:

> Woe to you Chorazin! Woe to you Bethsaida! for if the mighty works done in you had been done in Tyre and Sidon, they would have repented long ago in sackcloth and ashes. But I tell you, it shall be more tolerable on the day of judgment for Tyre and Sidon than for you. And you, Capernaum, will you be lifted up to heaven? You shall be brought down to Hades. For if the mighty works done in you had been done in Sodom, it would have remained until this day. But I tell you, it shall be more tolerable on the day of judgment for the land of Sodom than for you.

The "mighty works," the miracles of Jesus, make faith reasonable. They remove any excuse that Chorazin or Bethsaida might offer for refusing faith, for failing the obligation. The utility of such signs of credibility for coming to know the fact of revelation has been defined.[9] We will return to this in more detail.

(8) Of course, precisely because faith is our most personal engagement with God, with Christ, and because it involves us in sharing the thoughts of God, and in trusting his word, and since it is a knowledge that depends on grace and lifts us above what we see clearly by the natural light of reason—for all of these reasons (but especially because it means relying on the God whom we cannot see), faith is obscure, or mysterious. This makes it hard to talk about, and we must watch out that we do not make what is obscure clearer than it is. The obscurity of faith is nicely expressed in that saying of St. Paul, "Now we see in a glass, darkly, but then, face to face" (1 Cor 13:12). Clarity is for heaven; now, in the time of faith, we see with difficulty and obscurely.

(9) Faith is personal not simply as coming from our personal center, but as responding to a person, the person of Christ. The New Testament has much to say about the relation of faith to Christ.

---

9. First Vatican Council, *Dei Filius* (1870), chap. 3, and the third canon for that chapter (Neuner and Dupuis, *The Christian Faith*, nos. 119, 127).

Faith and Christ

Much of the New Testament's teaching on faith can be summed up by saying that faith is Christocentric, Christo-teleological, and Christological.[10]

That faith is rightly said to be Christocentric does nothing except to return us to chapter 1, on the pattern of revelation. The pattern or economy of revelation figures forth Christ and is completed by Christ; its all-inclusive object of faith is Christ. Its "center" is Christ, as it were; and every radius goes from him to the circumference of the circle.

That the content of faith is Christ is evident from the creed itself. The second and most detailed article of the creed is about Christ; the first article speaks of the Father *of the Son*; the third article speaks of the Spirit *of Christ* and of the Church *of Christ*. St. Paul teaches that faith is Christocentric. As he tells the Corinthians, "I decided to know nothing among you except Jesus Christ and him crucified" (1 Cor 2:2). He could speak to them of Christ alone, because that was sufficient—"Christ" and "Christ crucified" contains all the other contents of faith, implicitly or explicitly. In explaining his apostolate, he speaks to the Galatians of his conversion, when God "was pleased to reveal his Son to me, in order that I might preach him among the Gentiles" (Gal 1:16). "His Son" contains the whole of revelation, and so it is enough that Paul preach him and his cross to the Gentiles (but of course with all the implications thereof). And he speaks of Christ as the one "in whom are hid all the treasures of wisdom and knowledge" (Col 2:3). If all the treasures of wisdom and knowledge are hidden in Christ, there is no content of faith that is outside of or beyond or in addition to him.

That Christ is the pattern and completion of revelation suggests correlatively that faith is Christo-teleological. The sense is that faith conforms us to Christ, and is ordered so to do. The Christo-teleological character of faith is expressed in the Seventh Preface for Sundays of the Roman Rite. According to this preface, we pray that God may see in us what he sees and loves in Christ. The goal of our life is to be conformed to Christ. St. Paul says this expressly: "those whom he [God] foreknew he also predestined to be conformed to the image of his Son, in order that he might be the first

10. Juan Alfaro, SJ, *Fides, Spes, Caritas: Adnotationes in Tractatum De Virtutibus Theologicis*, new ed. (Rome: Gregorian University, 1968), 495–96.

born among many brethren" (Rom 8:29). So, we are called to the "assembly of the first-born" (Heb 12:23), for, as his brethren, we are all to look like him, Christ, our elder brother. St. Paul tells the Galatians that "God has sent the Spirit of his Son into our hearts, crying 'Abba! Father!'" (Gal 4:6). We have the same relation to God as does Christ; we are like him; so, in the next verse, he says "through God you are no longer a slave, but a son, and if a son then an heir." We are sons conformed to the Son. We are taken up into the filial identity of the Son.

To speak of the Christo-teleological character of faith is to speak of the eschatological character of faith. It means that faith is oriented to the vision of God (Jn 17:3), to that face-to-face intimacy (1 Cor 13:12) that is the perfection of friendship. Christ was revealer as man because he beheld, as man, the infinite intelligibility and truth of the Godhead. For out of that abundance did he speak and act. And it is to that abundance that he means to lead us by faith. Now we see in a mirror, by faith, but then, as led by faith, face to face (again, 1 Cor 13:12). Our seeing in a mirror, now, is actively tending toward seeing face to face in heaven. Conformation takes place by "seeing." As St. Paul also says: "We all, with unveiled face, beholding [or reflecting; the Greek is *katoptrizomenoi*] the glory of the Lord, are being changed into his [Christ's] likeness from one degree of glory to another" (2 Cor 3:18). What we behold, we reflect; we are made like to what we see. But our being made like to Christ is a process; it is happening now, according as we look to Christ, but will be perfect only in heaven.

In the third place, faith is Christological, in the sense that the *logos* of faith comes from him, in that the preeminent and definitive revealer is Christ. In the act of faith, in saying "I believe," we are responding to the revelation of Christ, that is, to him revealing. "Christological"—that is, faith responds, as it were, to his word; we follow his "logic" and appropriate his way of construing things. "I believe" answers to his teaching, responds to him as teaching, obeys his command to "Repent and believe in the gospel." Faith is therefore trust in Christ, in his person; it is also assent to what he teaches. Faith is both fiducial and cognitive.

The Christological character of faith is to be discovered in St. Paul. At 2 Corinthians 3:18, 4:6, and 13:8, Christ speaks in the Apostle who asks for faith, and it is therefore Christ asking for faith in his word. And of course Paul speaks of his gospel as something he received "through a revelation of Jesus Christ" in Galatians 1:12, which is equivalently a revelation of God in 1:16. Thus, Christ is not only the content of faith, but also the one who reveals that content.

But it is especially John who expresses the Christological character of faith. To believe in Christ (*pisteuein* + *eis*) is to believe *that* he is the Son of God. Thus, in John 4:39, many Samaritans "believed in him," which is to say that they believe that he "is indeed the Savior of the world" (Jn 4:42). Again, at 11:25, Jesus says that the one who "believes in me" shall not die, which seems to be the equivalent, at 11:27, of Martha's believing "that you are the Christ, the Son of God, he who is coming into the world." Compare also 14:10 and 14:12.

Also, to believe him who is speaking (*pisteuein* + dative) is to believe him *as* the Son of God (the Savior, the One Sent, etc.) who is speaking. At John 5:38, not believing Jesus is not believing him as the one sent from the Father. Again, at 6:30, there is question of believing Jesus in the sense of believing that he is sent (6:29), and believing him *as* the One Sent.

So, in the end, to believe him (with the dative—indicating trust) makes one thing with believing that he is the Son. And the ground of this identity is the divine Filiation, the fact that he is indeed and in truth the Son. See John 6:29, 30; 8:30, 31; 9:35–37; 10:36–38; 14:10–11. Believing Jesus is believing him as the Son and believing that he is the Son, and believing that he is because he, the Son, says so.

This is why John's gospel distinguishes between believing that Jesus is the Son because Jesus the Son says so and believing the works. Believing the works is letting oneself be moved by the signs Jesus provides. But this is not sufficient; it does not attain his person. In language to be explained shortly, it does not fall under the adequate formal object of faith (Jn 10:37). Likewise, believing because the Father bears witness to Jesus through Jesus is distinguished from the witness John the Baptist bears him: radically, the testimony that Jesus receives is not from man (Jn 5:34).

Juan Alfaro describes the knowledge of God, the immediate and proper knowing of his Father, that the Fourth Gospel attributes to Jesus. Then in what follows he shows the implications of this for his testimony and our faith.

From this vital union with the Father, from this knowledge of God exclusively proper to Christ, it follows that his words ("my words") are the "word of God" in a new sense, unique and supreme (John 5:24; 8:44, 51, 55; 7:16; 14:19, 24; 17:6, 8, 14, 17; etc.). Here there is the foundation of the unique "testimony" of Jesus in the Fourth Gospel, particularly in Chapter 8. Jesus testifies of himself that he is the Son of God and demands to be believed because it is he, the Son, who testifies to it. Johannine faith implies that *believing that* Christ is the Son of God (*pisteuein eis*: John 3:36; 4:39; 8:30; etc.) is indivisibly *believing Christ* as the Son of God (*pisteuein* with the dative: John 4:21; 5:38, 46; 6:30; 8:31, 45, 46; 10:37–38; 14:11). The reason that Johannine faith implies that believing that Jesus is the Son of God is believing him as the Son of God is found in his divine sonship: Jesus speaks as the Son and it is precisely in the demand to believe him that he reveals his divinity (the prophets demanded that one "believe [the Lord]"). Therefore, according to the Fourth Gospel, Jesus is indivisibly the revealer and the revealed, the center and foundation of faith, and in the last analysis this is so because he is the personal Word of God incarnate. Incarnation and revelation are only two aspects of the same event; in the light of the Incarnation there can be understood what the revelation of God is.[11]

The Formal and Material Objects of Faith

To distinguish between believing what Christ says and believing him as we have done reading the Fourth Gospel, just as to distinguish the Christocentric and the Christological aspects of faith, is in effect to distinguish what we can call the "objects" of faith. The so-called material object is *what* is believed, that is, the things, the articles that are believed. But the formal object of faith is believing the Revealer who is enunciating for us what to believe, the material object.[12] The formal object is that by which we attain to the material object. For instance, we see colored objects within our sight, but we see them all only as actually illuminated. The colored books and doors and carpets can be seen only given the light. The colors we see are the material object of sight, but light is the formal object. We attain to things as colored only in that they are lit up. By analogy, then,

11. Juan Alfaro, SJ, *Esistenza Christiana*, 2nd ed. (Rome: Gregorian University, 1979), 63.

12. St. Thomas Aquinas, *Summa theologiae* II-II, q. 1, a. 1, c.; q. 2, a. 2, c. On the formal and material objects of faith, see Dulles, *Assurance of Things Hoped For*, 187–90.

we are saying that the formal object of faith is Christ-speaking, Christ-revealing. That is how we attain to the spoken, the taught, the revealed. And since Christ is the divine Son of God, we can say that the formal object of faith is *God*-speaking, *God*-revealing. Equivalently, the formal object of faith is God as First Truth.

In faith, then, we believe God, we believe Christ the Son of God. We believe the prophets, too—but they are leading up to Christ and anticipating what he will say and teach. We believe the apostles, of course (and the Church and the bishops), but only because and insofar as they repeat what he said. Faith is "divine faith;" that is to say, it is faith in God speaking.

The content of faith can be expressed in propositions. The content of the faith is expressed preeminently in the articles of the Creed, which are propositions. In fact, the content of faith must be expressed in propositions, else God is not speaking to *us*. For the properly human purchase on reality, and especially where this reality is not and cannot be an object of our immediate experience, is via the proposition.

Of course, since the assent to the proposition depends strictly on our trust in God, we can say, if we want, that faith as trust is more important than faith as assent. But without faith as assent to propositions, faith is as it were empty. If God wishes to communicate to us, to give us that knowledge of himself on which our supernatural love of charity in response to him depends, and that knowledge of our end which we must have if we are to attain it, the communication must be by way of propositions.

It was Liberal Protestantism or Catholic Modernism that lead people to deny or belittle or call into question the propositional character of revelation and faith. This is still very common, and we will visit it more at length in the next chapter. Apart from Liberal Protestantism or Catholic Modernism in their rank form, Christians are sometimes asked to credit some communication of revelation via religious "experience," where this experience is pre-predicative, pre-conceptual, a-linguistic. We have criticized this view in discussing the development of dogma. Revelation to us human beings according to our capacity to be in the truth makes use of language or does not exist. And news about what cannot be sensed must all the more be communicated in language, or not at all.

It is sometimes said that St. Thomas relativizes the propositional character of faith by saying that the act of faith terminates in the reality, not in the proposition. And this is taken to indicate something mystical about faith, or especially characteristic of faith as a gift of God. But it is not true that St. Thomas discounts the propositional character of faith, and he is not saying anything special about faith here. What he in fact is saying is that just as scientific knowledge (and for that matter, ordinary, everyday knowledge may be included too) is a purchase on, a cognitive possession of the real, so also is faith. "For we do not formulate propositions except that through them we might have knowledge about realities, *just as in science*," he says.[13] And just as the assent of science (or common sense) does not terminate in the proposition, so neither does the assent of faith. He is not saying anything *special* about faith here. He is adverting to the fact that *every* properly human cognitive possession of the real is via the proposition.

This is easily to be seen if we ask what it would mean for an assent to terminate in the proposition, and not in the reality the proposition speaks of. This would be to consider the proposition as merely proposed by someone, as possibly true, but not definitely as true. This happens both in science as well as in matters religious: "It could be that X is Y." Here, our cognitive possession terminates in the knowledge that some speaker or other proposes X as Y. The assent terminates in the proposition. But we have cognitive possession of X as Y, the reality spoken of, only when we assent to the proposition "X is Y" as true. Here, the assent terminates indeed in the reality. It does so, of course, only through and because of the proposition.[14]

The Supernatural Character of Faith

In faith, we rely on the speaking, the witness, the testimony of God in Christ. He offers us his truth and veracity as the guarantee of what we

13. St. Thomas Aquinas, *Summa theologiae* II-II, q. 1, a. 2, ad 2. In the *Quaestiones disputatae de veritate*, vol. 1 of his *Quaestiones disputatae*, ed. Raymund Spiazzi, OP (Rome: Marietti, 1949), q. 14, a. 8, ad 5, St. Thomas says that the object of faith can be considered in two ways, according as it exists outside of us, and according as it is in the knower. In the second way it is propositional: "the divine truth, which is simple in itself, is the object of faith; but our intellect receives it in its own way by way of composition"—that is, propositionally (my translation).

14. See Robert Sokolowski, *Introduction to Phenomenology* (Cambridge: Cambridge University Press, 2008), 99–101.

believe, of our being in the truth. This makes of faith something supernatural; it is not our standard operating procedure so to rely on the truth and veracity and infallibility of God for what we know.[15]

For the kind of things he wishes to tell us, however, it must be so. Faith can bear on things that we could figure out on our own (see above, chapter 5, on the *praeambula fidei*). But in its core, faith bears on things that no eye has seen nor ear heard, on things that have not entered into the heart of man (1 Cor 2:9). These things, beyond the natural capacity of man to know, beyond the capacity of any possible creature to know naturally, are therefore rightly called "supernatural truths." They are such things as that we are called to friendship with God (no way to deduce that from our nature or from God's goodness), and the Incarnation (no way to predict that from Creation, or from that fact that we are called to friendship with God, or even from how sin will be repaired).[16]

So, the content of revelation is supernatural. Further, the very manner of revealing it is supernatural. For prophets require the light of prophecy to prophesy. Apostles and hagiographers need to have a similar light of witnessing unerringly to the truth of Christ. And the humanity of Jesus is also raised above itself so that it can be the instrument of revelation. This happens in that the mind of Christ was always illumined by the immediacy of the intelligibility and truth of the divine nature.[17]

We should expect, therefore, that our appropriation of revelation in faith is similarly supernatural. Just as a prophet needs extra light to know and to speak the word of God, so we need extra light to receive that word. As was said just above, it is not our natural mode of knowing to know what we do relying on the divine testimony. In fact, faith requires that our conscious subjectivity be strengthened by grace in order for us to make the act of faith.[18] Some details of this will emerge shortly.

15. On the supernatural character of faith, see the wonderful and comprehensive treatment of Alfaro, *Fides, Spes, Caritas*, chap. 5.

16. See First Vatican Council, *Dei Filius* (1870), chap. 2 (Neuner and Dupuis, *The Christian Faith*, no. 114).

17. For the scriptural and patristic defense of Christ's human mind's immediate vision of God and for its systematic theological explanation, see Simon Francis Gaine, *Did the Saviour See the Father? Christ, Salvation and the Vision of God* (London: Bloomsbury, 2015).

18. St. Thomas Aquinas, *Summa theologiae* II-II, q. 6, a. 1.

Naturally, we rely on the light of the agent intellect, the light of being and the light of the first principles of being, in order to come to know the things of this world. But faith, as supernatural, is to rely on Subsistent Understanding, the Uncreated Light, the Principle beyond the first principles of common being. Faith therefore requires a modification of the human subject, a supernaturalizing of the human subject by grace. It requires some created grace operative in us in order that we can, as it were, punch above our weight, our cognitive weight, and come to share not only in what God knows but in the very way he knows it, relying on him and no other in the knowledge of faith.

The supernaturalized human subjectivity of faith is something consciously given, since human subjectivity, as engaged in knowing and willing, is conscious not only of the objects it intends but also of the acts by which it intends them and, indeed, of the human subject himself. When I look at a tree, I am aware not just of the tree, but of my act of seeing, and of me seeing it. So also, in the intellectual order, when I prove the Pythagorean Theorem, I am aware not only of the theorem, but of the act of proving it and understanding it, and myself as positing the acts of reasoning, of concluding, of being "behind" them. And just as I am aware of the physical light when looking at the tree, so in intellectual knowing, the light of being, the light of the "agent intellect," as St. Thomas styled it, the light that makes things intelligible—that light is also present to me. Of course, I am not aware of the act and of myself and of the light as I am of the object of the act—the presence of myself to myself, and of my acts to myself, and of the light to myself, does not come with the sharpness and discreteness of an object. They are more obscurely given, and that is why people make mistakes in reporting their consciousness of themselves as they do not in reporting their consciousness of birds and trees. It is easier to give a sharp description of the oak than it is to give a crisp description of consciousness.

If the supernatural character of faith means a supernaturalizing of our subjectivity, then, of our consciousness, how will this appear? There is a new object given us, one of the articles of the creed, say; and there is new formal object given us, God-speaking, the authority of God revealing, as the First Vatican Council puts it.[19] And the supernaturalizing in question affects our subjectivity in a nonobjective way. That is, it affects our subjectivity not in the way of proposing an object of sense (the colored picture on the wall), or memory (yesterday's trip to town), or imagination (my dog with wings), or thought (democracy in America), or faith (the incarnate Son), but in the very experience of grasping the object, of being present to it. And given the different objects, the experiences of the self in grasping the object are also distinguishable: I am not present to myself as sensing the way I am present to myself as picturing, or as thinking, or as arguing, or as believing God. However, these ways of being present to oneself in intentional, object-oriented experience, distinguishable as they must be, are not easy to describe in their distinctions from one another, except according as we advert to the objects themselves. So also, the supernaturalizing of our subjectivity in faith is not easily picked out from our ordinary and natural states of consciousness. Nonetheless and even so, this interior modification of our subjectivity shows up principally in two ways.

First, it shows up in the *desire* to believe, of the attractiveness of faith, which consists in the apprehension of the great good that faith is, that sharing in the mind of God is, that being friends with him in this way is. This is the so-called *instinctus interior* or *instinctus fidei*, a sort of interior inclination of our appetite, a supernatural inclination, proportionate to the supernatural good that is being preached to us.[20] A correlative of this first thing, within the process of conversion, can be a great weariness with our life unillumined by faith, a great distaste for the misery, cognitive and moral, of life apart from God. Second, the supernaturalizing of our subjectivity shows up in the *certainty* of faith, such that we hold what we hold by faith with a greater certainty than we do any other truth. For this, there must be an increased participation in the First Light, the *lumen fidei* or light of faith, by which we are made proportionate to and so receptive of faith's formal object, God-revealing.[21]

19. First Vatican Council, *Dei Filius* (1870), chap. 3 (Neuner and Dupuis, *The Christian Faith*, no. 118).

20. St. Thomas Aquinas, *Summa theologiae* II-II, q. 2, a. 9, ad 3; q. 5, art. 2, ad 2; Thomas Aquinas, *Super Evangelium Sancti Ioannis Lectura*, ed. Raphael Cai, OP (Rome: Marietti, 1952), no. 935.

21. St. Thomas Aquinas, *Summa theologiae* II-II, q. 2, a. 3, ad 2.

Faith is free, an act of freedom, which is to say an act of will, and it is an intellectual act, under the direction of the will; namely, the act of assent to the articles of the Creed. Therefore we must expect that our faculties, both intellect and will, will be aided to make the act of faith. The will is touched and strengthened by the *instinctus interior*; the mind is fortified by the *lumen fidei*.

The supernatural character of faith and the role of grace in faith do not destroy the freedom of faith. To the contrary, grace makes faith possible, but does not coerce as by violence. Grace moves freedom; it does not replace it or destroy it. When our freedom is moved by grace, it remains exactly what it is—freedom.[22]

The supernaturalizing of our subjectivity in faith occurs preeminently and precisely in conversion, and in making the act of faith by reciting the Church's Creed. But it ought not to be supposed that this supernaturalizing of consciousness is limited to such discrete moments. Above, the light of faith was likened to what St. Thomas, following Aristotle, called the light of the agent intellect—the light by which we make the potential intelligibility of the material things of the world actually intelligible. This is the light of being, for we make things intelligible by asking what they are and whether they exist in the way we say they do. This light, the natural light, is the light of wonder. It is the desire for an unlimited intelligibility and truth. When we give this desire the lead in our lives, then we perfect ourselves with the intellectual virtues of science and wisdom, and following the truth of our own nature, we perfect ourselves in the order of moral action with the virtues of justice and temperance and fortitude. We become, in Aristotle's sense, both a philosopher and a gentleman; we become, in Heidegger's sense, shepherds of being. There is a correlative scope in giving the light of faith the lead in our lives. We ask how all things fit together in the pattern of revelation and redemption. Even without the cultivation of theology, and with greater ease than Aristotle's philosopher attains to wisdom and science, we live more and more by the infused gifts of the Spirt, the gifts of wisdom and understanding. In the moral order, the light of faith brings with it the heat of charity, and with the ardor of the love of God above all

22. Ibid., I-II, q. 113, a. 3.

things and the love or our neighbor as ourselves, we become friends with all who are being saved, because first of all friends with God. Just as nothing the naturally virtuous man does is untouched, unillumined by the light of being, and he is attuned to see everything as a promised or actual manifestation of the intelligibility and truth of being, so for the mature Christian, all he does is illumined by the light of faith, our conscious experience of everything is modified because we know the One who is beyond being and that he has entered into the world; now, everything is a manifestation of God, his Creation and his grace, and all the works of the Christian are ordered by and ordered to charity. If the Christian remains a shepherd of being, it is because he himself is lead to his own pasture by the Good Shepherd.

Human Faith and Divine Faith

The contrast of divine faith and human faith is clarifying.[23] Two things especially jump out. The first thing is that while it is sometimes proper and indeed required of us to measure the credibility of a human witness, it is impossible for us to measure the credibility of God and, moreover, blasphemous to try to do so. In other words, God's testimony, Christ's testimony, is auto-credible, worthy of belief in and of itself.

By contrast, the testimony of a human witness is credible by reference to something outside itself. For ordinary testimony of ordinary things in ordinary life—exchanging news about the neighbors, reporting local news, repeating well-known facts of history and popular science—a person's testimony is ordinarily immediately accepted That it is right for the hearer to take what is said as true, and right for the one who testifies to expect to be believed, are sometimes taken as if they were basic truths for which for no apology can be made except by indicating the utility of such behavior for social intercourse and the madness of someone who asked for the credentials of everyone for every saying. This is not exactly true. These truths are indeed fairly basic, and the "rights" involved are natural. But speaking of natural rights indicates the ultimate warrant for the credibility of ordinary speech from ordinary speakers about ordinary things, and that is human

23. See Alfaro, *Fides, Spes, Caritas*, chap. 9, a. II, on human and divine testimony.

nature itself. We are built both to want to know the truth and to want to share it—that is our nature. When we accept the stranger's testimony at face value, we think the note backed up by the gold of a nature the speaker did not make. Other things being equal, the person's ordinary credibility is credible by reference to human nature—something "outside" of, which is to say in a way distinct from, the person himself.[24]

"Other things," however, are not always equal, and the hetero-credibility of the human being is manifest in situations where the truth and competence of the speaker or actor are more important. If the doctor tells me something about my lungs, I will believe him. But that is because of the diploma from the medical school on his wall: the university, something other than the doctor, vouches for the medical competence of the doctor. His testimony is made credible by an accrediting agency distinct from him. Furthermore, his status as someone who is not only competent to know the truth but veracious, which means inclined to tell the truth, is attested by his current membership in the American Medical Association and other appropriate medical associations, and perhaps by his having taken the Hippocratic Oath (if he takes it by appealing to some guarantor distinct from himself).

No human speaker is absolutely credible; no human speaker is always worthy of being taken at his word simply on the ground that he is giving out that word. So, for human witnesses, we sometimes legitimately and by right and duty enquire into their credentials: have they spoken the truth in the past? are they known to be of good and honest character? is there any reason for them to falsify the truth in this instance? is it probable or certain that they have knowledge whereof they speak?

With the divine testimony, however, things are quite different. God, just as he is absolute and subsistent being, and just as he is absolute and subsistent Truth, is absolutely and with no reference to anything outside of him worthy of being taken at his word. Therefore, when God says that X is Y, it is to be accepted on the sole authority of the God who is speaking, and his quality as a witness is not rightfully or without sin subject to any created or human criterion.

24. This is to say that the created person's credibility is credible by reference to the God who made it in his image.

It is just so that God in fact presents himself speaking to us, demanding to be taken at his word. So, in Isaiah 45:23, we read that it is by himself that God swears that he will save Israel. He swears "by himself," for there is no one or nothing greater than God by which he can swear. "Men indeed swear by a greater than themselves" (see Heb 6:13–18), but such is impossible for the God who is "that than which nothing greater can be thought."[25]

So we ought *not* to measure or test the credibility of God in Christ by some other thing. There is no right by which we can ask for a proof that God is competent or veracious and no possibility that there could be such a thing. He is the Creator, and so the cause of created things and created truth. But whatever proof there could be distinct from God revealing would be some created thing. And then we would be measuring the Creator by the creature. And just as he cannot be deceived about anything, so he cannot deceive, and we cannot ask anyone to attest to his veracity. How could a created person's attestation increase our confidence in the veracity of the uncreated God? In short, we cannot measure God as Subsistent Truth against our created reason.

In the Gospels, when the Lord preaches the nearness of the Kingdom of God, he demands acceptance of this message and the repentance of human beings which responds to it on the sole fact and authority that he says it. We adverted to this in chapter 6. Jesus acts as if his saying that the Kingdom of God is at hand is reason enough to think so. That is, he presents his word, his witness as needing no warrant outside itself, nothing beyond itself to back it up. He presents it as auto-credible. This very manner of proceeding, to be sure, is itself an implicit claim to a divinity like that of the God of Israel, transcendent to every created or human measure, and so unmeasurable by any created or human thing. And see chapter 8 in John's Gospel on Christ's testimony.

There is an analogy here to be drawn between God's causality and creaturely causality and God's credibility and creaturely credibility. Just as God does not and cannot share his power to create with any creature, in that the entire being of the creature remains dependent solely on God, and yet

25. St. Anselm, *Proslogion*, in *St. Anselm: Basic Writings*, trans. S. N. Deane, 2nd ed. (LaSalle, Ill.: Open Court, 1962), chap. 2

without prejudice to the reality of second causes, so God does not and cannot share his credibility, the Truth and Veracity with which he speaks, in that the entire faith of the believer remains dependent solely on God, and yet without prejudice to the reality and credibility of the apostles and heralds of his word. The power of created causes is a derived power, derived from God. So too, the credibility of apostle and bishop is likewise "borrowed." When we cash it in by believing what they teach, the belief ultimately terminates at the God who issues the apostolic and ecclesial bond.

When the Pharisees ask for a sign, some wonder that may vouch for his teaching, Jesus responds that it is an evil and adulterous generation that seeks for a sign. It is an evil and adulterous generation that seeks a sign from God, that puts God to the test (Mt 12:38). And he continues, "No sign shall be given this generation except the sign of Jonah the prophet" (12:39). This response is explained in a twofold way. First, the sign of Jonah is explained as the teaching of Jonah. "The men of Ninevah will arise at the judgment with this generation and condemn it; for they repented at the preaching of Jonah, and behold, something greater than Jonah is here" (12:41). The preaching of Jesus alone, greater than Jonah's, should be enough to move us to faith and repentance. Second, the sign of Jonah is explained as the resurrection: "For just as Jonah was in the belly of the whale three days and three nights, so will the Son of man be three days and three nights in the heart of the earth" (12:40). Do these explanations conflict? No, for while the resurrection is a sign, it is the sign of Jesus himself, restored to life, and so the re-presentation to us of the one whom we should take at his word. And, of course, the sign of the resurrection is not wholly apprehended or apprehensible outside of faith itself.

Evidently, both the divine testimony, and the supernatural faith that answers to it, can be but imperfectly understood by analogy to human testimony and human faith. As divine testimony is unique and incomparable, just as the God whose testimony it is, so divine faith is faith in a unique and absolute sense. "Faith," Emily Dickinson says, "is the Pierless Bridge/Supporting what We see/Unto the Scene that we do not."[26] It is "pierless," but we are supposed to hear the homonym, too, "peerless."

26. Emily Dickinson, *The Complete Poems of Emily Dickinson*, ed. Thomas H. Johnson (Boston: Little, Brown and Company, 1960), no. 915.

The incomparable nature of the divine testimony has an important implication for the certainty of faith, which must be more certain than any other faith, ordinary human faith, and more certain that any human knowledge, even scientific knowledge, even naturally apodictic knowledge.

Attaining to the Formal Object of Faith by Faith

There is a second important contrast of divine faith and human faith. When a man tells us something, over the backyard fence, or from the witness stand, or from the newscaster's desk, we may or may not believe what he tells us. But that he is telling us something is evident and undeniable. It is something we know, not something we believe on testimony.

In divine faith, however, we do not in the same way know that God is telling us something, that he is speaking to us, that he is revealing himself. That God is speaking, that God is revealing—that is an object of faith, too. It is in this way that divine faith is pure faith. In human faith, there is a mixture of knowledge, our reasoned assessment as needs be of the human witness's competence and veracity, and that knowledge and assessment go together with our consequent trust in what the man says, such that we assent to what he is telling us. But in divine faith, although we do not need to assess the witness's competence and veracity, we believe not only what God says, but that he is saying it.

Perhaps it will help if we try to think about things more concretely. Here is the story of the healing of the paralytic in Mark 2:1–12.

And when he returned to Capernaum after some days, it was reported that he was at home. And many were gathered together, so that there was no longer room for them, not even about the door; and he was preaching the word to them. And they came, bringing to him a paralytic carried by four men. And when they could not get near him because of the crowd, they removed the roof above him; and when they had made an opening, they let down the pallet on which the paralytic lay. And when Jesus saw their faith, he said to the paralytic, "My son, your sins are forgiven." Now some of the scribes were sitting there, questioning in their hearts, "Why does this man speak thus? It is blasphemy! Who can forgive sins but God alone?" And immediately Jesus, perceiving in his spirit that they thus questioned within themselves, said to them, "Why do you question thus in your hearts? Which is easier, to say to the paralytic, 'Your sins are forgiven,' or to say,

'Rise, take up your pallet and walk'? But that you may know that the Son of man has authority on earth to forgive sins"— he said to the paralytic —"I say to you, rise, take up your pallet and go home." And he rose, and immediately took up the pallet and went out before them all; so that they were all amazed and glorified God, saying, "We never saw anything like this!"

First, notice what is being revealed; namely, that "the Son of man has power on earth to forgive sins." This is a truth proposed for assent; it is a revealed truth to be assented to by faith. Second, there is a revealer, Jesus of Nazareth, who is to be believed and trusted. Next, note that there is a sign making such trust reasonable, and so making the assent to the proposal about the Son of man reasonable. "*That you may know....*" Fourth, the sign does not coerce trust, however, and so it does not coerce assent to the proposition. The Pharisees do not trust Jesus—they do not take him as the Son of man, divinely revealing something; and they do not believe (assent to) the proposition that the Son of man has power to forgive sins. Thus, the trust in Jesus, as well as the decision to assent to what he says, remain free. Fifth, we may add that the sign, the healing, though it leaves freedom intact, makes for culpability: not trusting Jesus, and not believing what he says, is sinful. See Matthew 11:20ff ("Woe to you, Chorazin!") or John 9 (the man born blind and the reaction of the authorities). Many of the elements of faith listed at the beginning of this chapter are nicely illustrated here, and even the need for interior grace is present by implication, in the contrast between the hard-heartedness of the Pharisees and the good heartedness of the crowd.

Suppose you are a part of the believing crowd, amazed and praising God for his Christ. What do you know, and what do you believe in faith? You believe that the Son of Man has power on earth to forgive sins. You believe also that Jesus *is* the Son of Man. Do you know that a revelation is being made—that is, that God is revealing himself in Christ, the way you know a man is speaking even if you disbelieve what he is saying? No. You know that there is a man named Jesus who is speaking and saying that the Son of Man has power to forgive sins. But you do not know he is the Son of Man. You believe that, and so you are believing, not knowing, that what he is saying is divine revelation.

Suppose you tell a third party, your cousin who was not there, what happened. And suppose you begin by telling him, "the Son of Man has power on earth to forgive sins." And suppose he asks you why you say that, why you believe that. You will say, because Jesus of Nazareth said so. And you will add that he is the Son of Man. But why, your cousin will ask, do you believe that he is the Son of Man, and so believe what he says? And you will say, "Well, there was this paralytic that was let down in front of him through the roof, and don't you know, Jesus healed him." The sign is what makes it credible to believe that there is a revelation being made. But the reason for believing that Jesus is the Son of Man and that the Son of Man has power on earth to forgive sins is that Jesus said so, and only that. That is, the material object, about the power of the Son of Man, is attained through the formal object, that Jesus said so, and both are attained by faith.

The sign offers no apodictic proof that Jesus is the Son of Man, the Christ. Else why would not the Pharisees also assent to what he says?[27] They saw the same miracle. The sign does not prove absolutely and metaphysically that there is a divine revelation occurring at Capernaum. The sign makes it credible—"able to be believed"—that Jesus is the Christ and so that he has power to forgive sin. "Able to be believed" here means "able to be *reasonably* believed." And, if we may split the infinitive even more, it means "able to be reasonably *and so in a morally praiseworthy way* believed."

The Role of the Signs of Credibility in Coming to Faith

The signs of the credibility of revelation, from the immensity and intricacy of the economy of revelation to the miracles and resurrection of Jesus, from the authority of his preaching to the beauty of dogma, and including the historical plausibility of the Gospels as eyewitness accounts and of the foundation of the Church—all these things make faith reasonable.[28] Their relation to faith, however, is difficult to state. There are two main errors to be avoided. The first error denies that the event and content of revelation need to be shown to be credible, or correlatively, that faith

27. St. Thomas Aquinas, *Summa theologiae* II-II, q. 6, a. 1.
28. Dulles, *Assurance of Things Hoped For*, chap. 10; Alfaro, *Fides, Spes, Caritas*, chap. 8.

needs to be shown to be reasonable. This first error is common in some forms of Protestantism. Just as there need be no possibility of establishing the existence of God prior to faith in order to ensure the reasonability of faith, and just so that the word of God meets us *without* sinful man's anticipation and deformation of it, so the attempt to show by signs that God has spoken and that therefore faith is reasonable in fact measures the word of God in just the illegitimate way reproved above when we compared human and divine faith. For Catholics, such a position seems to mean that God ignores the work of creation in perfecting it by grace. Protestants in general are not so attached to the idea that grace perfects nature as are Catholics, who baulk at the idea that, Kierkegaard and Tertullian notwithstanding, we believe something *quia absurdum est.*

The second error is to introduce the signs into the interior structure of faith, and in that way contaminate faith by reason in just the way some forms of Protestantism fear. This is done when one holds that the formal object of faith is attained, not by faith and faith alone, but by the signs of credibility. Then, knowing that revelation has taken place, we assent to what is revealed.

The Catholic view is that faith must indeed be reasonable, for it is an act commanded by God, who does not ask us to violate our nature, since he is its Maker. For the reasonability of faith, moreover, signs of credibility are certainly required. That is, there must be signs that revelation is credible, that it can reasonably be believed that God has revealed himself in the teaching of Christ and the Church. More simply, there must be rationally apprehensible signs of the "fact of revelation," as the First Vatican Council has it.[29] But how does this fit with saying that the formal object of faith is attained only by faith? The formal object is "God-speaking." Surely that is just another way to say "the fact of revelation." There are thus two questions we must ask. First, is there some difference between the formal object of faith and the fact of revelation? Second, if there is not, how can we now be saying that we have to be able to know the fact of revelation by reason, from external signs, such things as miracles and fulfilled prophecies?

29. First Vatican Council, *Dei Filius*, chap. 3, canon 3 (Neuner and Dupuis, *The Christian Faith*, no. 127).

As to the first question, the fact of revelation is expressed when we say, "God has spoken," or "God has revealed himself." And we express the formal object with the phrase "God-speaking" or "God-revealing." We use a phrase here, because we are indicating God as speaking *something*—some material object. The fact of revelation is expressed adequately in a whole proposition—"God has revealed himself." And this alerts us to the fact that revelation is itself an object of faith, and indeed revelation shows up as an object of faith in the Nicene-Constantinopolitan Creed, when we confess that the Holy Spirit has spoken through the prophets. What can that be except to take revelation itself, the fact of it, as an object of faith?

In one important way, therefore, there is no difference between the fact and the formal object. There is just one reality being referred to, the event of "God speaking." But if we consider this reality as the vehicle to *what* God says (the material objects), then we are thinking of it as the formal object of faith. On the other hand, if we want, we can think of this vehicle of other truths as itself something delivered to us, itself a truth, the truth "that God has spoken." And then we think of it in itself as an object like other material objects. So, there is a distinction to be made between the fact of revelation and the formal object of faith, but it is a distinction in how we are looking at one and the same thing.

As to the second question, when we think of the fact of revelation as distinct from the formal object of faith, we can think of it *also* insofar as it can be attained by reason and as known from signs. Why would we do this? Just in order to make faith reasonable. However, in coming in this way to apprehending the fact of revelation, we are not *proving* that revelation has happened. If we did this, we would not really need faith in the sense of trust, trusting in God, in order to assent to what he says. For if we know, with speculatively certain knowledge, that God has said *p*, then we know that *p* must be true—God can neither deceive nor be deceived. In this way, the freedom of the assent of faith would be destroyed.

We must be careful as to what question we are asking. Why is it reasonable to believe (with divine faith) that God has spoken, and so why is it further reasonable to assent (with divine faith) to what he says? The answer will be the signs of credibility. But why do I believe (with divine faith) that God has spoken? Because he has spoken; he has addressed me (through Christ and the Church). And by faith, I trust him. And so I assent (by faith) to what he says, and, if it should be useful, I assent as well to the proposition that he has spoken (and so affirm the fact of revelation). Only in such a way, moreover, can faith be certain.

The above two paragraphs can be combined in a single argument to show that the signs of credibility do not constitute part of the formal foundation, the formal object, of faith. If they did, the argument goes, then assent to the articles could not be free *and* certain at the same time. For the reasoning based on the signs is either demonstrative or not. If the reasoning is demonstrative, then the assent of faith will not be free. If it is not demonstrative, then the assent of faith will not be certain. On the contrary, the assent of faith is both free and certain; therefore, the knowledge of the signs does not form part of the formal object of faith. They rather give support to the judgment that it is credible—*believable*—that there is a revelation, that it is credible that God is speaking.[30] The formal object is the First Truth, God speaking-revealing, and that alone.[31]

A fortiori, we should not think that the signs enable us to know the "fact of revelation" independently and prior to what is being revealed.[32] They do not produce a knowledge that "God is speaking," given which formal object, we then attain, in a subsequent act, to the truth of the articles, of what is said. For again, if the signs did do this, then this fact of revelation, affirmed by reason, is known either demonstratively or not. In either case, the assent of faith cannot be *both* free and certain. Rather, the fact of revelation, taken as part of the material object of faith, cannot be attained outside of faith, and the fact understood as God-speaking and taken as the formal object of faith is affirmed in the same act as that in which the articles are affirmed. Therefore, the fact of revelation and what is revealed are attained in one and the same act. This can be expressed emphasizing either part, but both parts go together. I believe that God is speaking (and so assent to what he is saying). I assent to what God is

---

30. For this position, critical of the Old Innsbruck School, see Alfaro, *Fides, Spes, Caritas*, 427–28.

31. For discussion of Pierre Rousselot, see Dulles, *Assurance of Things Hoped For*, 110–12, 213–14; and Alfaro, *Fides, Spes, Caritas*, 416–18.

32. For this position, contrary to Louis Billot and Christian Pesch, see Alfaro, *Fides, Spes, Caritas*, 429–33.

saying (since I believe it is God who is speaking). This is simpler than it seems: if God is speaking, then he must be saying something; if nothing is being said, then he is not speaking.

Furthermore, if the fact of revelation, God speaking, and what is being said, were not attained in one and the same act, there would be an infinite regress. Suppose (1) no proposition is believed with divine faith unless on the supposition it is revealed. Suppose (2) that the believed proposition and the fact of its being revealed cannot be attained in the same act. Suppose also (3) that the fact of revelation must be believed. So:

I believe that God is three in one. Why?

It is revealed (that God is three in one).

Which proposition is to be believed on the supposition that it is revealed (from 1).

Which fact of revelation must be believed (from 3)

and must be attained in a distinct act (from 2).

↙

Which means I must believe:

It is revealed [that it is revealed (that God is three in one)].

Which proposition is to be believed on the supposition that it is revealed (from 1)

Which fact of revelation must be believed (from 3)

and must be attained in a distinct act (from 2).

↙

Which means I must believe:

It is revealed {that it is revealed [that it is revealed (that God is three in one)]}.

Which proposition is to be believed, etc.

If the infinite regress is to be stopped, then either (1) or (2) or (3) must be false. But not (1): divine faith is strictly correlative to divine revelation; the human "I believe" answers the divine "I testify." And not (3): for the fact is attained either by faith or by reason. If by reason, then the reasoning is either demonstrative or probable. If demonstrative, then faith is not free, which is false. If probable, then faith is not certain enough to arrange one's life around it, which is also false. Therefore, the fact of revelation is attained by faith. Therefore, (2) is false, and the fact of revelation and the revealed content are attained in the same act.

J. Alfaro cites John Capreolus responding to an objection of John Duns Scotus:

> J. Capreolus (†1444), the famous interpreter of the teaching of St. Thomas ... first expressly formulated the assertion that infused faith *in one and the same act* believed both the First Truth revealing and the revealed proposition, in such a way, however, that the assent of faith is brought to bear in the first place on divine revelation on account of itself, and secondarily and by reason of divine revelation on the revealed proposition: "through faith, I assent first and directly to this, 'God has revealed that God is three and one,' ... and secondly I assent to this, 'God is three and one' ... but nonetheless in one and the same act ... And when it is asked further: how do I assent to this, 'God has revealed this,' etc.—I say that faith assents to this on account of itself, and not on account of any other proposition, from assent to which is caused assent to this, 'God has revealed this.'"[33]

What the signs do, to repeat, is to support the judgment of credibility— "It is believable that God is speaking here." But the "I believe," in which we trust God who is speaking, and assent to what he is saying, that is directed not to the signs, but to the pure word of God alone. It is in this way that Catholic attention to the signs of credibility does not impugn that sovereignty of God that some forms of Protestantism have rightly been concerned to defend. Faith remains, as Dickinson says, a "pierless bridge"; just in itself, it is supported only by the pure word of God which also in its being spoken is attained only by faith.

The signs thus support a "judgment of credibility," and together with the working of grace, they support the so-called "judgment of credentity." Credibility: "It is reasonable for me to believe that God has revealed himself in Christ." Credentity (from *credendum*): "I ought to believe that God has revealed himself in Christ." The signs by themselves assuage reason; the signs together with the interior grace of God ground the perception of the obligatory character of faith for me.[34]

33. Alfaro, *Fides, Spes, Caritas*, 437; Alfaro is citing the *Defensiones Theol. divi Thomae Aquin.*, III, d. 24, 1, 3, no. 4.

34. St. Thomas Aquinas, *Summa theologiae* II-II, q. 1, a. 4, ad 2.

The Resurrection of Jesus as Sign, Content, and Event of Revelation

The signs of credibility are usually listed as miracles and fulfilled prophecies. We can also say, however, and more primitively, that the preeminent sign of faith is Christ himself, especially in his resurrection, and also in the "whole Christ" which includes the Church.

In the resurrection, the Christocentric, Christological, and Christo-teleological characters of revelation, as well as the reasonableness of faith, are all to be discerned together.

(1) That Jesus was raised is an object of faith, part of the material object of faith. But also, it is rightly seen as the original formula of faith that commits one to all the other contents of divine and catholic faith. That is, we might say, the first full and fully Christian confession is "the Lord is risen and has appeared to Peter." So, faith is Christocentric.

(2) In the very event of the resurrection, however, Jesus is also the revealer, the revealing, of this "object," simply in his presence to the disciples. He, the Risen One, shows himself and so the rising to his disciples. Faith is Christological.

(3) The resurrection of Jesus is the model of our own resurrection, to which we incline in hope, and in which we are perfectly conformed to Christ. Faith is Christo-teleological.

(4) In the event of the resurrection, he is also, in his appearing to them, the sign that makes reasonable their trust in him as communicating by his presence and word that he is who he said he is (the Messiah, the Son), and that he has been raised by God his Father. The appearance— that is, the presence of the risen Lord, the risen Lord himself—is also therefore the sign that makes trust in him as Risen Revealer, and belief that he has been raised by God his Father, reasonable. Christocentric and Christological faith is known to be reasonable because of Christ.

(5) We may add that Christ is also the one who breathes forth onto his disciples the Holy Spirit, the interior principle of their faith that strengthens their mind, and draws their freedom, to make the act of faith. Christocentric and Christological faith is also caused efficiently by Christ through his Holy Spirit.

The Church also provides a sign of credibility. In the ancient Church, this was understood to be a matter of the quality of life of the members of the Church, a matter of the holiness of life of Christians.[35]

Reprise: From the Signs of Credibility to the Assent of Faith

The elements of the act of faith, working backwards from the assent of faith are as follows. First, there is the assent itself; that is, the saying Yes to a proposition because it is revealed. "I believe that X is Y because God says so." Equivalently: "I believe God is speaking, and so of course I accept what he says as true." This is indivisibly an act of both trust (believing God, *credere Deo*) and intellectual assent (believing that X is Y; *credere Deum*). This assent requires the grace of the light of faith.

Second, prior to the assent, there is the free act of the will choosing to believe in the sense of both choosing to trust and choosing to assent. This free choice is evidently a cause of the act of assent. Faith is something we are commanded by God. This supposes that in some respect, it is something within our power, our freedom, to do or not do. This choice requires the grace of the interior instinct.

Third, prior to the free choice of the will, there is a judgment that it is good to do so, that I ought to do so: "I ought to believe that God is speaking, I ought to assent to the articles of the Creed." This is the so-called judgment of credentity or practical judgment of credibility. It is nothing more than the act of intellect that must be supposed to be made prior to the choice to believe. Freedom embraces the good; the good is something first known by the mind before the heart can embrace it. This judgment is made under the influence of the grace of the interior instinct.

Fourth, prior to the practical judgment of credibility, there is the speculative (theoretical) judgment of credibility: "it is credible that there has been a revelation." This judgment need be only implicit. This judgment is ordinarily based on external signs of credibility. This judgment, whether

35. See Ephraim Radner, "Apologetics and Unity: Confessing the One Lord," in *Hope among the Fragments: The Broken Church and Its Engagement of Scripture* (Grand Rapids, Mich.: Brazos, 2004), 161–75.

explicit or implicit, is ordinarily *already* under the internal influence of grace, although strictly speaking according to our natural capacity it need not be. This judgment is not a cause of the assent of faith, but rather only a condition of its reasonableness. And that faith be reasonable follows from the idea that faith is a perfection of man, who is the rational animal. But faith could not perfect us, and precisely in the order of knowledge, of "assents," if it were contrary to or even indifferent to reason.

To take things in the order of their occurrence: (4) "It is believable that God has spoken here"; (3) "I ought to believe that God has spoken, and so believe what he has said"; (2) "I will so to believe"; (1) "I believe."

CHAPTER 8

THEOLOGY

God speaks to us, and his speaking demands an answer; he accomplishes our salvation in history, and that accomplishment commands a response. The first answer is the prayer of the Church in praise and thanksgiving, in words first taught to us by God in the Psalms; the first response is a re-actualization of the work of salvation in the liturgy, especially in Baptism and the Eucharist. A second response is the repetition of the word of God in evangelizing and catechesis and preaching, and the extension of God's salvation of us in the works of love we do for others. These works, the works of mercy, are enabled by the charity that is the ultimate effect of the Eucharist; they do not discriminate between Christian and non-Christian, since all belong to the Church at least potentially.

There is also a third response to the word of God and the work of salvation. That response is "theology," which is our word about God's word spoken to us in Christ and mediated to us by the Church in Scripture and Tradition, and in her own magisterial determination of its content in dogma.

The Necessity of Theology

There are three reasons why theology is necessary. First, there are still, as there have always been, enemies of the cross of Christ (Phil 3:18). These enemies challenge both the content and the credibility of Christianity. They challenge the content by alleging that one or another article of faith is not possibly true or by alleging that the articles together are incoherent or by alleging that Christian faith is inhuman, leads to the diminishment of human dignity, and conduces to unhappiness individually and communally. They challenge the credibility of Christianity by arguing, for instance, that the Gospels are late and distantly related to the historical Jesus, or by claiming that dogmas like the Trinity or the Real Presence of Christ in the Bread and Wine are not really found in Scripture. Since some of these challenges are sophisticated, it takes an equal sophistication to show they are sophistic. This is the sophistication of theology.

Second, Christianity makes an absolute claim about the nature and possibilities of human happiness. But all the human arts and sciences are concerned, one way or another, with human happiness. What then are the relations of the acquired to the infused moral virtues and the supernatural virtues of faith, hope, and charity? What, for instance, is the relation of the findings of physical anthropology to Genesis? How do or should the workings of the Church and the political community help one another? To show how the gospel relates to, agrees with, governs, and corrects the deliverances of the arts and sciences, practical and theoretical, the word of revelation has to be expressed in an equivalently artful and scientific way. Such expression of the word of revelation is theology.

Third, just as Christianity makes an absolute claim about human happiness, so also it speaks authoritatively about the ultimate Principle of reality and that Principle's will for the world and for us in Christ and the Spirit. These two things, the end of man and the first Principle of all things, frame the whole of human thought about everything whatsoever. There are no more fundamental things to think with. But the gift of the knowledge of fundamental things provokes wonder. Revelation is this gift. The corresponding wonder, while it gives rise to praise and thanksgiving, also gives rise to contemplation. According as this contemplation is complete, it beholds the intelligibility of God and of God's ordering of the universe, practically and speculatively, such as he has disclosed these things to us. This contemplation, when fully expressed, is theology, which gives joy to the heart.

The Nature of Catholic Theology in the Twentieth Century

Why "in the twentieth century"? If Catholic theology is one thing—since it contemplates one revelation whose one pattern is Christ, and which revelation is necessarily expressed coherently both in the one book of the Scriptures and in a consistent set of what are in principle trans-cultural dogmas, and since theology serves one Church in both her single mind and her action united by the one love of charity—must it not therefore have one nature? And once that nature is discovered and defined, would it not be good for all times and seasons? Theology may have parts and properties, but it does not seem that it could be many-natured. Nonetheless, the nature of theology is contested. All may agree with the hallowed formula that theology is faith seeking understanding. But the nature of faith is contested because the nature of revelation is contested. Nor is there a common understanding of understanding. It would be unfair not to alert any beginners to this contestation. For the sake of introductory clarity, therefore, three positions on the nature of theology put forth in the twentieth century will be set out, necessarily with broad strokes. Comparison and contrast will make the nature of theology—which of course is one—stand out more clearly.

Modernism: Theology as the Articulation of the Practical Consequences of Ineffable Revelation

In chapter 5, we recalled Kant's assertion of the limitation of human knowledge to the things of our experience. Karl Barth accepted this conclusion of Kant's First Critique. He re-affirmed the use of our language to speak of God and the things of God, as we reported, but only on the condition that that language is first used by God. There was another response to Kant, however, prior to Barth's, that of Friedrich Schleiermacher (d. 1834), just as important and perhaps more influential. It is time to take up this response.

Schleiermacher's view of revelation was developed by so-called Liberal Protestantism and can be found in some Catholic Modernists, George Tyrrell (d. 1909) notably.[1] Moreover, it, or at least what follows from it, has re-emerged very strongly within Catholic theology in the last forty years. On this view, revelation is in the first place a wordless encounter with God, a consciousness of our dependence on him, as Schleiermacher originally formulated it, and one ordered to the continuing prosecution of an ever more perfect human flourishing.

The idea that revelation in itself is a wordless encounter with God must be taken quite seriously. It follows that whatever we say about God, whatever the Church says about God and divine things, publicly and communicably in words, is but a human word responding to a revelation which is not, in itself, the delivery of a divine word to us. Moreover, language that seems to speak of God, whether the language of revelation itself in Scripture or the language of the Church in liturgy and dogma or the language of theology never really does in fact speak about God. Rather, it always only retails our response to God, our response to the wordless event of revelation. All the words that this event generates come from us, from the recipient of what is strictly an ineffable event, an encounter with an unknowable God.

Why does the Liberal Protestant and Catholic Modernist view of Christian language about God give us to understand that, in the end, we are always only speaking about ourselves? There were two arguments for this position. The first, as mentioned, is the Kantian critique of human knowledge, in the light of which we cannot really speak meaningfully and truthfully about God as he really is, although in order to make sense of our moral experience, we need to postulate his existence. God turns out in this way to be a necessary principle of the human good. He makes us good, not by grace (of which reason knows nothing), but by standing as the guarantor of the moral law and the one who rewards its keeping. The second argument is the alleged contradictoriness embedded within the history of the constitution of the biblical text or within the history of the Church's dogma. So, for Alfred Loisy (d. 1940), there is an unbridgeable gap in the

1. George Tyrrell, "Revelation," in Tyrrell, *Through Scylla and Charybdis, or the Old Theology and the New* (London: Longmans, 1907), 264–307, esp. pt. 2.

New Testament between what Jesus of Nazareth claimed about himself, and what Paul and John say about him.[2] For Tyrrell, there are unbridgeable gaps in the history of Church dogma.

Both the New Testament and Church teaching, however, have had good effects on those who embraced them and lived by them; they conduce to good morals and to holiness. Perhaps, then, that is the point of revelation: it is not God telling us about himself and our relation to him in Christ; it is not something that can be captured in concept or reported in words. More than a collection of propositions, revelation is simply the experience of God, an experience itself ineffable, but powerful enough to introduce into human history a movement toward human authenticity and community—a movement to the good. The propositions of Scripture and Tradition do not have a cognitive content. Their meaning is practical and mystical. And that is pretty much just where Édouard LeRoy (d. 1954) left the modernist theological experiment in the first decade of the twentieth century.[3] And that is the second controlling idea of this view of theology, second after the first idea that revelation is ineffable experience. If revelation is first of all and primordially some experience of the divine, mystical, or ecstatic as you please, and not necessarily rare (for some theorists, it is given to every man), its point is not to inform us about God. The point of the experience, vouchsafed as it is by God, is a more perfect human flourishing within and by means of religious forms embedded in the languages and cultures of man. The goal of revelation and the aim of religion is thus practical.

There remains yet a third point. The languages and cultures of man vary from age to age and from culture to culture, and so do the religious forms embedded in them. These religious forms find first expression in narrative, as in the Bible, and final expression in statements about God and in statements that describe the practices that will lead to a better human life, doctrines both (seemingly) speculative and (expressly and truly) practical. The words of the narrative, and the words of the statements, are supplied from those who first had the experience, or who are custodians

2. Alfred Loisy, *Autour d'un petit livre*, 2nd ed. (Paris: Picard et Fils, 1907), part 4.
3. Édouard Le Roy, "Qu'est-ce qu'un dogme?" in *Dogme et critique* (Paris: Librairie Bloud et Cie., 1907), 1–34, esp. at 25–26.

of their accounts, and not from God, to be sure. But ever-changing cultures and religious forms mean there is a work of translation to be performed. The goal of theology, then, is to translate for another age the first response to revelation such as we have it in Scripture (where we already find translations of prior expressions).[4] For our age, this includes taking account of all the translations of the original response to revelation, although we need not and should not exclude the recognition of on-going revelatory experiences given to the holy people of God. The course of theology, therefore, is the course of translation from Hebraic culture to Hellenism, from Hellenism to Late Antiquity, and then on to the Middle Ages, the Reformation, the Enlightenment, and today, to a culture informed by post-Modernism (or however we are to divide things up).

Now, because this first position envisages the cultural differences as very great, it anticipates great changes in the doctrine and practice of the Church. The changes can be so great that doctrines of later ages contradict doctrines of former ages, and practices of later ages are inconsistent with practices of former ages. Thus we have the explanation of the alleged fact of contradictions and inconsistencies within Catholic tradition. The existence of such contradictions means that revelation cannot consist in a divine discourse once delivered to the Church. Revelation, therefore, must be noncognitive and so concerned with practice. In fact, it is "super-cognitive," it consists in the confession of the unknowability of an incomprehensible God who cannot be rightly spoken of by men, but the encounter with whom leads us to a better version of ourselves.

On this account, the goal of theology is to aid in the translations that the Church must make every time an age of man is to be buried or there is some cultural divide to cross. What we know now, however, past the historical studies of the eighteenth and nineteenth centuries, is that the real control of such translation is not some original deposit of teaching, but the goal of aiding human flourishing. The "translation," therefore, can be very loose, for the only thing in the end that controls it is what conduces here and now to human flourishing. The only thing that is normative, it might be said, is the continual call to make the translation, to negotiate

4. Tyrrell, "The Rights and Limits of Theology," in Tyrrell, *Through Scylla and Charybdis*, 200–241, esp. 211–12.

cultural gaps again and again.[5] Of course, no less an authority than Pope John XXIII proposed a theological task of bringing ecclesial things "up to date," and including doctrine. But there is a difference between what he took and what this first position takes as the origin and status of the word that is to be translated. Is it ultimately a divine word (in human expression) or a purely human word responding to an event or experience?

Theology as an Aristotelian Science

One of the more vigorous theological responses to Modernism began with emphasizing just that point, to wit, that revelation is really and truly a word spoken to us by God; it is God's word spoken to us by him in our words (so that we can hear it). So did Ambroise Gardeil, OP, respond to Tyrrell, arguing for the publically communicable character of revelation in human words from the social nature of man, and defending the trans-empirical scope of human language when it is used analogically.[6] Kantian strictures on human knowledge were criticized in the name of a metaphysics whose subject is being, and the breaks in the history of doctrine alleged by the Modernists were addressed with an extended presentation of a theory of the logical development of doctrine. Gardeil furthermore extended his reply unto a vindication of St. Thomas's position that theology is a *science*.

The goal of theology is not translation, in the sense of a finding of equivalent terms in another culture, another language, for the same message; its goal is not some trans-temporal re-negotiation of Christian teaching as the times and seasons require. It is, however, trans-cultural and trans-temporal in another sense. Theology aims to find real definitions of divine realities, insofar as that may be done given the transcendence of God and his action, and from which may be deduced their properties. Faith and charity, for instance, can be truly defined. And these definitions will find expression in philosophically articulated concepts, whose point of departure is to be found in the common and basic notions of being

5. For a post-conciliar statement of this position, arrived at from hermeneutical theory, see Edward Schillebeeckx, OP, *The Understanding of Faith: Interpretation and Criticism*, trans. N. D. Smith (Dutch, 1972; New York: Seabury Press, 1974), esp. chaps. 2 and 4.

6. Ambroise Gardeil, OP, *Le donné révélé et la théologie*, 2nd ed. (Paris: Cerf, 1932).

familiar to all humanity, and so will be accessible to every culture and all ages.[7]

Gardeil's view of theology takes inspiration more from metaphysics than from history and hermeneutics. It does not think of the sciences as falling into two groups, *Naturwissenschaften* and *Geisteswissenschaften*, where the first can be understood in terms of Kant's First Critique and the second in terms of a theory of cultural development and dialectic (a governing principle befitting Modernism's view of things). Rather, it repairs to a much older theory of science, that of Aristotle, where the science of *X* is the certain knowledge of the causes of *X*. In other words, St. Thomas's view that theology is a science, more purely a science that any Aristotle knew of, is true, and not itself an accommodation of Christian teaching to some temporary exigence of the thirteenth century. Envisaging theology as a science was a permanent advance. And there are permanent explanatory advances within theology that remain true always and forever. The way to become a theologian is not to learn a language into which one wishes to translate revelation, but to learn the fundamental causes and principles that are the foundation of our capacity to express the objective intelligibility of the revealed mysteries of the Trinity, Incarnation, Church, and Sacraments. The goal of theology is the perfect apprehension of the intelligibility of revealed mystery insofar as this is possible in this life.

However, it is by no means true that Gardeil ignored the contemporary claims of historical studies. For him, the *first* part of theological endeavor, prior to the properly "scientific" part, is simply to establish what has in fact been revealed, to establish what he called "*le donné théologique.*" This is not simply the contemporary teaching of the Church, but rather this teaching brought back to its sources in the fonts of revelation and brought forward in its development to its contemporary expression.[8] This is "positive theology," "positive" because laying down what revelation proposes to us as to be received by faith, theology because and insofar as the

---

7. For a more complete theory of these common notions of being, the notions articulated by Aristotle and St. Thomas, see Reginald Garrigou-Lagrange, OP, *Le sens commun. La philosophie de l'être et les formules dogmatiques*, 3rd ed. (Paris: Nouvelle Librairie Nationelle, 1922).

8. Gardeil, *Le donné révélé*, 209.

historical reconstruction of Church doctrine is always guided by faith. Congar explains as follows:

> The method of positive theology, because it is theology, will then be "regressive" according to the term proposed by Fr. A. Gardeil. Positive theology takes its departure from the present, from the actual teaching in the Church, but it tries to enrich that teaching with a knowledge obtained by putting to work all the resources of historical reason as well as the total teaching of the Church ... which comprises together with Scripture ... all the development and all the expressions which Revelation has received in the Church through time and space.[9]

Just as theology in the thirteenth century took the philosophy of Aristotle for its handmaid, it now takes other servants into its household, the modern historical sciences. Just as metaphysics enriches the contemplation of the interior structure of the mysteries and their relation to one another as realities, so the historical sciences enrich the understanding of just what is being affirmed in the teaching of the Church—why it was taught in the first place, why it took the form it did, what false paths were being avoided by the form adopted. And just as faith corrects metaphysical error, so also it recognizes what historical reconstructions are faulty even before the historical sciences show that.

"La Nouvelle Théologie"

The idea of theology as a science, just as St. Thomas worked it out in the thirteenth century, proposed for modern times by Pope Leo XIII in the nineteenth century, and defended by Gardeil in the first decade of the twentieth, was the default position for how to think about theology embraced by most Catholic theologians for the next fifty years. It is what they said theology was, even if they did not always practice it in that form. But it did not survive as the default position past the Second Vatican Council.[10] There were three reasons for this.

9. Yves Congar, OP, *A History of Theology*, trans. and ed. Hunter Guthrie, SJ (French, 1938–39; Garden City, N.Y.: Doubleday, 1968), 236–37. Thus, whatever Juan Alfaro means by "regressive method" and reproves, it is not altogether commensurate with what Gardeil, as understood by Congar, means by that tag; see Juan Alfaro, SJ, "Il Tema biblico nella teologia sistematica," in Alfaro, *Cristologia e Antropologia* (Assisi: Citadella Editrice, 1972), 11–45, esp. 27.

10. There are several versions of this story. I recommend starting with Aidan Nichols, OP, "Thomism and the Nouvelle Théologie," *The Thomist* 64 (2000): 1–19. Fergus Kerr's *Twentieth-*

First, there was indeed a failure always accurately and fully to reappropriate St. Thomas's practice of theology. Article 8 of question 1 of the *prima pars* of the *Summa theologiae* could be interpreted in such a way that the goal of theology as a science can be adequately understood as the deduction of conclusions from revealed premises. Such deduction can be relatively easy, if tedious, but it may also be altogether ignorant of the synthetic acts of understanding that St. Thomas deployed in the *Summa*, the fruit of his own contemplation, the thing that makes his theology a living, organic whole.[11] These acts are such things as the deployment of the idea of law, analogically understood, in the *prima secundae* to relate and compare laws, eternal, natural, and human, all the better to understand the law of the Old Covenant and how the New Law surpasses it in the dispensation of grace. Or again, there is the extensive deployment of the idea of instrumental causality that unites our understanding of the humanity of Christ and the sacraments, including their ministers, and which is open to an understanding of the Church in the same order.[12] There is the protean grasp of virtue, again in *secunda pars*, that distinguishes and unites acquired virtue and infused virtue, virtue proportioned to our natural end and virtue that moves us to our supernatural end.[13] There is, as a last example, the over-arching understanding of divine distinction, Trinitarian distinction, as the ground of the distinction of the things of the world, an understanding that makes the manifold of creatures distinct in number and kind just as such good, and very good for us to behold, and is

Century Catholic Theologians (Oxford: Blackwell Publishing, 2007) discusses many of the key figures; the first chapter provides an overview up to the Second Vatican Council, and chapter 5, on Henri de Lubac, is important. There is also *Ressourcement: A Movement for Renewal in Twentieth-Century Catholic Theology*, ed. Gabriel Flynn and Paul D. Murray (Oxford: Oxford University Press, 2012). More philosophically focused is Gerald McCool's *From Unity to Pluralism: The Internal Evolution of Thomism* (New York: Fordham University Press, 1989).

11. Bernard Lonergan, *The Triune God: Systematics*, trans. Michael Shields (Toronto: University of Toronto Press, 2007), 49: "Nothing is easier than to conclude correctly: once the premises are posited, the conclusion either follows necessarily or it does not ... In contrast, a judgment about a theological understanding is not easy; it is extremely difficult. What is in question is not a conclusion but a principle." For more extended remarks on "conclusions theology," see ibid., 53–59.

12. St. Thomas Aquinas, *Summa theologiae* III, q. 19, a. 1 (instrumentality of the humanity of Christ); q. 62, aa. 1 and 4 (instrumentality of sacraments of the New Law); q. 63, a. 2 (instrumentality of sacramental character).

13. Ibid., I-II, q. 55, a. 4; q. 61, a. 5, q. 62, a. 1, q. 63, aa. 1–4. See Thomas M. Osborne Jr., "Perfect and Imperfect Virtue in Aquinas," *The Thomist* 71 (2007): 39–64.

itself the most powerful argument *ex convenientia* for the divine desire to include created persons, redeemed and graced, into Trinitarian communion.[14] While St. Thomas's own theological conclusions were often ably explained and defended in the renewed scholasticism following Leo XIII, a participation in and extension of his wisdom was not always attained.

Second, there was the formidable and not easily met challenge systematically and consistently to come to grips with contemporary historical sciences as touching Scripture and dogma. This was one of the issues of Modernism, of course, and we have seen how Gardeil addressed it. The excellent and wide-ranging historical studies of Thomas himself in the twentieth century alerted theologians to a like possibility and profit in matters scriptural and doctrinal. But this possibility was only slowly realized, as the difficulties Marie-Joseph Lagrange experienced in prosecuting it in Scripture studies bear witness. It is consequently harder to find a broad and deep theological achievement engaging and therefore judging in any detail the offerings of modern historical studies. So, for instance, there is, in the twentieth century, a reviviscence of the positions opposed to each other in the sixteenth-century controversy *De auxiliis*. But it is more difficult to do the historical work which situates this controversy not only against St. Thomas's own view of grace, which is an exercise in both history and metaphysics, but against Scripture and the Fathers. The appropriation of historical methods got better and better as the twentieth century wore on, and contributed to excellent theological work in the 1950s and 60s. But by then it was too late.

Third, there was an equally understandable failure fully to execute Leo XIII's program of restoration, which was more difficult than dusting off the commentaries and syntheses of Cajetan and John of St. Thomas, valuable though that could be. To be sure, Leo wanted the wisdom of St. Thomas employed to refute prevailing error,[15] but he also envisaged that new things might perfect the old.[16] The restoration was to be a resto-

---

14. See Gilles Emery, OP, *La Trinité créatrice: Trinité et création dans les commentaires aux Sentences de Thomas d'Aquin et de ses précurseurs Albert le Grand et Bonaventure* (Paris: Vrin, 1995), 445–554.

15. Leo XIII, encyclical *Aeterni Patris, On the Restoration of Christian Philosophy* (August 4, 1879), no. 31.

16. Ibid., no. 24.

ration not just of a philosophical and theological doctrinal content, but of an ethos according to which the medievals themselves were hospitable to pre-Christian an even extra-Christian thought and philosophy. Were this, too, reproduced, it would bring with it the advantage of making old things, newly perfected, take their place in modern philosophical and political conversation and in that way make the Church herself more present to the contemporary age. And indeed, there is the accomplishment of men like P. Rousselot (d. 1915), Désiré Mercier (d. 1926), and Joseph Maréchal (d. 1944), A. Sertillanges (d. 1948), Jacques Maritain (d. 1973), and É. Gilson (d. 1978) in philosophy. Likewise, in theology, there is Gardeil (d. 1932) himself and R. Garrigou-Lagrange (d. 1964), especially when he turned to the philosophical impediments to the knowledge of God's existence and his revelation. On the theological front, however, Yves Congar lamented, in 1935, the general isolation of theology from modern science and contemporary concern.[17]

A little over a decade later, Jean Daniélou made the same lament over the isolation of theology from contemporary life and culture. His programmatic "Les orientations de la pensée religieuse" is rightly taken as a sort of charter of what came to be called "la nouvelle théologie."[18] Daniélou argued for *ressourcement*, attention to modern philosophical currents, and engagement with contemporary problems especially as impacting the life of ordinary Christians.

As to the first, a better cultivation of the relation of theology to its fonts in Scripture, the Fathers, and the liturgy was needed to make the immediacy of the first and galvanizing revelation of God's transcendence and freedom more present to theology. Scholasticism, by contrast, insulated itself from a thorough possession of these fonts by too narrow a focus on dogma. Modern New Testament studies and a renewed access to the Fathers and contemporary liturgical excavation abolish this insularity.[19]

Second, Daniélou thought scholasticism especially ill-equipped to

17. Yves Congar, OP, "Déficit de la théologie," *Sept* (January 18, 1935).

18. Jean Daniélou, SJ, "Les orientations présentes de la pensée religieuse." *Études* 79 (1946): 5–21.

19. Daniélou himself, together with Henri de Lubac and Claude Mondésert, served importantly to increase access to the Fathers with the foundation of *Sources chrétiennes* in 1942 at Editions du Cerf and which since then has published new editions of hundreds of patristic works with French translation.

handle modern appreciations of the historicity of culture and thought, and so truly modern appreciations of dogma and theology, and of the modern turn to the subject, one manifestation of which Daniélou found in then-popular existentialism. Third, neither were the immediate pastoral needs of married people and lay spirituality addressed by scholastic theology.

Meeting these needs would break the stranglehold of neo-scholasticism on Catholic theology. In the arrangement of the symphony of theology, it would mean sending St. Thomas from the director's podium to a place in the orchestra, and not necessarily that of the first violin.

Today, it is no longer obvious why "scholasticism" could not integrate all of these concerns of Daniélou into such theological wisdom as St. Thomas conceived it. It is not obvious, for example, why the contemporary cultured despisers of Christianity cannot figure more prominently in the objections to the *quaestio*, especially where the *quaestiones* are more theologically fundamental, than in the past. In that respect, the new theologians were saying that all theology has to be written with an apologetic aim, even if one is writing in the first place for Christians, beleaguered as they will doubtless be by the surrounding culture. Howsoever, conciliar *aggiornamento* came to mean in many institutions of theological learning not the bringing of old things up to date, perfecting the old with the new, as Leo XIII had it, but the abandonment of much that was valuable.

Assessing Modernism

According to the deliverances of Scripture and Tradition, the first position, Modernism, is ruled out. Modernism is ruled out both by the nature of revelation, if how we have described it in chapter 1 is right, and by the nature of Scripture and dogma, if how we have described them in chapters three and four is correct, and by the express condemnation of Modernism by Pius X.

Modernism, it will be recalled, rested on two arguments: the Kantian denial that, strictly speaking, we can know God; and the alleged contradictions within Scripture (Loisy) and the history of doctrine (Tyrrell). The Kantian argument was touched on, if only briefly, in chapter 5. To the argument from the alleged contradictions within Scripture one has to be able to reply with a robust view of how the New Testament was constructed by weaving the warp of Jesus' history and self-understanding into the woof of Old Testament prophecy and figure, after Jesus' own pattern, such that it becomes evident that (allegedly) independent "Christologies" organized around now one and now the other of the titles of Jesus do not contradict one another. To the argument from the alleged contradictions in the history of doctrine, one has to be able to show how the prophetic and figurative reading of Scripture was continued by the Church in a more summary and theoretic mode, in the production of doctrine within a culture informed by the Greek philosophical ambition of being able to find a trans-cultural language for describing and analyzing the real. The idea that there is a trans-cultural language for describing and analyzing revealed reality has been embraced by the magisterium, and not just at the time of Modernism, as was also noted in chapter 4 and argued for in chapter 5.

There is also the problem for Modernism of determining the human good toward which revelation is supposed to move us. Revelation itself *says* nothing—it is no real word of God. What therefore gives content to the human good that revelation is supposed to promote and by which we are to judge the adequacy of doctrine? It would seem to be just us. Or, it would seem to be the theologians and masters of contemporary culture who will tell us what is good for us.

Now the view of theology inherent in Modernism is by no means dead but has enjoyed a great revival in the last forty years, pretty much as if the council's vindication of the *nouvelle théologie* was taken to be a vindication of Catholic Modernism, which would have surprised Garrigou-Lagrange, the inveterate enemy of both Modernism and the "new theology." But some contemporary apologists for the "new theology" think exactly that.[20] The truth, both historically and theologically, is quite other, since the vindication of the "new theology" was not a vindication of Modernism, at least according to such figures as H. de Lubac, nor did the council's *Dei Verbum*—"*Word* of God"—reduce revelation to a wordless mystical engagement.

20. For this view, see Jürgen Mettepenningen, *Nouvelle Théologie—New Theology: Inheritor of Modernism, Precursor of Vatican II* (London: T and T Clark International, 2010), esp. 21, 36.

Still, the idea that experience is a font of theology, whether alone or in conjunction with Scripture and Tradition, has been argued for or simply assumed by many theologians today. Scripture and Tradition and the Church's teaching, and also our own experience, are sources whence we draw what we say about God and the things of God. Where theology is conceived wholly as a work of translation, translating Scripture or the gospel or prior Church teaching into such a form as men can hear it today, there is a certain plausibility about the proposal: just as one must know the first and original language of Scripture etc., so one must know the target language, "the language of the men of today" or "the language of post-modern Western culture" or "the language of generation X" or whatever. But since the languages are in some manner expressions of the experience of those who speak them, then experience enters into the theological project. And, it is sometimes urged, the theologian's own experience enters into his theological project, whether he is aware of it and attends to it or not. Better, then, to be aware and conscious of it.

Of course, if theology is not fundamentally a work of translation, then the first reason does no work to establish experience as a font of theology. The second reason, too, is not very telling. There is a sense—hard to define—in which one's experience enters into one's considered expression of the meaning and possibilities and end of human life. Fine. But our extra-Christian, pre-Christian human experience that governs what we say about these things cannot be drawn without mediation into theology. This is because our human experience just as such is conditioned by sin—the sin of Adam, making us ignorant, and personal sin, making us stupid—distorting what we see and how we see it. So our experience cannot enter into theology until it is criticized by the tenets of the gospel and by the teaching of the Church and until it is disciplined by the practical directives of life in Christ. But then, this is to say that the obvious sources of theology—Scripture, Tradition, Dogma—trump whatever our unpurified experience gives us to say, and we are back to the original list of fonts.

There is another reason people give for listing experience as a font of theology, and that is the theology of Karl Rahner and what he calls the "supernatural existential."[21] On this view, God modifies our fundamental

21. Karl Rahner, SJ, "Concerning the Relationship between Nature and Grace," in Rahner,

spiritual orientation to him; he changes the horizon of our spiritual activities of knowing and loving and so of our encounter with all the objects within that horizon, all the objects of the world and especially our fellow human beings, because he makes himself in his own immediacy to himself the ultimate goal of all our spiritual activities. Whether this modification be conceived of as the always available offer of actual grace or in some other way need not detain us. The idea is that the framing parameters of our knowing and willing have been changed by the God of grace who is always nearer to us than we think. Therefore, our experience, our experience of ourselves and our experience of God and our experience of the neighbor, are always already touched by grace or at least the offer of grace, and so show themselves to be a font of what we want to say about God, that is, a font of theology.

Supposing everything that Rahner says at this point is right and true, it does not make experience a font of theology. The attempt to make it one comes up against the same criticism to the argument that our personal experience is always a factor in our theologizing. Suppose that our experience of God and our world and ourselves is graced from stem to stern. Still, this is a transcendental experience—like the presence to us of the light of the agent intellect—prior to every category, prior to words. And it is an experience conditioned by sin and the results of sin that we encounter in ourselves and in the world. Therefore, however we try to shape it up, it cannot play a role in theology until it is cleaned up and criticized by the word that we know certainly has come from God, the word of Scripture mediated to us by Tradition and interpreted by dogma. In chapter 4, we recalled Newman's ready admission that there may be revelation granted throughout the world and the world's history to every human conscience, and especially to those who seek God with a pure heart, revelation bearing on moral conduct and the course of God's providence. However this may be, such revelation cannot function as an addition to or standard of the revelation of Christ that comes to us *publicly*, and, as

Theological Investigations, vol. 1, trans. Cornelius Ernst, OP (German, 1950; Baltimore: Helicon, 1961), 297–317; Rahner, "The Experience of God Today," in Rahner, *Theological Investigations*, vol. 11, trans David Bourke (German, 1970; New York: Seabury, 1974), 149–65; Rahner, "Experience of Self and Experience of God," in Rahner, *Theological Investigations*, vol. 13, trans. David Bourke (German, 1972; New York: Seabury, 1975), 122–32.

was argued in chapter 1, comes to us expressly as *closed*, and whose canon of New Testament Scripture, as was noted in chapter 3, similarly comes to us with advertisements that we should expect no further apostolic word. It is difficult, therefore, to find a role for "experience" that would make it an independent font of theology, something that we would appeal to as we appeal to the Gospel according to John or to the Fourth Lateran Council or to St. Augustine's *De Trinitate*.

What we can say about experience relative to theology is the following. There is an experience of grace in the act of faith: the light of faith is something consciously given, and the *instinctus fidei* is something consciously felt, such that, enlightening us we are impelled to believe, and once moved to believe we are further enlightened.[22] The indwelling of the divine persons in the hearts of the faithful is also something experienced. There is, moreover, a kind of connatural knowledge of what we love by charity since charity makes us like these divine things and so, a connatural knowledge of the things concordant or discordant with them. But none of these things are words. And it is words that originally and necessarily constantly convey revelation to us.[23] None of these things, in other words, is an original cognitive source of what God is, who the divine Persons are, what they did, what they are doing. It was not the feeling of the Lord, or the breath of the Lord that came to Elijah, but a "still, small voice." And the Lord himself, when he lived among us, was preeminently and obviously a rabbi, a *teacher*. He has something to tell us, and he tells us by teaching. Also by doing, yes. But without the words, the meaning of the deed is opaque. What would driving the money changers out of the Temple mean unless the Lord interpreted it? Christ also has something to give us, too. But we do not know what it is unless he tells us what it is.

It is sometimes said, as we have already mentioned, that revelation ought not to be conceived of as a list of propositions. Well, no, not a list. Although, to be sure, there are genealogical lists in Genesis and Exodus, and there are lists of proverbs in Proverbs, and there are lists of rules in the

---

22. Juan Alfaro, *Fides, Spes, Caritas*, thesis 10.

23. For the unsubstitutable role of language in mediating revealed reality to us, see Robert Sokolowski, "God's Words and Human Speech," *Nova et Vetera* (English) 11 (2013): 187–210; and Olivier-Thomas Venard, OP, "Scriptural Hermeneutics and the Thomistic Making of a Doctrine of God," *Nova et Vetera* (English) 12 (2014): 1091–123.

paranetic sections of Paul's letters. But in the main, not a list. Narratives are not lists. But there is no narrative without propositions. There are also commands and questions in the written word of God. But in the main, they are contextualized by propositions, by statements in the indicative mood.

It is sometimes said that revelation ought not to be conceived of as propositional at all, but rather as the act of imparting a reality, even, Reality, to us. But this mistakes the human way of possessing reality. What we possess, just as men, or according to what defines us as men, is what we possess cognitively. And the instrument of our cognitive possession of any reality is the proposition. The act of faith, St. Thomas says and as noted in the previous chapter, terminates not in the proposition but in the reality.[24] And that is true not just of the act of faith, but of the act of any other cognitive habit, whether natural or infused. The chemist's assertion that table salt is mostly sodium chloride terminates, not in the proposition just enunciated, but in what is on the counter, in the shaker. But apart from the proposition, no reality, chemical or divine, is given to us as seekers of truth.

It is because this way, the propositional way, is the only way for us that the Church takes the care she does about enunciating dogma, about formulating her traditions, about the exegesis of Scripture, indeed, about establishing the letter of the text of Scripture, about the text of the liturgy. If there were some other way of possessing reality, intelligently grasping the intelligibility of what is possessed, truthfully and so grasping the truth of what is possessed, then the language, the words, the propositions would not matter so much. But there is not. And so they do.

Theology as Science

The second position, the one beholden to how St. Thomas thought about theology, has been endorsed frequently by the magisterium.[25] It is endorsed by the Second Vatican Council in its Decree on the Training of Priests, *Optatam Totius*. More recently, it seems to be broadly approved

24. St. Thomas Aquinas, *Summa theologiae* II-II, q. 1, a. 2, ad 2.
25. See the collection of magisterial material in Santiago Ramirez, OP, *The Authority of St. Thomas* (Washington, D.C.: The Thomist Press, 1952); and more recently Bruno M. Shah, OP, "The Promise of a Unitary Sacred Theology: Rereading *Aeterni Patris* and *Fides et Ratio*," *Nova et Vetera* (English) 11 (2013): 147–86.

and recently recommended by the pontifically chartered and appointed International Theological Commission.[26]

The council's view is briefly articulated in *Optatam Totius*, no. 16.

Dogmatic theology should be so arranged that these biblical themes [i.e., "the great themes of divine revelation"] are proposed first of all. Next there should be opened up to the students what the Fathers of the Eastern and Western Church have contributed to the faithful transmission and development of the individual truths of revelation. The further history of dogma should also be presented, account being taken of its relation to the general history of the Church. Next, in order that they may illumine the mysteries of salvation as completely as possible, the students should learn to penetrate them more deeply with the help of speculation, under the guidance of St. Thomas, and to perceive their interconnections. They should be taught to recognize these same mysteries as present and working in liturgical actions and in the entire life of the Church. They should learn to seek the solutions to human problems under the light of revelation, to apply the eternal truths of revelation to the changeable conditions of human affairs and to communicate them in a way suited to men of our day.[27]

We might divide "dogmatic theology" here into the treatment of the Trinity, Christ, the Church, the Sacraments, and theological anthropology. Those would be "integral parts." The concern, however, is method. The idea is that theology is first a matter of listening to the Bible, the Fathers, and Church dogma. This is "positive theology," in the sense that it seeks to locate those truths "posited" in revelation and formulated by the Church. It is a matter of listening to what Scripture, the Fathers, and the dogmatic tradition of the Church say about Christ, or the Trinity, the Church or some sacrament. This is theology as gathering evidence for determining what really has been revealed. Still, "positive theology" remains theology because it is a history of doctrine and exegesis of Scripture submitted to the authority of revelation. Historical deliverance and scriptural interpretation are thus auxiliary and subordinate sciences. They do not deliver their results to the theologian for his use except as judged by theology.[28]

---

26. International Theological Commission, *Theology Today: Perspectives, Principles, and Criteria* (Washington, D.C.: The Catholic University of America Press, 2012).

27. This is the translation at the Vatican website, http://vatican.va.

28. St. Thomas Aquinas, *Summa theologiae* I, q. 1, a. 6.

What this means in practice is that the excavation of biblical themes and what the Fathers made of them is guided by the theologian's knowledge of where many of the most important of these themes and developments have ended, namely in some defined dogma. Knowing the end of things helps us determine its often obscure beginning, just as Cardinal Newman said.[29] The program, in other words, is the "regressive method" of Gardeil.[30]

That positive theology consists in gathering up what the Scriptures teach and what the Church declares is obvious enough from what we have said about the nature of Scripture and dogma both. But why have the Fathers the position they do in Catholic theology? Joseph Ratzinger's answer to this question is very convincing.[31] No word is spoken unless it is heard. Hearing, moreover, is responsive, giving answer to the heard word. This is true of the word of God, too. Now, the word of God is not spoken wholly except it is completed by the word of Christ and the apostolic witness to that word and its accompanying deed. Thus, the first hearer of the entire word of God, the word of God in its integrity, is the Church. And the Church answers that word in the mouths of the Fathers of the Church. Patristic response, recapitulation, and commentary on the word of God therefore is an essential moment of the event of revelation itself. Consequently, it is not simply a matter of the antiquity of patristic witness that is important, but it is important as the first answer to the first fully heard word of God. Patristic witness to the sense of Scripture, to doctrine, to Christian mores, to Christian worship has therefore a sort of privileged, preeminent authority to it, never to be surpassed. The echo of the word of God in the ears of the undivided Church, in the ears of the Fathers, has an unmatched ability to help us determine the genuine content of that word, its tonality, its emphases, its unity, and its fecundity. We could say that the dialogic character of inspiration that Ratzinger

29. John Henry Newman, *An Essay on the Development of Christian Doctrine*, 6th ed. (Notre Dame, Ind.: University of Notre Dame Press, 1989), chap. 1, sec. 1, no. 7.

30. Bernard Lonergan, SJ, *Early Works on Theological Method 1*, ed. Robert M. Doran and Robert C. Croken (Toronto: Lonergan Research Institute of Regis College, 2010), 409; Andrew Meszaros, "The Regressive Method of Ambrose Gardeil and the Role of *Phronesis* and *Scientia* in Positive and Speculative Theologies," *Ephemerides Theologicae Lovaniensis* 89, no. 4 (2013): 307.

31. Joseph Ratzinger, "Importance of the Fathers for the Structure of Faith," in *Principles of Catholic Theology: Building Stones for a Fundamental Theology*, trans. Sister Mary Frances McCarthy, SND (San Francisco: Ignatius Press, 1987), 133–52.

champions, according to which the word is not originally spoken except in dialogue with Israel and her prophets and sages and priests, or again except in dialogue with the Church and her apostles and evangelists, is repeated at another level, the level not of constituting the word of God in Scripture, but the level of first interpreting the word of God, and that level is that of the Fathers.

Optatam Totius gives us a sort of threefold division of the fonts of theology, namely, Scripture, the Fathers, and dogma, which latter bespeaks in the first place the authority of ecumenical councils. The authority of Scripture and the Fathers as proper to theology is explicitly recognized by St. Thomas.[32] The Fathers themselves recognize this twofold authority, and the authority of dogma. So, for instance, at the Council of Ephesus, the orthodoxy of the Christology of Nestorius is settled not only on the authority of Scripture, but also on the authority of Nicaea. And the authority of prior patristic witness is evidenced by the *patristic* Church already in the fourth century.

After determining what has been revealed and received in the Church, there is, second, the "speculative penetration" of the revealed mysteries. What it amounts to is a comprehensive understanding of some revealed reality, so encompassing that the whole of the reality is embraced, such that its composing moments are seen in right relation to one another, and its integrity rightly related to the other revealed mysteries and the supernatural end of man, as the First Vatican Council taught. For instance, once positive theology delivers us the teachings of Ephesus, Chalcedon, Constantinople II and III as arising from Scripture and the Fathers, then we are possessed of what is first in the order of being, namely, that Christ is a divine person subsisting in two natures, human and divine, and we are possessed of this just in order to explain Christ's work of revelation and salvation, which come to completion in the Cross and Resurrection and Pentecost. These works of Christ in the order of revelation and salvation are what are first given to us in Scripture; they are what is most evident to us from the pages of Scripture and in the celebrations of the liturgy. But these mysteries are "illuminated" by the theoretic insight of St. Thomas.

32. St. Thomas Aquinas, *Summa theologiae* I, q. 1, a. 8, ad 2.

Thus, we explicate, say, the work of the cross when we understand it as the obedient action in suffering of one who is wholly divine and wholly human, whose human sorrow for sin is more intense than that of any other because of his human knowledge of the divine goodness and whose charity in suffering for our good and in our stead is a charity than which no greater can be conceived, and when we understand how the human charity and obedience of Christ both reveal his personal identity as Son, and at the same time satisfy for sin and merit the grace of our own inclusion in Christ and his work. This is a matter, then, of seeing the intelligibility of revealed mysteries, an intelligibility expressed in terms of causes and principles, powers and habits and acts, and the Second Vatican Council recommends doing so with the help of St. Thomas. This part of theology is usually called "systematic theology."

Third, there is "pastoral theology," the pastoral communication of the mysteries to today's people (variously cultured, of course) and the pastoral application of the mysteries so known and understood to contemporary affairs. The role assigned to systematic theology, of "illuminating" the mysteries, "penetrating them more deeply" is evidently strategic: it provides understanding of the truths gathered in listening, and so prepares for communicating and applying them. Such a role for understanding the mysteries, such as we can, was articulated already by the First Vatican Council in *Dei Filius*, and repeated after the Second Vatican Council by John Paul II in *Fides et Ratio*. This is the idea of theology as *scientia*.

It seems obvious that the intellectual virtue governing pastoral theology is prudence: the particularities of those who are to hear, the contingencies of the people and institutions to be managed, call for the finesse of what Aristotle called *phronesis*, the virtue that governs the application of general norms to concrete situations. If speculative or systematic theology really is a "science," then we know already what virtue presides over its activity, although the conciliar dicta about the illumination and penetration of the mysteries suggests rather the virtue of *intellectus* as presiding over the work of systematics, and directs us to those synthetic acts of Thomist understanding celebrated by Bernard Lonergan.

But what virtue presides over positive theology? It is another form of prudence. Historical judgment about the course of the emergence of doctrine—what the key factors were, why the path went this way instead of that—is just as much a matter of mastering particularities and contingencies as the pastoral application of theology. Except in this instance, it is a matter not of changing the future, but understanding the acts of understanding and decisions of the past.[33]

The "New Theology"

Finally, there are Henri de Lubac and Hans Urs von Balthasar and company, the "new theologians." In fact, this company is mixed, and there can be no uniform assessment of all the founding figures and their inheritors. Marie-Dominique Chenu, Karl Rahner, and Edouard Schillebeeckx, for instance, all drifted off at the end of their careers, if not before, into a kind of dogmatic historicism or relativism.[34]

Such was emphatically not the case for Henri de Lubac and Balthasar, however.[35] De Lubac's theological expertise, competence, and achievement were endorsed by John XXIII, who appointed him to the Preparatory Theological Commission for the Second Vatican Council, and by Pope Paul VI, who appointed him to the council's Theological Commission and wanted to make him a cardinal. Jean Daniélou, de Lubac's close theological associate, Paul VI did make a cardinal. As for Balthasar, Paul VI appointed him to the International Theological Commission, and John Paul II wanted to give the red hat to him, too. Joseph Ratzinger was very open about his appreciation of Balthasar's work. These considered

33. Andrew Meszaros, "The Regressive Method of Ambrose Gardeil," 307–11.

34. M. D. Chenu, OP, "Vérité évangélique et métaphysique wolfienne à Vatican II," *Revue des Sciences Philosophiques et Théologiques* 57 (1973): 632–40; Karl Rahner, SJ, "Yesterday's History of Dogma and Theology for Tomorrow," in *Theological Investigations*, vol. 18, trans. Edward Quinn (German, 1977; New York: Crossroad, 1983) 3–34; Rahner, "The One Christ and the Universality of Salvation," *Theological Investigations*, vol. 16, trans. David Morland (German, 1975; London: Darton, Longman & Todd, 1979), 199–224. See the critical comments on these articles by Hans Urs von Balthasar, "Human Religion and the Religion of Christ," in *New Elucidations*, trans. Sister Mary Theresilde Skerry (German, 1979; San Francisco: Ignatius Press, 1986), 74–87; Schillebeeckx, *The Understanding of Faith: Interpretation and Criticism.*

35. For de Lubac, see his "The Council and the Para-Council," in de Lubac, *A Brief Catechesis on Nature and Grace,* trans. Richard Arnandez, FSC (San Francisco: Ignatius Press, 1984), 235–60, esp. 257. In "The 'Sacrament of the World'?" also in *A Brief Catechesis on Nature and Grace,* 191–234, he rebukes Schillebeeckx.

signs of approbation are very important given that one of the aims of de Lubac, Daniélou, and Balthasar was not only to recover a more lively patristic presence in contemporary theology, but also to break the hold of Thomism on Catholic theology that had been in place since Leo XIII.[36] Should we rather say merely that they wanted to break the almost *exclusive* hold of the Thomism *of their day* on Catholic theology? If that was the aim, it was successfully carried through.

It is easier to say what the "new theologians" disliked, namely neoscholasticism and its exercise of hegemony—than what they were for, beyond saying "*ressourcement*" and "contemporary relevance." How should we describe what Henri de Lubac and Hans Urs von Balthasar were attempting to do? What was the point of de Lubac's endless exhumation of patristic and medieval witnesses in such a book as *The Splendour of the Church*— but not excluding citations from the Roman School and Bossuet?[37] The catholicity of the witnesses across time is strategic, and formal to what he is doing; it amounts to a genuine method. He did not begin with the questions about the Church asked by Bellarmine and the Reformation. Rather, he was trying to show us the phenomenon of the Church as she must appear in every age. He was trying to show us the Church just as she originally appears and gives her reality to believing eyes, as she first and always thereafter normatively showed herself to the Fathers, as a communion of charity made by the Eucharist, manifesting her true reality most patently there, and also how she subsequently gave herself to the long meditation of the monks, who saw in the Church Mary writ large and in Mary the outline of ecclesial reality, and third, the Church who could yet be perceived as what she really is in seventeenth-century France. In this way, he was doing something more in tune with what the Fathers and

36. Fergus Kerr, *Twentieth-Century Catholic Theologians*, 86, speaking of de Lubac: "It is hard to believe that he did not plan his books in order to destroy neoscholastic theology. That was the effect, for better or worse ... yet he seems never to have seen, let alone intended, it that way." Ratzinger's own relation to St. Thomas is noteworthy. He never warmed to St. Thomas (as he did to St. Bonaventure). There is not a single reference to St. Thomas in his *Introduction to Christianity* (San Francisco: Ignatius Press, 2004). This book originated as series of university lectures in the late 1960s, and it is difficult to believe that the absence of reference to St. Thomas is not both studied and strategic.

37. Henri de Lubac, SJ, *The Splendor of the Church*, trans. Michael Mason (French, 1953; San Francisco: Ignatius Press, 1986).

monks themselves paid attention to, the very way the Church shows up as a communion of charity, as a communion formed by the Eucharist and as a Marian reality. This sort of showing is prior to thinking out definitions and properties, structures and norms, although it is not opposed to that.

Or again, what is Balthasar doing in *The Glory of the Lord*? He is showing us the form of revelation, which is the form of Christ, how that form is beheld and the conditions of beholding it. For this "theological aesthetics," the beautiful is the "attractiveness" and "self-evidence" of the good and the "cogency" of truth, "the language of light" in which Being finds attractive and convincing expression.[38] He shows us the beautiful form in an (almost, it seems) infinite series of comparisons and contrasts that enlist Christian Scripture, the Fathers and the great theologians, pagan artists and philosophers, and post-Christian and even anti-Christian poets and philosophers. The form of Christ shows up by an endless circling around and around the cross, seeing what all these witnesses either anticipated, reported directly, or mis-described. Those who hit the target and those who miss all in their own way contribute to our own chances to see. There are apologetic reasons for this way of proceeding, but we would be mistaken if we did not first behold it as the report of and inducement to a sort of ecstatic rapture before the revelation of the Trinity in the crucified and risen Christ.

We might say that the goal of such a way of theologizing is the renewed manifestation of revelation for a given age, our own, but only by way of taking account of the artistic and moral and philosophical and theological appearances of the same reality across all the ages. In this way, therefore, de Lubac and Balthasar prosecute a form of theology that Robert Sokolowski calls "the theology of disclosure."[39] It is a form of theology that supposes a firm grasp on Church doctrine, for that is the measure of how to weigh what each of the crowd of witnesses says that revealed

38. Hans Urs von Balthasar, *The Glory of the Lord: A Theological Aesthetics*, vol. 1, *Seeing the Form*, trans. Erasmo Leiva-Merikakis (German, 1961; San Francisco: Ignatius Press, 1982), 19.

39. See Robert Sokolowski, *The God of Faith and Reason: Foundations of Christian Theology* (Notre Dame, Ind.: University of Notre Dame Press, 1982), chap. 8; and Sokolowski, *Eucharistic Presence: A Study in the Theology of Disclosure* (Washington, D.C.: The Catholic University of America Press, 1994), chaps. 1 and 13; and Sokolowski, "The Theology of Disclosure," *Nova et Vetera* 14 (2016): 409–23.

things are. However, it is rather a form of theology that attends to *how* Christ and Christian things appear to us. It is interested in how they *must* appear to us, if the very thing to be seen really is seen. It is interested therefore in the essential structure of revealing and beholding what is revealed. But it is not interested in a causal analysis of what manifests itself except insofar as that can help us (and sometimes it does) see how things must appear. Causal analysis is more the concern of the second position on the nature of theology, theology as science.

If it is true that de Lubac and Balthasar owe something to the patristic sensitivity to the manner of *appearing* of sacred things, it is all the more important to figure out how they can be imitated. For it has to be admitted that in one respect de Lubac and Balthasar are not easily imitable at all. Insofar as the "method" of both men consisted in a sort of encyclopedic knowledge of the prior theological tradition and contemporary philosophical positions and concerns and schools, it is not really helpful to a beginner to say "Learn everything ever said by Christians about God, and everything ever said by non-Christians about what Christians said about God, and then come back to me." However, insofar as de Lubac and Balthasar are incipient practitioners of what Sokolowski calls "the theology of disclosure," then there is something very definite to learn in order to imitate them. That thing is the rudiments of phenomenological method: learning how things appear to us, as wholes that have parts; learning that things have essences that can be discovered by imaginative variation of their properties and parts and relations to other things; learning how to make a distinction; learning the role of the vague and the confused in our coming to see things distinctly and crisply. Thus, if Husserl can teach us how to intuit an essence, then he can teach us how to intuit a theologically relevant essence.[40] Insofar as it is true that de Lubac and Balthasar are interested in how Christian things manifest themselves to us, then their inheritors are perhaps to be identified today with the French theo-phenomenologists like Jean-Luc Marion and Jean-Yves Lacoste and company.[41] Evidently, however, and by the many

40. See Robert Sokolowski, "Knowing Essentials," *Review of Metaphysics* 47 (1994): 691–709; and chapters 7 and 8 of his *Phenomenology of the Human Person* (Cambridge: Cambridge University Press, 2008).

41. See Dominique Janicaud, Jean-François Courtine, Jean-Louis Chrétien, Michel Henry,

references to his work, I have tried throughout this volume to indicate the fruitfulness for fundamental theology of a theology of disclosure as articulated and practiced by Robert Sokolowski.

The Unity of Theology

But if what St. Thomas and his followers and as endorsed by the magisterium are doing is theology, and if what de Lubac and Balthasar are doing is theology, how can the unitary nature of theology be defended? As was intimated at the beginning of this chapter, must not theology be one thing, have one nature? The answer has to do with the relation of manifestation to what is manifested, with the relation of intellect to reality, with the relation of the true to being. Neither term of each pair is understood without reference to the other. They stand or fall together. So, in attending to what is manifested, to its objective and intrinsic intelligibility in terms of essence and properties and powers and operation, I presuppose that it has been manifested to me truly, and that the real has not been deformed in my description and understanding of it. The study of being *qua* being covers the same territory, with the same fundamentality, under the head of a transcendental term of equivalent comprehension, being, as does the true—which builds into its content attention to how being appears to us. There is, then, a profound harmony (not without tensions) between Aristotle and Husserl. Sokolowski explains: "whereas Aristotle's first philosophy examines being as being, Husserl's examines intellect as intellect."[42]

In explaining St. Thomas's importance for Catholic theology generally, it is usually the case that one invokes him as a master of the causal, theoretical analysis of the mysteries. The councils who used him, the popes

---

Jean-Luc Marion, and Paul Ricoeur, *Phenomenology and the "Theological Turn": The French Debate* (New York: Fordham University Press, 2000). For Marion more particularly, see Christina M. Gschwandtner, *Reading Jean-Luc Marion: Exceeding Metaphysics* (Bloomington, Ind.: Indiana University Press, 2007).

42. Robert Sokolowski, "How Aristotle and Husserl Differ on First Philosophy," in *Life, Subjectivity, and Art: Essays in Honor of Rudolf Bernet*, ed. Roland Breeur and Ullrich Melle (Dordrecht: Springer, 2012), 1–28. See also Robert Sokolowski, "Husserl on First Philosophy," in *Philosophy, Phenomenology, Sciences: Essays in Commemoration of Edmund Husserl*, ed. Carlo Ierna, Hanne Jacobs, and Filip Mattens (Dordrecht: Springer, 2010), 3–23.

who recommended him, moreover, were not staying safely behind fortress walls, but were advancing thought with the very distinctions between creature and Creator, nature and grace, natural and supernatural knowledge, given classical, which is to say perennial expression by St. Thomas, and without which today it is impossible to imagine a Catholic thought in continuity with its past, biblical, patristic, and modern. Not skipping St. Thomas certainly means learning the metaphysics and philosophy of man that are presupposed on every page of his corpus.

However, this ignores St. Thomas's own attention to how the mysteries *appear*. That is to say, he is himself very attentive to the very ways in which the revelation reveals—the structures and modes of it, all as suited to revealing what is revealed *to us*. So, for instance, he asks about the manifestation of the Lord's resurrection, its epistemic structure, and its details as fitting that structure.[43] In treating the life of Christ, he asks about the fittingness of his baptism, of his temptation, of his manner of teaching, of his miracles, of his transfiguration, and these questions are exercises in how the mystery of Christ is disclosed to us.[44] Many of these questions were unique to Thomas and his treatment of the life of Christ in his own day, and were not asked again after him. Just as his own theological work includes positive and systematic theology in intimate union, it is also hospitable to the theology of disclosure.

Perhaps it is worthwhile to say a word about the nature of this hospitality. Thomism is broadly hospitable to any thinker or philosophy on two conditions. First, there must be no denial of any of the *praeambula fidei*. The inability to meet this condition rules out much of seventeenth- and eighteenth-century European philosophers, such as Hobbes, Hume, and Kant. Whatever insights they still convey to us, they cannot be taken neat. Second, there must be no denial of any of the *articuli fidei*. It is this condition that German Idealism generally fails. Hegelian insights may be taken up into Catholic theology, but not Hegel himself, although, with a thinker of such power and a system of such integrity, it is not easy to taste just a little Hegel. But Husserl meets both conditions. There is in him a sort of indeterminacy, like that of Plato and Aristotle, relative to the

43. St. Thomas Aquinas, *Summa theologiae* III, q. 55.
44. Ibid., III, q. 39, a. 1; q. 41, a. 1; q. 42; qq. 43–44; q. 45, a. 1.

determinate claims of the gospel. Husserl does not have to be re-fashioned to prove theologically useful. Sokolowski himself has given some thought to the ways Thomism and phenomenology can profitably collaborate and converge in the very practical endeavor of seminary education.[45]

If the remarks of this chapter have any truth in them, then what seems to promise life for the future of Catholic theology is the continuing recovery of the theology of St. Thomas, interrupted for thirty years after the council, and pushing forward the theology of disclosure. The collaboration of both could go far to meet the challenges of contemporary historicism and positivism.[46] More than that, however there is the deep satisfaction of the desire to know the causes of things and the ordering of reasons, prior and posterior, that Thomism provides for the contemplation of the Christian mysteries. And there is the constantly renewed delight at beholding the way the mysteries first present themselves to a greater than philosophic wonder that the theology of disclosure gives us.

45. Robert Sokolowski, "Philosophy in the Seminary Curriculum," *Homiletic and Pastoral Review* 104 (2004): 14–22.

46. For these challenges, see Robert Sokolowski, "Intellectual Formation in Catholic Seminaries," *Seminarium* 46 (2006): 827–46.

BIBLIOGRAPHY

Alfaro, Juan, SJ. *Fides, Spes, Caritas: Adnotationes in Tractatum De Virtutibus Theologicis*. New edition. Rome: Gregorian University, 1968.

———. "Il Tema biblico nella teologia sistematica." In Alfaro, *Cristologia e Antropologia*, 11–45. Assisi: Citadella Editrice, 1972.

———. *Esistenza Christiana*. 2nd ed. Rome: Gregorian University, 1979.

Allison, Dale. "Explaining the Resurrection: Conflicting Convictions." *Journal for the Study of the Historical Jesus* 3 (2005): 117–33.

Alonso-Schökel, Louis, SJ. *The Inspired Word: Scripture in the Light of Language and Literature*. Translated by Francis Martin. New York: Herder and Herder, 1965.

Anselm. *Proslogion*. In *St. Anselm: Basic Writings*. Translated by S. N. Deane. 2nd ed. LaSalle, Ill.: Open Court, 1962.

Aristotle. *Basic Works of Aristotle*. Edited by Richard McKeon. New York: Random House, 1941.

Augustine. *The City of God*. Translated by Marcus Dods. New York: Modern Library, 1950.

———. *Commentaire de la première épître de saint Jean*. Edited by Paul Agaësse. Sources chrétiennes 75. Paris: Les Éditions du Cerf, 1994.

———. *The First Catechetical Instruction*. Translated and annotated by Joseph P. Christopher. Ancient Christian Writers 2. New York: Newman Press, 1946.

———. *The Literal Meaning of Genesis*. Vol. 1. Translated by John Hammond Taylor, SJ. Ancient Christian Writers 41. New York: Paulist Press, 1982.

———. *Of True Religion*. In *Augustine: Earlier Writings*, edited and translated by J. H. S. Burleigh. Philadelphia: Westminster Press, 1953.

———. *On Free Choice of the Will*. Translated by Thomas Williams. Indianapolis: Hackett, 1993.

———. *Teaching Christianity: De Doctrina Christiana*. Translated by Edmund Hill, OP. Hyde Park: New City Press, 1996.

Balthasar, Hans Urs von. *The Glory of the Lord: A Theological Aesthetics*. Vol. 1, *Seeing the Form*. Translated by Erasmo Leiva-Merikakis. San Francisco: Ignatius Press, 1982.

———. *Origen: Spirit and Fire, A Thematic Anthology of His Writings*. Translated by Robert J. Daly, SJ. Washington, DC: The Catholic University of America Press, 1984.

———. "Human Religion and the Religion of Christ." In *New Elucidations*, translated by Sister Mary Theresilde Skerry, 74–87. San Francisco: Ignatius Press, 1986.

———. *The Glory of the Lord: A Theological Aesthetics*. Vol. 7, *Theology: The New Covenant*. Translated by Brian McNeil, CRV. San Francisco: Ignatius Press, 1989.

———. *The Glory of the Lord: A Theological Aesthetics*. Vol. 5, *The Realm of Metaphysics in the Modern Age*. Translated by Oliver Davies et al. San Francisco: Ignatius Press, 1991.

———. *The Glory of the Lord: A Theological Aesthetics*. Vol. 6, *Theology: The Old Covenant*. Translated by Brian McNeil and Erasmo Leiva-Merikakis. San Francisco: Ignatius Press, 1991.

———. "Holy Scripture." Translated by Jeremy Holmes. *Nova et Vetera* (English) 5 (2007): 707–24.

Barth, Karl. *Church Dogmatics*. Translated by G. W. Bromiley, T. H. L. Parker, et al. Edinburgh: T and T Clark, 1956–1975.

Barton, John. "Biblical Studies." In *The Blackwell Companion to Modern Theology*, edited by Gareth Jones, 18–33. Oxford: Blackwell Publishing, 2007.

Bauckham, Richard. "For Whom Were the Gospels Written?" In *The Gospels for All Christians: Rethinking the Gospel Audiences*, edited by Richard Bauckham, 9–48. Grand Rapids, Mich.: Eerdmans, 1998.

———. "Reading Scripture as a Coherent Story." In *The Art of Reading Scripture*, edited by Ellen F. Davis and Richard B. Hays, 38–53. Grand Rapids, Mich.: Eerdmans, 2003.

———. *Jesus and the Eyewitnesses: The Gospels as Eyewitness Testimony*. Grand Rapids, Mich.: Eerdmans, 2006.

Behr, John. *The Way to Nicaea*. Crestwood, N.Y.: St. Vladimir's Seminary Press, 2001.

———. *The Mystery of Christ: Life in Death*. Crestwood, N.Y.: St. Vladimir's Press, 2006.

Benedict XV, Pope. *Spiritus Paracletus, Commemorating the Fifteenth Centenary of the Death of St. Jerome*. Encyclical letter. September 15, 1920.

Benedict XVI, Pope. *Jesus of Nazareth: From the Baptism in the Jordan to the Transfiguration*. Translated by Adrian J. Walker. New York: Doubleday, 2007.

———. *The Word of God in the Life and Mission of the Church: Verbum Domini*. Postsynodal apostolic exhortation. Frederick, Md.: The Word Among Us, 2010.

Benoît, Pierre, OP. *Aspects of Biblical Inspiration*. Translated by J. Murphy-O'Connor, OP, and S. K. Ashe, OP. Chicago: Priory Press, 1965.

Bradshaw, Paul F. *Ordination Rites of the Ancient Churches of East and West*. New York: Pueblo, 1990.

Brown, Raymond, SS. "Hermeneutics." In *The Jerome Biblical Commentary*, edited by

Raymond E. Brown, SS, Joseph A. Fitzmyer, SJ, and Roland E. Murphy, OCarm. Englewood Cliffs, N.J.: Prentice-Hall, 1968.

———. *The Critical Meaning of the Bible*. New York: Paulist Press, 1981.

Burridge, Richard. *What Are the Gospels? A Comparison with Graeco-Roman Biography*. Cambridge: Cambridge University Press, 1992.

Calvin, John. *Calvin: The Institutes of the Christian Religion*. 2 vols. Translated by Ford Lewis Battles. Library of Christian Classics 20 and 21. Philadelphia: Westminster Press, 1956.

Cassian, John. *The Conferences*. Translated by Boniface Ramsey, OP. Ancient Christian Writers 57. New York: Newman Press, 1997.

Chadwick, Owen. *From Bossuet to Newman*. 2nd ed. Cambridge: Cambridge University Press, 1987.

Chenu, Marie-Dominique, OP. "Vérité évangélique et métaphysique wolfienne à Vatican II." *Revue des Sciences Philosophiques et Théologiques* 57 (1973): 632–40.

Congar, Yves, OP. "Déficit de la théologie." *Sept* (January 18, 1935).

———. *La Foi et la Théologie*. Tournai: Desclée, 1962.

———. *Tradition and Traditions: An Historical Essay and a Theological Essay*. Translated by Michael Naseby and Thomas Rainborough. New York: Macmillan, 1966.

———. *A History of Theology*. Translated and edited by Hunter Guthrie, SJ. Garden City, NY: Doubleday, 1968.

Congregation for the Doctrine of the Faith. *Mysterium ecclesiae*, Declaration in Defense of the Catholic Doctrine on the Church against Certain Errors of the Present Day. June 24, 1973.

———. *Dominus Iesus, Declaration on the Unicity and Salvific Universality of Christ and the Church*. August 6, 2000.

Cunningham, Conor. *Darwin's Pius Idea: Why the Ultra-Darwinists and Creationists Both Get It Wrong*. Grand Rapids, Mich.: Eerdmans, 2010.

Cyril of Alexandria. *Commentary on the Gospel according to S. John*. Vol. 2. Translated by Thomas Rendell. Library of the Fathers 48. London: Walter Smith, 1885.

———. *Commentary on John*. Vol. 1. Translated by David R. Maxwell. Downers Grove, Ill.: IVP Academic, 2013.

Daniélou, Jean, SJ. "Les orientations présentes de la pensée religieuse." *Études* 79 (1946): 5–21.

De la Potterie, Ignace, SJ. *La vérité dans saint Jean*. 2 vols. Rome: Biblical Institute Press, 1977.

De Lubac, Henri, SJ. *The Sources of Revelation*. Translated by Luke O'Neill. New York: Crossroad, 1968. Reprinted as *Scripture in the Tradition*. New York: Crossroad, 2000.

———. *La Révélation divine*. 3rd ed. Paris: Cerf, 1983.

———. "The Council and the Para-Council." In de Lubac, *A Brief Catechesis on Nature and Grace*, translated by Richard Arnandez, FSC, 235–60. San Francisco: Ignatius Press, 1984.

————. "The 'Sacrament of the World'?" In de Lubac, *A Brief Catechesis on Nature and Grace*, translated by Richard Arnandez, FSC, 191–234. San Francisco: Ignatius Press, 1984.

————. *The Splendor of the Church*. Translated by Michael Mason. San Francisco: Ignatius Press, 1986.

————. *Medieval Exegesis*. 3 vols. Translated by Marc Sebanc and E. M. Macierowski. Grand Rapids, Mich.: Eerdmans, 1998–2000.

————. *History and Spirit: The Understanding of Scripture According to Origen*. Translated by Anne Englund Nash. San Francisco: Ignatius Press, 2007.

Dickinson, Emily. *The Complete Poems of Emily Dickinson*. Edited by Thomas H. Johnson. Boston: Little, Brown and Company, 1960.

Dulles, Avery, SJ. *The Assurance of Things Hoped For: A Theology of Christian Faith*. Oxford: Oxford University Press, 1994.

————. "Vatican II on the Interpretation of Scripture." *Letter & Spirit* 2 (2006): 17–26.

————. *Magisterium: Teacher and Guardian of the Faith*. Ave Mara, Fla.: Sapientia Press, 2007.

Emery, Gilles, OP. *La Trinité créatrice: Trinité et création dans les commentaires aux Sentences de Thomas d'Aquin et de ses précurseurs Albert le Grand et Bonaventure*. Paris: Vrin, 1995.

————. *Trinity in Aquinas*. Ypsilanti, Mich.: Sapientia Press, 2003.

————. "The Personal Mode of Trinitarian Action in St. Thomas Aquinas." In Emery, *Trinity, Church, and the Human Person*, 115–53. Naples, Fla.: Sapientia Press, 2007.

————. "Trinity and Truth: The Son as Truth and the Spirit of Truth in St. Thomas Aquinas." In Emery, *Trinity, Church, and the Human Person: Thomistic Essays*, 73–114. Naples, Fla.: Sapientia Press, 2007.

Farkasfalvy, Denis, OCist. "Theology of Scripture in St. Irenaeus." *Revue Bénédictine* 78 (1968): 319–33.

————. "How to Renew the Theology of Biblical Inspiration?" *Nova et Vetera* (English) 4 (2006): 231–54.

————. *Inspiration and Interpretation: A Theological Introduction to Sacred Scripture*. Washington, D.C.: The Catholic University of America Press, 2010.

Fastiggi, Robert. "Communal or Social Inspiration: A Catholic Critique." *Letter and Spirit* 6 (2010): 247–63.

Ferguson, Everett. "*Paradosis* and *Traditio*: A Word Study." In *Tradition and the Rule of Faith in the Early Church: Essays in Honor of Joseph T. Lienhard, SJ*. Edited by Ronnie J. Rombs and Alexander Y. Hwang, 3–30. Washington, D.C.: The Catholic University of America Press, 2010.

Feser, Edward. *Philosophy of Mind*. London: Oneworld, 2006.

————. *The Last Superstition: A Refutation of the New Atheism*. South Bend, Ind.: St. Augustine's Press, 2008.

―――. "Motion in Aristotle, Newton, and Einstein." In *Aristotle on Method and Metaphysics*, edited by Edward Feser, 236–58. New York: Palgrave Macmillan, 2013.

Flynn, Gabriel, and Paul D. Murray, eds. *Ressourcement: A Movement for Renewal in Twentieth-Century Catholic Theology*. Oxford: Oxford University Press, 2012.

Francis, Pope. *Laudato Si': On Care of Our Common Home*. Frederick, Md.: The Word Among Us Press, 2015.

Gaine, Simon Francis. *Did the Saviour See the Father? Christ, Salvation and the Vision of God*. London: Bloomsbury Publishing, 2015.

Gardeil, Ambroise, OP. *Le donné révélé et la théologie*, 2nd ed. Paris: Cerf, 1932.

Garrigou-Lagrange, Reginald, OP. *Le sens commun. La philosophie de l'être et les formules dogmatiques*, 3rd ed. Paris: Nouvelle Librairie Nationelle, 1922.

―――. *De Revelatione per Ecclesiam Catholicam Propositam*. 2 vols. 5th ed. Rome: Desclée et Socii, 1950.

Gerhardsson, Birger. *The Reliability of the Gospel Tradition*. Peabody, Mass.: Hendrickson Publishers, 2001.

Giambrone, Anthony, OP. "The Quest for the *Vera et Sincera de Jesu*: *Dei Verbum* no. 19 and the Historicity of the Gospels." *Nova et Vetera* (English) 13 (2015): 87–123.

Giussani, Luigi. *The Religious Sense*. Translated by John Zucchi. Montreal: McGill-Queen's University Press, 1997.

―――. *At the Origin of the Christian Claim*. Translated by Viviane Hewitt. Montreal: McGill-Queen's University Press, 1998.

Graves, Michael. *The Inspiration and Interpretation of Scripture: What the Early Church Can Teach Us*. Grand Rapids, Mich.: Eerdmans, 2014.

Greer, Rowan. "The Christian Bible and Its Interpretation." In Rowan Greer and James Kugel, *Early Biblical Interpretation*, edited by Wayne A. Meeks, 107–208. Philadelphia: Westminster Press, 1986.

Gregory the Great. *Homilies on the Book of the Prophet Ezekiel*. Translated by Theodosia Tomkinson. Etna, Calif.: Center for Traditionalist Orthodox Studies, 2008.

Gschwandtner, Christina M. *Reading Jean-Luc Marion: Exceeding Metaphysics*. Bloomington, Ind.: Indiana University Press, 2007.

Guarino, Thomas G. *Vincent of Lérins and the Development of Christian Doctrine*. Grand Rapids, Mich.: Baker Academic, 2013.

Habermas, Gary, and Antony G. N. Flew. *Did Jesus Rise from the Dead? The Resurrection Debate*. Edited by Terry L. Miethe. San Francisco: Harper and Row, 1987.

Harrison, Brian. "Restricted Inerrancy and the 'Hermeneutics of Discontinuity.'" *Letter and Spirit* 6 (2010): 225–46.

Hart, David Bentley. *Atheist Delusions: The Christian Revolution and Its Fashionable Enemies*. New Haven, Conn.: Yale University Press, 2010.

Hays, Richard. *Reading Backwards: Figural Christology and the Fourfold Gospel Witness*. Waco, Tex.: Baylor University Press, 2014.

Healy, Mary. "Inspiration and Incarnation: The Christological Analogy and the Hermeneutics of Faith." *Letter and Spirit* 2 (2006): 27–41.

Hengel, Martin. "The Titles of the Gospels and the Gospel of Mark." In *Studies in the Gospel of Mark*, translated by John Bowden, 64–84. Philadelphia: Fortress Press, 1985.

Henry, Michel. *Words of Christ*. Translated by Christina M. Gschwandtner. Grand Rapids, Mich.: Eerdmans, 2012.

Hertling, Ludwig, SJ. *Communio: Church and Papacy in Early Christianity*. Translated with introduction by Jared Wicks, SJ. Chicago: Loyola University Press, 1972.

Huizenga, Leroy. "The Matthean Christ, Center of Salvation History." *Letter and Spirit* 9 (2014): 11–29.

Hume, David. *An Inquiry Concerning Human Understanding*. Edited by Charles W. Hendel. Indianapolis: Bobbs-Merrill, 1980.

Innerst, Sean. "Divine Pedagogy and Covenantal Memorial: The Catechetical *Narratio* and the New Evangelization." *Letter and Spirit* 8 (2013): 161–88.

International Theological Commission. *Theology Today: Perspectives, Principles, and Criteria*. Washington, D.C.: The Catholic University of America Press, 2012.

Irenaeus of Lyons. *On the Apostolic Preaching*. Translation and introduction by John Behr. Crestwood, N.Y.: St. Vladimir's Press, 1997.

————. *Against Heresies*. In *The Ante-Nicene Fathers*, vol. 1, edited by Alexander Roberts, James Donaldson, and Arthur Cleveland Coxe. New York: Cosimo Classics, 2007.

Janicaud, Dominique, Jean-François Courtine, Jean-Louis Chrétien, Michel Henry, Jean-Luc Marion, and Paul Ricoeur. *Phenomenology and the "Theological Turn": The French Debate*. New York: Fordham University Press, 2000.

John Paul II, Pope. *Fides et Ratio, on the Relationship between Faith and Reason*. Encyclical letter. September 14, 1998. http://vatican.va.

————. *Restoring Faith in Reason, A New Translation of the Encyclical Letter Faith and Reason of Pope John Paul II together with a commentary and discussion*. Edited by Laurence Paul Hemming and Susan Frank Parsons. Notre Dame, Ind.: University of Notre Dame Press, 2003.

Kant, Immanuel. *Religion within the Limits of Reason Alone*. Translated by Theodore M. Greene and Hoyt H. Hudson. New York: Harper and Row, 1960.

————. *Critique of Pure Reason*. Translated by Norman Kemp Smith. New York: St. Martin's Press, 1965.

Kasper, Walter. *Dogma unter dem Wort Gottes*. Mainz: Matthias-Grünewald Verlag, 1965.

Kerr, Fergus, OP. *Twentieth-Century Catholic Theologians*. Oxford: Blackwell Publishing, 2007.

Kierkegaard, Søren. *Philosophical Fragments*. Edited and translated by Howard V. Hong and Edna H. Hong. Princeton, N.J.: Princeton University Press, 1985.

Kugel, James. "Early Interpretation: The Common Background of Late Forms of

Biblical Exegesis." In James Kugel and Rowan Greer, *Early Biblical Interpretation*, edited by Wayne A. Meeks, 9–106. Philadelphia: Westminster Press, 1986.

Kugel, James, and Rowan Greer. *Early Biblical Interpretation*. Edited by Wayne A. Meeks. Philadelphia: Westminster Press, 1986.

Lamont, John R. T. *Divine Faith*. Aldershot, UK: Ashgate, 2004.

Leo XIII, Pope. *Aeterni Patris, on the Restoration of Christian Philosophy*. Encyclical letter. August 4, 1879. http://vatican.va.

———. *Providentissimus Deus, on the Study of Scripture*. Encyclical letter. November 18, 1893.

Le Roy, Édouard. "Qu'est-ce qu'un dogme?" In *Dogme et critique*, 1–34. Paris: Librairie Bloud et Cie., 1907.

Levering, Matthew. *Christ's Fulfillment of Torah and Temple*. Notre Dame, Ind.: University of Notre Dame Press, 2002.

———. *Scripture and Metaphysics: Aquinas and the Renewal of Trinitarian Theology*. Oxford: Blackwell Publishing, 2004.

———. *Mary's Bodily Assumption*. Notre Dame, Ind.: University of Notre Dame Press, 2015.

Lewis, C. S. *Miracles: A Preliminary Study*. Revised edition. New York: HarperCollins, 2001.

Lienhard, Joseph, SJ. *The Bible, the Church, and Authority: The Canon of the Christian Bible in History and Theology*. Collegeville, Minn.: Liturgical Press, 1995.

Loisy, Alfred. *Autour d'un petit livre*. 2nd edition. Paris: Picard et Fils, 1907.

Lonergan, Bernard, SJ. *The Triune God: Systematics*. Translated from *De Deo Trino: Pars systematica* (1964) by Michael Shields. Toronto: University of Toronto Press, 2007.

———. *The Triune God: Doctrines*. Translated from *De Deo Trino: Pars dogmatica* (1964) by Michael Shields. Toronto: University of Toronto Press, 2009.

———. *Early Works on Theological Method 1*. Edited by Robert M. Doran and Robert C. Croken. Toronto: Lonergan Research Institute of Regis College, 2010.

Luther, Martin. *Lectures on Romans*. Translated by Walter G. Tillmanns and Jacob A. O. Preus, edited by Hilton Oswald. Luther's Work 25. St. Louis: Concordia, 1972.

Mankowski, Paul, SJ. "Language, Truth, and *Logos*." In *The Oxford Handbook of Christology*, edited by Francesca Aran Murphy, 9–20. Oxford: Oxford University Press, 2015.

Mansini, Guy. "Apologetics, Evil, and the New Testament." *Logos* 4 (2001): 152–68.

———. "Error, Guilt, and the Knowledge of God: Questions about Robert Sokolowski's 'Christian Distinction.'" *Logos* 5 (2002): 116–36.

Marin-Solà, Francisco, OP. *L'évolution homogène de dogme catholique*. 2 vols. 2nd ed. Fribourg: Librarie de l'Oeuvre de Saint-Paul, 1924.

Marion, Jean-Luc. "'They Recognized Him; and He Became Invisible to Them.'" *Modern Theology* 18 (2002): 145–52.

Martin, Francis. "Election, Covenant and Law." *Nova et Vetera* (English) 4 (2006): 857–90.

———. "Revelation and Its Transmission." In *Vatican II: Renewal within Tradition*, edited by Matthew L. Lamb and Matthew Levering, 55–75. Oxford: Oxford University Press, 2008.

May, Gerhard. *Creatio Ex Nihilo: The Doctrine of "Creation out of Nothing" in Early Christian Thought*. Translated by A. S. Worrall. London: T and T Clark International, 1994.

McCabe, Herbert, OP. "Creation." In McCabe, *God Matters*, 2–9. Springfield, Ill.: Templegate Publishers, 1987.

McCarthy, Dennis J., SJ. "Personality, Society, and Inspiration." *Theological Studies* 64 (1963): 553–76.

McCool, Gerald, SJ. *From Unity to Pluralism: The Internal Evolution of Thomism*. New York: Fordham University Press, 1989.

McDonald, Lee Martin. *The Biblical Canon: Its Origin, Transmission and Authority*. Peabody, Mass.: Hendrickson Publishers, 2007.

McEvoy, James, "Commentary on *Fides et Ratio*." In *Restoring Faith in Reason,* A New Translation of the Encyclical Letter *Faith and Reason* of Pope John Paul II together with a commentary and discussion, edited by Laurence Paul Hemming and Susan Frank Parsons, 175–98. Notre Dame, Ind.: University of Notre Dame Press, 2003.

McKenzie, John L., SJ. "The Social Character of Inspiration." *Catholic Biblical Quarterly* 24 (1962): 115–24.

Meszaros, Andrew. "The Regressive Method of Ambrose Gardeil and the role of *Phronesis* and *Scientia* in Positive and Speculative Theologies." *Ephemerides Theologicae Lovaniensis* 89, no. 4 (2013): 279–321.

———. *The Prophetic Church: History and Doctrinal Development in John Henry Newman and Yves Congar*. Oxford: Oxford University Press, 2016.

Mettepenningen, Jürgen. *Nouvelle Théologie—New Theology: Inheritor of Modernism, Precursor of Vatican II*. London: T and T Clark International, 2010.

Metzger, Bruce. *The Canon of the New Testament: Its Origin, Development, and Significance*. Oxford: Clarendon Press, 1987.

Meynell, Hugo. "The Intelligibility of the Universe." In *Reason and Religion*, edited by Stuart C. Brown, 23–43. Ithaca, N.Y.: Cornell University Press, 1977.

Miller, Ed. *God and Reason: A Historical Approach to Philosophical Theology*. New York: Macmillan, 1972.

Morerod, Charles, OP. *The Church and the Human Quest for Truth*. Washington, D.C.: The Catholic University of America Press, 2008.

Murray, John Courtney, SJ. *The Problem of God*. New Haven, Conn.: Yale University Press, 1964.

Nagel, Thomas. *Mind and Cosmos: Why the Materialist Neo-Darwinian Conception of Nature Is Almost Certainly False*. Oxford: Oxford University Press, 2012.

Neuner, J., SJ, and Jacques Dupuis, SJ, eds. *The Christian Faith in the Doctrinal Docu-*

ments of the Catholic Church. 7th revised and enlarged edition. New York: Alba House, 2001.

Newman, John Henry. *An Essay on the Development of Christian Doctrine.* 6th ed. Notre Dame, Ind.: University of Notre Dame Press, 1989.

Nichols, Aidan, OP. *The Shape of Catholic Theology.* Collegeville, Minn.: The Liturgical Press, 1991.

———. "Thomism and the Nouvelle Théologie." *The Thomist* 64 (2000): 1–19.

———. *Lovely Like Jerusalem: The Fulfillment of the Old Testament in Christ and the Church.* San Francisco: Ignatius Press, 2007.

O'Connor, Timothy, and Hong Yu Wong, "Emergent Properties." In *The Stanford Encyclopedia of Philosophy,* summer 2015 ed., edited by Edward N. Zalta. http://plato.stanford.edu/archives/sum2015/entries/properties-emergent/.

O'Keefe, John and R. Reno. *Sanctified Vision: An Introduction to Early Christian Interpretation of the Bible.* Baltimore: Johns Hopkins University Press, 2005.

Osborne, Thomas M., Jr. "Perfect and Imperfect Virtue in Aquinas." *The Thomist* 71 (2007): 39–64.

Pannenberg, Wolfhart. *Jesus—God and Man.* 2nd ed. Translated by Lewis L. Wilkins and Duane A. Priebe. Philadelphia: Westminster Press, 1977.

Pascal, Blaise. *Pensées.* Translated by W. F. Trotter. New York: Modern Library, 1941.

Paul VI, Pope. *Mysterium Fidei, on the Holy Eucharist.* Encyclical letter. September 3, 1965. http://vatican.va.

Percy, Walker. "The Message in the Bottle." In Percy, *The Message in the Bottle: How Queer Man Is; How Queer Language Is; and What One Has to Do with the Other,* 119–58. New York: Farrar, Straus and Giroux, 1982.

Pidel, Aaron, SJ. "Joseph Ratzinger on Biblical Inerrancy." *Nova and Vetera* (English) 12 (2014): 307–30.

Pitre, Brant. "The 'Ransom for Many,' the New Exodus, and the End of Exile: Redemption as the Restoration of All Israel (Mark 10:35–45)." *Letter and Spirit* 1 (2005): 41–68.

Pius XII, Pope. *Divino Afflante Spiritu, on Promoting Biblical Studies.* Encyclical letter. September 30, 1943. http://vatican.va.

———. *Humani generis, Concerning Some False Opinions Threatening to Undermine the Foundations of Catholic Doctrine.* Encyclical letter. August 12, 1950. http://vatican.va.

Plato. *Phaedrus.* Translated by R. Hackforth. In *Plato: The Collected Dialogues,* edited by Edith Hamilton and Huntington Cairns. Bollingen Series 71. Princeton, N.J.: Princeton University Press, 1961.

Pontifical Biblical Commission. "On the Historical Truth of the Gospels." *Sancta Mater Ecclesia.* Instruction. April 21, 1964.

———. *The Jewish People and Their Sacred Scriptures in the Christian Bible.* Boston: Pauline Books and Media, 2003.

———. *The Inspiration and Truth of Sacred Scripture.* Translated by Thomas Esposito and Stephen Gregg. Collegeville, Minn.: Liturgical Press, 2014.

Radner, Ephraim. "Apologetics and Unity: Confessing the One Lord." In Radner, *Hope among the Fragments: The Broken Church and Its Engagement of Scripture*, 161–75. Grand Rapids, Mich.: Brazos, 2004.

Rahner, Karl, SJ. "Concerning the Relationship between Nature and Grace." In Rahner, *Theological Investigations*, vol. 1, translated by Cornelius Ernst, OP, 297–317. Baltimore: Helicon, 1961.

———. "Inspiration in the Bible." Translated by Charles H. Henkey, revised by Martin Palmer, 7–86. In Rahner, *Inquiries*. New York: Herder and Herder, 1964.

———. "The Experience of God Today." In Rahner, *Theological Investigations*, vol. 11, translated by David Bourke, 149–65. New York: Seabury, 1974.

———. "Experience of Self and Experience of God." In Rahner, *Theological Investigations*, vol. 13, translated by David Bourke, 122–32. New York: Seabury, 1975.

———. "The One Christ and the Universality of Salvation." In Rahner, *Theological Investigations*, vol. 16, translated by David Morland, 199–224. London: Darton, Longman and Todd, 1979.

———. "Yesterday's History of Dogma and Theology for Tomorrow." In Rahner, *Theological Investigations*, vol. 18, translated by Edward Quinn, 3–34. New York: Crossroad, 1983.

———. *Hearer of the Word*. Translated by Joseph Donceel, SJ. New York: Continuum, 1994.

Ramage, Matthew. "Violence Is Incompatible with the Nature of God: Benedict, Aquinas, and Method C Exegesis of the 'Dark' Passages of the Bible." *Nova et Vetera* (English) 13 (2015): 273–95.

Ramirez, Santiago, OP. *The Authority of St. Thomas*. Washington, D.C.: The Thomist Press, 1952.

Ratzinger, Joseph. *Principles of Catholic Theology: Building Stones for a Fundamental Theology*. Translated by Sister Mary Frances McCarthy, SND. San Francisco: Ignatius Press, 1987.

———. *Called to Communion: Understanding the Church Today*. Translated by Adrian Walker. San Francisco: Ignatius Press, 1996.

———. *Milestones: Memoirs, 1927–1977*. Translated by Erasmo Leiva-Merikakis. San Francisco: Ignatius Press, 1998.

———. *God and the World: Believing and Living in Our Time*. San Francisco: Ignatius Press, 2002.

———. "What Is Theology?" In Ratzinger, *Pilgrim Fellowship of Faith: The Church as Communion*, translated by Henry Taylor, 29–36. San Francisco: Ignatius Press, 2002.

———. *Introduction to Christianity*. San Francisco: Ignatius Press, 2004.

Ratzinger, Joseph, Alois Grillmeier, and Béda Rigaux. "Dogmatic Constitution on Divine Revelation." Translated by William Glen-Doepel. In *Commentary on the Documents of Vatican II*, vol. 3, edited by Herbert Vorgrimler. New York: Herder and Herder, 1969.

Schillebeeckx, Edward, OP. *The Understanding of Faith: Interpretation and Criticism.* Translated by N. D. Smith. New York: Seabury Press, 1974.

Schlier, H. "Kerygma und Sophia." In *Die Zeit der Kirche: Exegetische Aufsätze und Vorträge,* vol. 1, 4th ed., 206–32. Freiburg: Herder, 1966.

Seitz, Christopher. *Figured Out: Typology and Providence in Christian Scripture.* Louisville, Ky.: Westminster John Knox Press, 2001.

———. *The Goodly Fellowship of the Prophets: The Achievement of Association in Canon Formation.* Grand Rapids, Mich.: Baker Academic, 2009.

———. "The Rule of Faith, Hermeneutics, and the Character of Christian Scripture." In Seitz, *The Character of Christian Scripture: The Significance of a Two-Testament Bible,* 191–203. Grand Rapids, Mich.: Baker Academic, 2011.

Shah, Bruno M., OP. "The Promise of a Unitary Sacred Theology: Rereading *Aeterni Patris* and *Fides et Ratio.*" *Nova et Vetera* (English) 11 (2013): 147–86.

Sokolowski, Robert. *Presence and Absence: A Philosophical Investigation of Language and Being.* Bloomington, Ind.: Indiana University Press, 1978.

———. *The God of Faith and Reason: Foundations of Christian Theology.* Notre Dame, Ind.: University of Notre Dame Press, 1982.

———. *Eucharistic Presence: A Study in the Theology of Disclosure.* Washington, D.C.: The Catholic University of America Press, 1994.

———. "Knowing Essentials." *Review of Metaphysics* 47 (1994): 691–709.

———. "Formal and Material Causality in Science." *American Catholic Philosophical Quarterly* 69 (1995): 57–67.

———. *Introduction to Phenomenology.* Cambridge: Cambridge University Press, 2000.

———. "Soul and the Transcendence of the Human Person." In *What Is Man, O Lord? The Human Person in a Biotech Age,* edited by Edward J. Furton, 49–63. Boston: National Catholic Bioethics Center, 2002.

———. "Philosophy in the Seminary Curriculum." *Homiletic and Pastoral Review* 104 (2004): 14–22.

———. "Intellectual Formation in Catholic Seminaries." *Seminarium* 46 (2006): 827–46.

———. *Phenomenology of the Human Person.* Cambridge: Cambridge University Press, 2008.

———. "God the Father: The Human Expression of the Holy Trinity." *The Thomist* 74 (2010): 33–56.

———. "Husserl on First Philosophy." Husserl Memorial Lecture, 2009. In *Philosophy, Phenomenology, Sciences: Essays in Commemoration of Edmund Husserl,* edited by Carlo Ierna, Hanne Jacobs, and Filip Mattens, 3–23. Phaenomenologica 200. Dordrecht: Springer, 2010.

———. "How Aristotle and Husserl Differ on First Philosophy." In *Life, Subjectivity, and Art: Essays in Honor of Rudolf Bernet,* edited by Roland Breeur and Ullrich Melle, 1–28. Phaenomenologica 201. Dordrecht: Springer, 2012.

———. "God's Word and Human Speech." *Nova et Vetera* (English) 11 (2013): 187–210.

———. "The Theology of Disclosure." *Nova et Vetera* 14 (2016): 409–23.

Staudt, Jared. "Aquinas and the Exegesis of Benedict XVI." *Nova et Vetera* (English) 12 (2014): 331–63.

Steiner, George. *Errata: An Examined Life*. New Haven, Conn.: Yale University Press, 1998.

Strauss, Leo. *Natural Right and History*. Chicago: University of Chicago Press, 1953.

Tanner, Norman P., SJ. *Decrees of the Ecumenical Councils*. 2 vols. London: Sheed and Ward, 1990.

Tertullian. *The Prescription against Heretics*. Translated by Peter Holmes. In *The Ante-Nicene Fathers*, vol. 3, edited by A. Roberts and J. Donaldson. Grand Rapids, Mich.: Eerdmans, 1980.

Thomas Aquinas. *Summa Contra Gentiles*. Rome: Marietti, 1934.

———. *Quaestiones disputatae de veritate*. In *Quaestiones Disputatae*, vol 1, edited by Raymund Spiazzi, OP. Rome: Marietti, 1949.

———. *Questiones disputatae de potentia Dei*. In *Quaestiones Disputate*, vol. 2, edited by P. Bazzi, M. Calcaterra, et al. Rome: Marietti, 1949.

———. *Quaestiones Quodlibetales*. Edited by Raymund Spiazzi, OP. 8th ed., revised. Rome: Marietti, 1949.

———. *Summa theologiae*. Edited by Peter Caramello. 3 vols. Rome: Marietti, 1952.

———. *Super Evangelium Sancti Ioannis Lectura*. Edited by Raphael Cai, OP. Rome: Marietti, 1952.

———. *Super Epistolam ad Hebraeos*. In *S. Thomae Aquinatis Super Epistolas S. Pauli Lectura*, vol. 2, edited by Raphaele Cai. Rome: Marietti, 1953.

———. *Summa Contra Gentiles, Book One: God*. Translated by Anton Pegis. Notre Dame, Ind.: University of Notre Dame Press, 1975.

———. *Summa Contra Gentiles, Book Two: Creation*. Translated by James F. Anderson. Notre Dame, Ind.: University of Notre Dame, 1975.

———. *Summa Contra Gentiles, Book Three: Providence, Part I*. Translated by Vernon J. Bourke. Notre Dame, Ind.: University of Notre Dame, 1975.

———. *Summa Contra Gentiles, Book Three: Providence, Part II*. Translated by Vernon J. Bourke. Notre Dame, Ind.: University of Notre Dame, 1975.

———. *Summa Contra Gentiles, Book Four: Salvation*. Translated by Charles J. O'Neil. Notre Dame, Ind.: University of Notre Dame, 1975.

———. *Summa Theologica*. Translated by the Fathers of the English Dominican Province. 5 vols. Westminster, Md.: Christian Classics, 1981. This is a reprint of the Benziger Brothers edition of 1948, itself a reprint of the original 1911 English edition.

———. *Thomas Aquinas: Selected Writings*. Edited and translated by Ralph McInerny. New York: Penguin Books, 1998.

Turner, Denys. *Faith, Reason and the Existence of God*. Cambridge: Cambridge University Press, 2004.

Tyrrell, George. "Revelation." In Tyrrell, *Through Scylla and Charybdis, or the Old Theology and the New*, 264–307. London: Longmans, 1907.

———. "The Rights and Limits of Theology." In Tyrrell, *Through Scylla and Charybdis, or the Old Theology and the New*, 200–241. London: Longmans, 1907.

Vall, Gregory. "Psalm 22: *Vox Christi* or Israelite Temple Liturgy?" *The Thomist* 66 (2002): 175–200.

———. "Word and Event: A Reappraisal." *Nova et Vetera* (English) 13 (2015): 181–218.

Vansina, Jan. *Oral Tradition as History*. Madison, Wis.: University of Wisconsin Press, 1985.

Vatican I. *Dei Filius; Pastor Aeternus*. In *Decrees of the Ecumenical Councils*, vol. 2, *Trent to Vatican II*, ed. Norman P. Tanner, SJ. London: Sheed and Ward, 1990.

Vatican Council II. *Dogmatic Constitution on Divine Revelation (Dei Verbum)*. In *Decrees of the Ecumenical Councils*, vol. 2, *Trent to Vatican II*, edited by Norman P. Tanner, SJ, 971–79. London: Sheed and Ward, 1990.

Vatican Council II. *Dogmatic Constitution on the Church (Lumen Gentium)*. In *Decrees of the Ecumenical Councils*, vol. 2, *Trent to Vatican II*, edited by Norman P. Tanner, SJ, 849–900. London: Sheed and Ward, 1990.

Venard, Olivier-Thomas, OP. "Scriptural Hermeneutics and the Thomistic Making of a Doctrine of God." *Nova et Vetera* (English) 12 (2014): 1091–123.

Vincent of Lérins. *The Commonitory*. Translated by C. A. Heurtley. In *The Nicene and Post-Nicene Fathers*, 2nd ser., vol. 11, edited by Philip Schaff and Henry Wace. Grand Rapids, Mich.: Eerdmans, 1982.

Wahlberg, Mats. *Revelation as Testimony: A Philosophical-Theological Study*. Grand Rapids, Mich.: Eerdmans, 2014.

Waldstein, Michael. "*Analogia Verbi*: The Truth of Scripture in Rudolf Bultmann and Raymond Brown." *Letter and Spirit* 6 (2010): 93–140.

White, Thomas Joseph, OP. *Wisdom in the Face of Modernity: A Study in Thomistic Natural Theology*. Washington, D.C.: The Catholic University of America Press, 2009.

———. "'Through Him All Things Were Made' (John 1:3): The Analogy of the Word Incarnate according to St. Thomas Aquinas and Its Ontological Presuppositions." In *The Analogy of Being: Invention of the Antichrist or the Wisdom of God?* edited by Thomas Joseph White, OP, 246–79. Grand Rapids, Mich.: Eerdmans, 2011.

———. "Trust Witness." A review of *Revelation as Testimony* by Mats Wahlberg. *First Things* (November 2015): 60–62.

———. *Exodus*. Grand Rapids, Mich.: Brazos Press, 2016.

Wicks, Jared, SJ. "Six Texts by Prof. Joseph Ratzinger as *Peritus* before and during Vatican Council II." *Gregorianum* 89 (2008): 233–311.

Wright, N. T. *Jesus and the Victory of God*. Minneapolis: Fortress Press, 1996.

———. *The Resurrection of the Son of God*. Minneapolis: Fortress Press, 2003.

Wright, William. "Patristic Biblical Hermeneutics in Joseph Ratzinger's *Jesus of Nazareth*." *Letter and Spirit* 7 (2011): 191–207.

INDEX

Alfaro, Juan, SJ, 193n13, 214, 219n10, 221–22, 225n15, 229n23, 235n28, 238nn30–32, 240, 252n9, 260n22

Allison, Dale, 197

Alonso-Schökel, Louis, SJ, 81, 82, 90, 92

analogy of names, 175–78, 250

Anselm of Canterbury, St., 134, 210

Aquinas, Thomas, St., 1, 21n21, 25n29, 32n37, 33n39, 40n43, 61n14, 83, 87n59, 100, 104, 114, 127, 128, 161n35, 171n46, 208, 211; and analogy, 176–77, 178; and apostolic witness, 199–200, 202; authority of in theology, 256, 261, 262, 270, 272; on faith, 215, 222n12, 223–24, 225n18, 226, 227nn20–21, 228, 235n27, 240, 261; and God, 166n40, 167n43, 168n44; and inerrancy of Scripture, 103nn109–10, 113; and inspiration, 79n42, 87n60, 90n68, 96–98; on name of God, 11n6, 12, 13n10, 212; and natural theology, 148, 151; and onto-theology, 178; and Ratzinger, 267n36; and senses of Scripture, 23n27, 64, 66–67, 91–92nn72–73, 93–94; and theology, 4n3, 250–52, 253, 254, 261, 264–65, 271

Aristotle, 1, 17n18, 114, 127, 133, 148, 151, 212, 213, 252, 252, 265, 271; and Husserl, 270; and mind, 159, 163, 228; and onto-theology, 176n55; and trans-cultural weight of, 178, 179, 182

Arius, 120, 121–22

Athanasius, St., 121, 148,

Augustine, St., 17, 19n19, 25, 26, 42, 96n85, 104, 134, 148, 163, 175n54, 211, 260; and

apologetics, 188, 190; and inspiration, 82, 85, 97; and pattern of revelation, 28, 29, 31; and senses and interpretation of Scripture, 51, 57

authority of Jesus' word, 190–95

Balthasar, Hans Urs von, 31–33, 55n1, 95n82, 174, 190, 210, 270; and "new theology," 266–69

Barth, Karl, 99n93, 147–48, 149, 171, 246

Barton, John, 203n33

Bauckham, Richard, 27n31, 59n9, 200n27, 202n30, 204n35

Behr, John, 49n12

Benedict XV, Pope, 101n105

Benedict XVI, Pope. *See* Ratzinger, Joseph

Benoît, Pierre, OP, 79n43, 81n49, 98n92

Billot, Louis, 238n32

Brown, Raymond, SS, 93n75, 99, 101n106

Bultmann, Rudolph, 30, 99n93, 199, 204n34

Burridge, Richard, 204n35

canon of Scripture, 68–78; as self-closing, 73–78; principle of, 70–73

Capreolus, John, OP, 240

Cassian, John, 67n22

"catholic (trans-cultural) categories," 123–24, 133, 178–83

Catholic Modernism, 41, 223, 246–50, 251, 254, 256–61; on dogma, 248–49; on revelation, 247–48; revival of, 257; on theology, 249

Chadwick, Owen, 127n30

Tertullian, 47, 48, 120, 236

theology: dogmatic, 262; and Fathers of the Church, 263–64; fundamental, 2–5; necessity of, 245–46; pastoral, 265; positive, 251–52; as science, 265, 269; at Vatican II, 261–64, 265–66; speculative (systematic) theology, 264–65

theology of disclosure, 268–72

Troeltsch, Ernst, 146

truth, 134–37

Turner, Denys, 166n40

Tyrrell, George, 247–49, 250, 256

Vall, Gregory, 16n16, 38n41, 94n77

Vansina, Jan, 55n2, 56n4, 204n34

Vatican Council I, 39, 69n24, 80n45, 82, 101n104, 103, 116, 126n28, 133, 134, 143, 144, 148, 152, 178, 181, 186, 216n3, 218n9, 225n16, 227, 236, 264, 265

Vatican Council II, 266; *Dei Verbum*, 2n2, 9, 10n2, 24n28, 44–45, 58, 67n22, 69, 74n38, 84, 88n61, 101, 126, 130n34, 205; *Lumen Gentium*, 113, 117, 118n14; *Optatam Totius*, 261, 265

Venard, Olivier–Thomas, OP, 13n9, 260n23

Verbum Domini (Benedict XVI), 24n28, 81n46, 84n54, 95nn82–83, 100n102, 104n114

Wahlberg, Mats, 11n7, 16n14, 99n93, 147n6, 191nn8–9, 198n20, 198n22

Waldstein, Michael, 99

White, Thomas Joseph, OP, 103n108, 148–51, 166n40, 176n55, 198n22

Wicks, Jared, SJ, 85n55, 85n58

Wong, Hong Yu, 159n31

words (language), 10–16, 129–30, 173, 260; of Christ, 190–94

Wright, N. T., 197–98, 206n39

ALSO IN THE SACRA DOCTRINA
SERIES

An Introduction to Vatican II as an Ongoing Theological Event
Matthew Levering

Fundamental Theology was designed in Garamond, with Scala Sans and Garda Titling display type, and composed by Kachergis Book Design of Pittsboro, North Carolina. It was printed on 60-pound House Natural Smooth and bound by Sheridan Books of Chelsea, Michigan.